# CROATIA: A HISTORY

*'Povijest Hrvata'* (The History of the Croats), sculpture by
Ivan Mestrovic, 1932 outside the University of Zagreb

IVO GOLDSTEIN

# Croatia
## A History

TRANSLATED FROM THE CROATIAN BY
NIKOLINA JOVANOVIC

HURST & COMPANY, LONDON

First published in the United Kingdom by
C. Hurst & Co. (Publishers) Ltd.,
41 Great Russell Street, London, WC1B 3PL
© Ivo Goldstein, 1999
Second impression, 2001
Third impression, 2011
All rights reserved.
Printed in India

A catalogue data record for this volume is available
from the British Library.

ISBN: 978-1-85065-525-1 *paperback*

**www.hurstpub.co.uk**

# FOREWORD

By the fifteenth century, humanist circles congregated in Croatian cities along the eastern Adriatic coast were already interested in the history of Croatia. The first survey of its kind, *Six Books on the History of Croatia and Dalmatia*, written by Ivan Lučić and published in Amsterdam in 1667, typified the erudite historiography then dominant. The writing of Croatian history has been pursued ever since and flourished especially after the mid-nineteenth century. Despite this outpouring, books dealing with the entire span of Croatian history, detailing its major periods, were few and far between.

Until the beginning of the twentieth century the task of writing Croatian history was often taken up by Hungarian, Italian and Austrian historians since areas of Croatia formed part of their countries' territory at the time. After the creation of Yugoslavia in 1918, interest in the subject among non-Croats subsided and relatively few histories of the long and complex Croatian past were published abroad. This was partly because Yugoslavia was considered its own entity and interest in its history tended to focus on Serbia. Thus in order to respond to what we saw as a gap in the historiography of Croatia, the range of this book is from antiquity to the present.

I wrote it in the tumultuous period of the formation of an independent and democratic Croatian state and its struggle for survival. Of course, anything written during this period would have to take those events into account, but the book contains much more than the resolution of the Croatian national question, important though that question is. Instead, it focuses on how a small European nation has attempted for half a millennium to fortify its links with central and western Europe; how it has aspired to achieve the living standards enjoyed by its western and northern neighbours; and its compelling architectural and literary cultural production. I have tried to track these major developments.

I must thank my late friend Ivan Djurić (1947-97), Serbian historian and politician, who persuaded me to write the first draft of this book. I also thank Dr Mirjana Gross, my professor at the

University of Zagreb, who kept me informed of new trends in historiography and whose own methodologies I always try to follow. Last but not least, I thank my father, Slavko, who helped me prepare for the foreign reader some chapters of the book, particularly those dealing with the period of the Second World War, of which he had direct and painful experience.

*Zagreb, June 1999*                          IVO GOLDSTEIN

# CONTENTS

# MAPS

# 1

# INTRODUCTION

## Historical outline

In the fourth century AD the Roman empire was partitioned and became the Eastern and Western empires. In the Balkans the boundary between the two stretched from the Montenegrin coast up the river Drina to the confluence of the Sava and the Danube, and then further north. This boundary has remained more or less unchanged in overall European perception for a full 1,500 years. The European West ended and the East began, and *vice versa*, on South Slav territory. Frontier changes, economic contacts and cultural influences may have been of no great importance for Europe as a whole, but they had a crucial impact on the destiny of the small Slav peoples who lived in the area between what is today Italy and Austria, and Greece. There were and still are ethnic similarities between the peoples on the two sides of the divide, but their culture and history are fundamentally different. Regional developments have often focused on the Croats and Croatia, traditionally linked with the present-day Hungarian, Italian and German regions, and with Western Europe. Croatia is also a Mediterranean country whose shores have been strongly influenced by the rhythm of Mediterranean events.

Over the centuries different territories have been called 'Croatia' in historical sources. In the early Middle Ages the name designated the area in the hinterland of the central Dalmatian cities of Split, Trogir and Zadar, although the Slav tribe of Croats settled a much wider region, including Pannonia and probably what is today Montenegro. Later the territory called Croatia broadened to include areas to the north and west, but after the Ottoman conquests of the sixteenth and seventeenth centuries it was restricted to a narrow belt between Slovenia in the west, the vast Ottoman empire in the east, the Drava river and the Hungarian border in the north, and the Adriatic Sea in the south. As the

1

Ottomans withdrew from Europe, Croatia regained its former territory.

Croatian history unfolded under various kinds of foreign influence – there were Greek colonists in the fourth century BC, Arabian and Ottoman conquests, and Italians, Normans, Hungarians, Austrians, Germans and French. Their influence in different provinces varied, creating marked regional differences.

For a long time Croatia, as part of the triune kingdom of Croatia, Dalmatia and Slavonia, meant only the north-western part of the present state, and Dalmatia and Slavonia were distinct provinces in their own right. Today Croatia includes Istria, which for centuries was under the rule of various Habsburg or Italian masters, and the territory of Dubrovnik, which was long an independent republic. Croats who inhabited Bosnia and Hercegovina, and the Serbian provinces of Vojvodina and Kosovo, also belong to the Croatian ethnic corpus, but their history and the circumstances under which they live are very different from conditions in Croatia.

Political regionalism also developed as a result of different climatic and economic circumstances, the location of traffic routes, and historical influence.

## Topography

At first sight the topography of Croatia seems relatively simple, and to consist of three divisions – the littoral, the mountain backbone and the peri-Pannonian region – each with its own special features. Croatia's topography is closely related to the processes of its history.

In the north-west the spurs of the Alps stretch into Croatia, in the south-east rise the towering Dinaric mountains. They combine to make a rampart between the coastal region and the Pannonian plain between the Sava, Drava and Danube rivers. The great height of the north-western mountains and the karst nature of the Dinaric mountains emphasise their role as a boundary. The population of the interior, especially inhabitants of the Pannonian plain, were always attracted by the gentle Mediterranean, and the main route from Pannonia to the Mediterranean and back led through the pass between the Alps and the Dinarics. The negotiable valley of the river Una, the pastures of south Lika and the north Dalmatian plateau facilitated north-south links. The mountain passes are much lower than 1,000 metres. They are approached through the areas of Banija, Kordun, Gorski Kotar, Lika and the Dalmatian hinterland, which were traditionally more sparsely populated and relatively poor. Coastal Croatia stretches fanlike from the Slovenian border in the north of Istria, through the Croatian littoral centred on Rijeka in the north, Dalmatia centred on Split, and Dubrovnik in the south-east and the Bokakotorska gulf by the border with Montenegro. The importance of the coast is increased by the many islands, thirty of them covering more than 10 square km., and forty-five inhabited at the end of the twentieth century.

North Croatia, the area between the Sava, Drava and Danube, is part of a larger region, the Pannonian plain, whose northern part lies in Hungary and eastern part in the Serbian province of Vojvodina. Croatia's north-east is called Slavonia. It is mountainous in the centre, but is generally flat; its largest town is Osijek. In the north-west is the Croatian capital city, Zagreb. Several smaller towns developed in a radius of 100 km. around Zagreb, making this the most important industrial zone of Croatia. This region, bordering Slovenia and Hungary, is traditionally the most densely populated and has good connections with Slovenia, Austria and Italy.

## Climate

Croatia's climate results from its position on the Adriatic sea, with a mountain barrier stretching down the Adriatic shore, and the Pannonian Plain in the continental hinterland. Although Croatia is reached by both polar and tropical air currents, it is strictly divided into the Mediterranean and continental climatic regions. The first is limited to the low-lying narrow belt along the Adriatic and the islands, while the second affects the entire mainland hinterland.

The Mediterranean climate has mild rainy winters and dry, sunny and hot summers. Winters are short – usually no longer than four months, five at most. In the coldest month the average temperature does not fall below 5°C. In the northern part between Rijeka and Zadar the Mediterranean belt is very narrow because of the climatic barrier of Mount Velebit. Cold continental air currents sometimes reach the sea, penetrating through mountain passes where they gain in ferocity. This causes the unpleasant *bura* wind and a resulting significant drop in temperature. Snow sometimes falls in the northern part of the littoral, but rarely settles.

The northern Croatian lowlands and the karst *poljes*, the enclosed valleys of the Dinaric range, have a moderate continental climate with a pronounced winter and average sub-zero temperatures. The summers are hot, but cooler in areas closer to the Dinaric mountains. The highest mountains have an alpine climate with fresh summers and very cold winters, and much snow that lies for a long time. The mountain passes, which are so important for communications, are usually spared such extreme weather.

## Water

The rivers of Croatia flow into the Black Sea and the Adriatic, and the watershed between the two basins lies along the Dinaric range. In the north it is only 18 km. from the Adriatic coast, but further south the distance increases. The Black Sea river basin, especially in the lowlands of northern Croatia, is well developed. The rivers have backwaters and dry riverbeds, and meander on an unstable course. The Croats and the peoples who lived on the territory of Croatia before them traditionally built settlements and towns beside rivers, which played an important role in their everyday work and life. They were used for fishing, roads were usually built along their banks, and even if there were no roads it was easier to travel along river valleys. However, water was not always a blessing because many of the river valleys were marshy. As much as 8 per cent of Croatian territory is potentially marshland. Land improvements in the nineteenth century, which wiped out the malaria anopheles mosquito and provided more agricultural land, made life in these areas much easier.

The Dinaric mountains have much more rainfall than the lowlands, but even so a lack of water has fundamentally affected life in this region for centuries. Although there are rivers, many of them are sink rivers that emerge from the karst, have a short surface course and then disappear down swallow-holes that lie around the edges of karst valleys or in the valleys themselves. Because the swallow-holes cannot quickly absorb large quantities of water when the water-level is high, the karst valleys are frequently flooded. This is one of the reasons why for centuries settlements were built on the enclosing slopes of the valleys that faced the sun instead of in the valleys themselves. Another reason was that building towns and villages in the valleys would reduce the availability within them of precious and sparse fertile.

Most of the lakes in Croatia are in the karst region. Their surface area is small and their water-level fluctuates during the year, but they never dry out; this was important at times when the possibilities for transporting water were limited. In the lowlands of northern Croatia lakes usually developed in abandoned or meandering riverbeds, and during the centuries seemed more like ponds near the large lowland rivers. In the twentieth century many of them were drained or turned into recreational areas.

Thus throughout history the inhabitants of coastal areas and of the karst hinterland often lacked water, while those living in northern regions did not know how to get rid of it. While travellers to Dalmatia mostly had to concentrate on avoiding mountains and finding the easiest and lowest mountain pass, in Pannonia they had to know the best river crossings. All this determined routes and the location of settlements.

*Plant and animal life*

Like the rest of Europe, Croatia was densely forested for a long time. At the end of the eleventh century a French Crusader described Dalmatia as a land 'of mountains, forests and pastures, spreading far and wide, so there is very little cultivated land'. From the Middle Ages to the twentieth century forests were systematically felled and cleared, and some of them have ceased to exist altogether. In other places, as on Velebit, human activities added to the natural process of soil erosion to wash away the fertile mountain soil, resulting in today's bare and rugged landscape. More recently, acid rain has brought dangerous chemicals from distant industrial centres, which even threatens some primeval virgin forests.

A very characteristic species cultivated by man is the olive tree. For all practical purposes the region of the Mediterranean climate coincides with the areas of olive cultivation, and in places olive trees have been grown along the Croatian coast and islands for over 2,000 years. The grape vine has been grown in the same region since Greek colonisation, perhaps since the fourth century BC. Several centuries later the Romans brought it to the Pannonian plain.

Pannonian soil is exceptionally fertile, and always gave above-average yields, especially of cereals. The mountain and coastal regions, on the other hand, were not good for growing cereals but the mild climate fostered the growth of all kinds of fruit and vegetables. Two harvests could even be had in a year, which in hard times helped stave off food shortages and famine. In some areas potatoes and tobacco have been important crops for centuries – thus Columbus's discovery of America had a great effect on everyday life in these passive regions. The modern age and contemporary agricultural technology have brought plantations of citrus fruit to coastal areas.

Animal life in Croatia changed with the passage of time, mostly as a result of human activities. In the nineteenth century, as forests and marshes disappeared, and settlements and cultivated land spread, some wild animals had to flee from the most exposed places, but most of them did not die out. At the end of the twentieth century there are still bears, many wild boar, and deer in the depths of Croatian forests; wolves are known to attack isolated settlements in winter and slaughter sheep; and mountain crags are still the home of chamois and eagles.

For centuries raising livestock was one of the fundamentals of survival, especially in the highlands. There and on the coast and islands people kept sheep and goats, and used horses and donkeys as pack animals. In the northern lowlands the horse and cow traditionally predominated. Shepherds continued to spend summers with their animals in the high mountains of Bosnia and Hercegovina and come down in winter to the lowlands of north Croatia almost till the end of the twentieth century. They probably migrated in that way for centuries, if not for millennia.

## Special regional features

Much of the central region and the entire coast is a karst area, which strongly affected people's lives. Although the region's traffic and geographical position makes it important, in itself it offers only limited possibilities for a better life. For centuries houses were built of stone, even dry-stone, while wood was used for construction in the more northerly regions.

Mentality reflects regional characteristics. Although it is always dangerous to draw generalised psychological parallels, it is a fact that the coastal and island population have a typically Mediterranean outlook – they tend to be open by nature and have a culture of living in the streets and squares, outside the house. In the mountains the harsh climate and many centuries of frontier existence have resulted in a predominantly patriarchal attitude, and in the low lying north of Croatia the way of life and mentality are similar to those in central Europe.

There are other differences among Croatian regions which, while seeming trivial at first glance, reflect a deeper historical background. The cooking, besides specifically Croatian dishes, shows a diversity of regional influences: Mediterranean-Italian on the coast, Central European in the north, and typically Hungarian in the north-east (Slavonia). To all this must be added, especially in the second half of the twentieth century, the influence of typical oriental-Turkish dishes and ways of cooking (barbecue, *ćevapčići*). Croatia is similarly divided in many other features of everyday life, like music, dancing and folk costume.

There are also great differences in the way people built their settlements, because over the centuries this necessarily had to adapt to given circumstances. Lowland villages stretch out beside roads, are very long and usually have several thousand inhabitants. In mountain regions the villages are scattered, houses are built beside rivers and meagre cultivable land, usually on the slopes of karst valleys which receive the ways of the sun. On the coast agriculture was of prime importance for centuries and many villages were built beside cultivable land, sometimes as much as several kilometres from the sea, but in time the increasing development of the maritime economy, especially tourism in more recent times, brought people closer to it. However, cities and some other settlements have existed beside the sea for millennia, and in some cases their function of fortification, port and trading centre has lasted since antiquity.

For centuries relief determined migration; people left mountain regions and settled on the shore or in the fertile plains of the north, and this is still the trend. 'They settled a hundred lands, but are still not empty,' people say of those mountain regions.

## The sea

The sea holds a special place in Croatian history. In prehistoric times it was the route that brought the first seeds of European and Mediterranean influence. It brought many immigrants from various places, and took even more Croats away on their voyages of emigration. Goods also came by sea, and so did the most diverse influences. In times of famine the sea and the food that came from it sustained many coastal people.

Countless generations have been fishermen, but people also earned money by diving for sponges and pearls, and in trade. Robbery and piracy were often an important source of income for the poor communities of the eastern Adriatic coast, which considered these activities completely legitimate. Seaside tourism began to develop in Croatia from the late nineteenth country onwards, slowly at first and since the 1960s intensively. It is a significant source of revenue considering the size and overall wealth of the country and the number of coastal inhabitants.

The sea is of great and increasing importance for Croatia today.

# 2

# CROATIAN LANDS IN ANTIQUITY

*Croatian territory at the dawn of history: Illyrians, Celts and Greeks*

The beginnings of most European peoples reach into the early Middle Ages or into the last centuries of antiquity, and this is true of the Croats. Nevertheless, their history in the early Middle Ages and in later periods owes much to the culture, civilisation and ethnic, economic and political situation they encountered in the region they settled.

The population inhabiting the territory of what was to become Croatia was heterogeneous, mixed by frequent migrations, wars and assimilation. The Illyrians were the oldest Balkan population and they preserved their identity, at least to some degree and in some places, until the early Middle Ages. At first only one tribe, still unidentified, on the northern borders of classical Greece was called 'Illyrian' but later the name expanded to include a large number of ethnically, linguistically and culturally related Indo-European tribes in the west and central Balkans. Some of the tribes that lived in what is today Croatia (who seem not to have had much to do with the Illyrians) must be singled out: the Histri, who gave their name to the peninsula of Istria, and the Delmatae, whose long-lasting resistance to Roman legions made their name an eponym for the new Roman province of Dalmatia.

In the fourth century BC the Celts came to the Balkans from the north-west and somewhat changed the ethnic structure to their advantage. They also brought with them the potter's wheel – previously unknown to the Illyrians. Almost at the same time colonists from Greek cities arrived from the south-east and founded their first colonies on the mainland and islands of the eastern Adriatic, exerting an economic, cultural and social influence on the whole region.

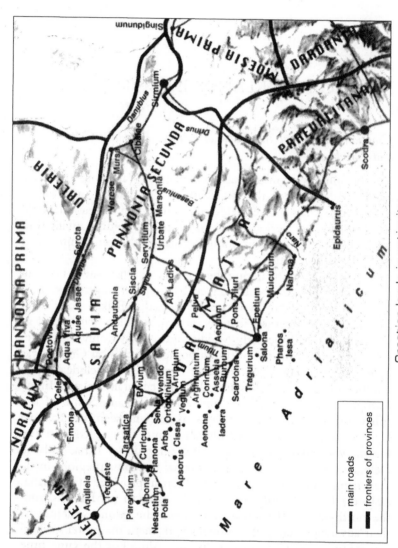

Croatian lands in antiquity

*Creating the first landscape of civilization: the Romans*

Early in the second century BC the Romans began to conquer
the region and took a full 200 years to do so completely. Istria
was subdued first and became part of Italy, and the other areas
were included in the provinces of Illyricum, Dalmatia and Pannonia.
Although the Romans brought many of the fruits of their civilisation, Illyrian resistance continued for a long time in all the fields
where this was possible. The indigenous Illyrian culture, or at
least elements of it, could long be discerned in symbiosis with
the imported classical culture, almost until the end of antiquity.
More basic changes in ethnic structure happened only in towns
and administrative centres that required the presence of a class of
officials, but Roman influence was felt not so much in the over-
whelming presence of the Roman (or Italic) population as in the
predominance of the Latin language. The Illyrians continued to
live according to their ancient customs and regulations with varying
degrees of success, jealously guarding local cults and retaining old
local names. They managed this better in regions further inland
from the Adriatic. Thus the Illyrian element certainly played an
important part in the Croatian ethnogenesis.

Economically Illyricum and Pannonia contributed greatly to
the Empire. In pre-Roman times the region was widely known
for its natural resources, agriculture and stock breeding. Wood,
cereals, livestock, ores and other products, in which Italy was
deficient even in those times, were exported to Rome. Urbanisation
began. Salona (near Split), the capital of the Roman province of
Dalmatia, was the centre of gravity for the broader Balkan area,
Pannonia and the Adriatic coast, and many towns developed in
strategically and economically important places. Road construction
contributed to overall progress, with three routes being of major
importance for the Empire. One led from today's Trieste in Italy
along the eastern Adriatic coast to today's Albania and then turned
eastward to Constantinople. Another linked today's Italy via the
south Pannonian Plain with the east Balkans and Asia Minor.
The third connected the Pannonian *limes* (boundary) with the
Adriatic. There are fourth-century records of pilgrims using these
roads to travel from Burdigale (Bordeaux) to Jerusalem.

*Disappearance of the Empire: Barbarian invasions*

Late in the fourth century the Roman Empire and the Roman
way of life were deeply undermined in Pannonia and all Croatian
areas. The region's geographical position was such that whoever
wanted to travel from east to west in Europe had to pass at least
through its outer periphery. Vandals, Huns, Gepidae, Lombards,
Heruli all came and went without leaving any notable traces.

In the late fifth century the Ostrogoths founded their state in
Italy, Pannonia and Dalmatia. In 535 Byzantium easily defeated
the Ostrogoths in Dalmatia, although the war continued in Italy
for the next twenty years. The Byzantine authorities tried to
rectify the situation, which was almost hopeless: many refugees
from unsafe northern regions swarmed into areas further south,
especially the Adriatic shore, and the economy kept deteriorating
because of the overall depression in late antiquity. The late Roman
provincial organization, Roman administration and the achievements of Roman civilization faced an inevitable end.

# 3

# THE FIRST CENTURIES OF CROATIAN
# HISTORY AND THE ESTABLISHMENT OF
# THE CROATIAN STATE

## *The Slavs and Croats settle the Balkans*

In the second half of the sixth century the Slavs and a Mongol people, the Avars, finally began to settle the Pannonian Plain. Slav migrations did not take the form of destructive lightning invasions of warlike groups, as with the Germanic peoples. They were gradual and continued for a long time, the slowness probably resulting from the fact that most of the Slavs were farmers and shepherds. They crept southwards relentlessly, conquered the towns of Pannonia, overwhelmed the Byzantine empire's fortified lines on the Danube and peopled the entire Balkans. By about 600 they had already settled the Dinaric mountains, and they seem to have reached the Adriatic at some points in the early seventh century. The Croats arrived in the former Roman provinces of Pannonia and Dalmatia at about the same time. To clarify all the circumstances and consequences of their arrival, we must go deeper into the past.

The Croats' history began several centuries before they settled their present homeland. Little is known about it. In the early centuries AD the Croats seem to have been a relatively small nomadic or semi-nomadic community. They were carried through the Black Sea steppes, from the Caucasus to the Carpathians, on the wave of the tempestuous happenings around them during the great migrations of peoples. They were Slavs, but the earliest strata of folk tradition indicate contacts with non-Slavs in regions around the Caucasus, probably with Iranians. However, by the time the Croats arrived in Dalmatia and Pannonia, non-Slav influence in their culture had all but disappeared, and no traces of it can be found in remains of the material culture.

13

Croatia in the early Middle Ages

Living over a long period in symbiosis with the Slavs, the Croats were completely assimilated into the Slav environment; if there were racial or cultural differences between them, we do not known what these were. However, they retained their name and passed it to their Slav neighbours, sometimes even imposing it – not *vice versa.*

### The 7th and 8th centuries: inactivity

Only a very small amount of data, either written or archaeological, has survived from the first centuries of Croat life in the former Roman provinces of Dalmatia and Pannonia, and little is known about it. However, it is certain that classical values were mostly preserved along the Adriatic coast and in the islands – the territory that was under Byzantine suzerainty from late antiquity until the late eleventh century. In coming centuries the Byzantine political presence was to be essential for Croatia, although as time passed connections with the western world grew stronger and finally crowded out most of the Byzantine influence.

The complete disintegration of the Roman communications system and imperial government in the territory settled by the Croats (although it certainly survived on the local level in some segments of life and organisation) encouraged the establishment of a decentralised, 'segmented' society. Clans and families were independent and economically self-sufficient, and there was almost no trade. Outside pressure was occasional and in most cases probably affected only a limited number of communities. However, the beginning of the ninth century brought radical changes.

### The 9th century: conversion to Christianity and intensive development

In about 800 the spread of the Frankish state under Charlemagne and the restoration of Byzantine power triggered off the Byzantine-Frankish war on the Adriatic, and both sides cast acquisitive eyes on Croatian territory. The Franks had already subdued Istria, and after overturning the Avar khanate they spread to the Pannonian plain and annexed northern parts of Croatia. By the Treaty of Aix-la-Chapelle (Aachen) in 812, Byzantium retained the coastal Dalmatian belt and the Franks got the mountain hinterland and

Pannonia. The *Annales Regni Francorum* record that Ljudevit, Duke of Lower Pannonia, rebelled against the Frankish authorities in 819 and at first held back the stronger Frankish armies which invaded from Italy, Carinthia and Bavaria, but in 823 he had to give way. This is the last record of major military campaigns. After that economic and cultural developments came to the fore, the most important being conversion to Christianity. The first Croats and Slavs were probably converted immediately after settling the region in the early seventh century, but conversion on a larger scale did not begin till the ninth century, when the first missionaries from Byzantium, Italy and the Frankish state reached Croatian territory, usually through the cities of Byzantine Dalmatia. Christianisation was a complex social movement, a revolution that included varied and contradictory changes, went through alternating periods of relative quiet and escalation, and resulted in social and psychological upheaval. In this case conversion spread from two different centres, creating a particular set of circumstances. Pupils of the brothers Cyril and Methodius of Salonika brought to Croatia church rites in the Slav language and especially the Slav script which, in the Croatian lands, later developed into the Glagolitic script. At the same time the Latin language and liturgy were also spreading.

Although it is not clear how many Croats converted according to each rite, conversion brought Croatia into the embrace of European civilisation and triggered overall social development in the ninth century. Trade developed. Traditional products of the Croatian karst hinterland – livestock, leather, agricultural produce – were exchanged for the artifacts of more developed societies – jewellery, knives, Carolingian swords. There was an inflow of gold and other coinage, and particular attention was given to turning religious buildings of the late Roman period into churches and building new ones. Between the ninth and eleventh centuries about 100 churches were built whose very distinctive form and specific architectural solutions make up the Croatian pre-Romanesque style. Their chancel screens had the first inscriptions; the oldest, dating from the mid-ninth century, mentioned the current ruler – Duke Trpimir. In 852 Trpimir donated lands near Split to the church, as described in 'Trpimir's Deed of Gift', the oldest preserved document on the territory of medieval Croatia. The name of Duke Branimir, who ruled about thirty years later, appears on four stone inscriptions: one of them mentions the year AD 888, the other has the first reference to Croats in stone – 'Branimir, Duke of the Croats'. Pope John VIII wrote a letter to Branimir addressing him in that style the Croats', which shows that the eastern Adriatic shore had a ruler and a state worthy of the Pope's attention. Benedictine monasteries were built, and local lords raised fortifications at strategically important points from which they controlled communications and the surrounding area. As time passed the Croatian ruler centralised the state and extended his rule even to relatively distant places. A strong state organisation was created in the basin of the Dalmatian rivers Cetina, Krka and Zrmanja, in the hinterland of the Byzantine cities of Split, Trogir and Zadar. Smaller administrative units were formed in the region, namely counties (*županije*) headed by counts (*župani*). A county usually covered one karst valley. In this barren region the only cultivable land was in those valleys, and settlements developed on their sloping sides, along with graveyards and churches. Routes linking the valleys followed logical directions, often a survival from Roman times. On them, usually in the county centre, stood a fortified castle from which the local count ruled his territory. The Croatian authorities extended their rule deeper into the interior, controlling river communications that linked Dalmatia with the Pannonian plain (the valleys of the Una, Vrbas and other rivers). The Croats who settled the area between the Sava and the Drava also established a state, of which very little is known. There were always strong tendencies for the two states to unite, right up till their final and firm unification in the second half of the eleventh century.

All these processes show that by the late ninth or the early tenth century the level of development reached by Croatian society made possible its inclusion in West European civilisation on an equal footing. In the mean time the influence of the Byzantine and Frankish empires on Croatian territory had waned, mostly because of their internal problems. But a new power, Venice, loomed on the horizon. Control over the eastern Adriatic sea route was essential for the stability of Venetian trade with the East. Croatian ships and the those of other eastern Adriatic Slav communities (Sclaviniae) often attacked and robbed Venetian galleys, considering this the natural right of more poorly developed communities in their efforts to survive. The Venetians were not without guilt, either, because their most profitable trade was in slaves, and one of the places where they captured slaves was the eastern Adriatic shore. These slaves were then sold at high prices throughout the Mediterranean. The struggle between Venice and the Croats for domination over the eastern Adriatic coast continued till the early fifteenth century. In the late ninth century the Hungarians came to the Pannonian plain and soon began to plunder much of Europe, including Croatian territory. They conquered some Pannonian fortifications and seem to have tried unsuccessfully to reach the Adriatic and gain an outlet to the sea. At that time Bulgaria (ruled by Emperor Simeon, 893-927), after defeating Serbia, also wanted to spread its influence to Croatia. But the Croatian ruler Tomislav (reigned *c*. 910-*c*. 928) defeated both the Bulgarian and Hungarian armies and averted the danger.

In 925 church synods were held at Split at which it was decided to prohibit the Slav language in liturgy and the Glagolitic script, and to support only the Latin language and script. These prohibitions were mostly encouraged by Rome but they did not produce the results their champions expected. The church hierarchy knew that it was incomparably easier to communicate with its congregations in their mother-tongue. In future centuries Glagolitic literacy and literature became important in Croatian cultural life.

When Tomislav died, a crisis began in Croatia, with civil wars that did not die down until the end of the tenth century. Then Držislav was granted the title of eparch and 'patrician' by Constantinople and the appropriate symbols of dignity were bestowed on him; thereafter Croatian rulers called themselves kings. Držislav and his heirs married into the Dalmatian patriciate and Venice. By his time, Croatian rulers had built a monumental complex of churches and tombs in Solin near Split, where many of them were buried and some were crowned.

## The 11th century: maturity of the Croatian Early Middle Age

After about 1000, Croatian society gradually recovered, like much of Europe. This culminated with Croatia's rise in the second half of the eleventh century under Petar Krešimir IV (1058-74) and Dimitrije Zvonimir (1075-89). Zvonimir strengthened the nation's international position because Pope Gregory VII conferred on him the title king of Croatia and Dalmatia. At that time he already had a court of a respectable size and was served by officials with Croatian names. Slowly but surely Croatia annexed the territory of Byzantine Dalmatia, and many of the cultural and ethnic differences between the Byzantine coast and the Croatian hinterland disappeared, although differences will always exist because of the different economy and way of life. Under Krešimir the Pannonian and Dalmatian parts of Croatia united into a single state. At the same time some Croatian towns showed signs of developing into commercial centres where goods were exchanged for money. The coastal regions, especially the cities of Split, Trogir and Zadar, profited greatly from their excellent position on sea and land routes leading from western Europe to Constantinople and, further on, to Jerusalem, the final goal of all the Crusades. A powerful but relatively small class of newly-rich citizens developed in the towns, its wealth coming from trade and the purchase of land, which was becoming increasingly precious. In the whole country, and especially in Dalmatia, monasteries were founded and grew strong as they acquired great estates of cultivable land. The process heralded the establishment of feudal relations, which became dominant in all Croatian lands in the twelfth century. This led to the disintegration of the traditional county system, which was reorganised on completely different principles in the high Middle Ages. After the 1060s monastery scriptoria issued a wealth of new documents, and the growing educated class espoused the written culture. The first inscriptions in the Glagolitic script and the Croatian language were carved in the late eleventh century. Although Glagolitic is a formal script reserved chiefly for religious writing and unsuitable for widespread use, these monuments are nevertheless the beginning of vernacular literacy and literature among the Croats. Architecture also went through a surge and embraced new forms that foreshadowed, and in the twelfth century finally grew into, the Romanesque style.

Croatian social development in the early Middle Ages thus peaked at the end of the eleventh century. The country began to resemble contemporary Europe in many external and internal characteristics. Early medieval development was firmly rooted in the traditions of antiquity, and it was crucially important that the main role should be played by the Slav, i.e. the Croatian, ethnicity. Pre-existing cultures in the region grew into the Croatian culture and became part of it, and culturally different regions on the newly-created Croatian ethnic territory slowly blended into an integral area of Christian civilisation with some regional features: the latter continued for a long time, and some still exist. The main elements of the Croatian early Middle Ages are thus the merging of the indigenous and the newly-arrived populations, the integration and complementary development of their cultures, the swelling force of Christianity, and the influences that reached Croatia from various parts of Europe. It was in the early Middle Ages, therefore, that the Croats defined the ethnic, political, territorial and cultural fundamentals that have remained essential right up to the present.

At the end of the eleventh century, kings of Croatian blood, members of the Trpimirović dynasty named after its founder Trpimir, disappeared and the Hungarian Arpad dynasty obtained the right to the Croatian crown through Zvonimir's widow who was sister to Hungarian princes. Knights of the First Crusade, mostly from France, travelled to Jerusalem through Croatia, and their description of it at that time is sombre. One reason for this impression was probably the struggle for the throne. The Hungarians did not manage to secure it till 1097, when they defeated the Croatian pretender Petar on Mount Gvozd (known today as Petrova Gora) in the Dinaric mountains.

# 4

# THE 12TH – 16TH CENTURIES: HUNGARY AND CROATIA UNITED UNDER ONE KING

## *Arpad Kings on the Croatian throne: the rise of feudalism*

In 1102 Coloman Arpad was crowned king of Dalmatia and Croatia, and the Arpad dynasty inherited the rights of Croatian kings. All the lands that made up the Croatian state – Croatia, Dalmatia, the duchy of Neretva and Slavonia (north of the Dinaric range) – were united under the Arpads. Byzantine authority over the coastal cities disappeared finally in the twelfth century. Both the Croats and the Venetians had always coveted those cities and the entire area of Byzantine Dalmatia, and now their fighting and disputes intensified. By that time the cities were almost completely Slavicised, with strong ties to the Croatian interior as well as close commercial and cultural connections with Italy. Control over the eastern Adriatic was of crucial importance for Venice because it secured command over an important section of the route to Byzantium and the eastern Mediterranean. The kings of Hungary-Croatia also wanted direct control over the coast and its hinterland, but this was often impossible, partly because the region was so distant from their seat in the Pannonian plain.

Hungarian influence was stronger in the north of Croatia (Slavonia). When the Arpads assumed the Croatian throne, they bestowed land in Slavonia on the Hungarian nobility, on whom they logically relied. Nevertheless Slavonia, like Croatia and Dalmatia, was separated from Hungary both territorially and organisationally, and a *ban* was appointed to rule it in the king's name. This separation became even more apparent when Slavonia was ruled by the king's brother or son with the title of *herceg* (duke); feudal forms of government modelled on those in Hungary were gradually introduced there. The old tribal counties (*županije*) and

21

their elders were replaced by royal counties as territorial units, and a sheriff (*župan*) was appointed to govern them and to command the county's army.

Only the king could grant land in Hungary and Croatia. The nobles on whom he conferred land came under his immediate authority and were tied to him by the fief and the obligation of military service. A fief was a separate economic, administrative and judicial unit, exempt from the authority of the *župan* – which conditions in general weakened, with the result that the king was forced to grant fiefs. This aided the rise of the Croatian nobility in the early thirteenth century, especially the Frankapan and Šubić families, some of whose branches remained important in the nation's history till 1671. In southern Croatia the great noble families grew so strong that they ruled almost independently of the Arpad kings, and began to seize land from others. The king turned a blind eye to this, but on the other hand he deliberately devalued the currency. This and other forms of oppression provoked the lower nobility into rebellion, and in 1222 they forced King Andrew II to issue the Golden Bull, a charter limiting the royal authority. Every year he had to convene an assembly (*sabor*) of the armed nobility and hear complaints and requests, and the nobility had the right to resist if he did not respect their privileges. In this way the lower nobility began to organise into an estate with political rights and judicial and administrative authority over the serfs. In 1273 in Zagreb the first *sabor* of 'All Slavonia' was held (today this region is Croatia north of the mountain of Gvozd (today known as Petrova Gora) and the Sava river). The nobility voted for various legal regulations and were clearly ambitious to rule alongside the king in accordance with the 1222 charter. The *ban* approved the assembly's conclusions. There was no great difference between these events and what was happening at the same time elsewhere in Europe.

By the twelfth and thirteenth centuries, towns had grown quite strong in Italy and Germany, and in Hungary and northern Croatia (Slavonia) the king and great lords granted various kinds of privileges and financial concessions to Italian and German craftsmen and merchants to attract them to the country. Part of the immigrant wave that swept through central Europe at this time reached Croatia: the newcomers were called guests (*gosti, hospites*), and joined with local people to build settlements along important routes, by crossroads and in the surroundings of castles where they practised their trade. They were under the king's protection and under the immediate authority of the *župan*. When the counties began to disintegrate, the powerful lords threatened to turn the communities of 'guests' into serfs. Because this was not in the king's interest, he supported the creation of free 'guest' communes subject to his direct authority. In the thirteenth century about fifteen Slavonian cities received royal charters granting municipal freedom, which some of them used to develop into major centres while others remained insignificant settlements. After the Mongolians devastated Hungary and Croatia in 1241-2, King Bela IV issued an especially large number of such charters to encourage faster development. The commune of 'guests' elected the city judge, who had administrative power, and the king granted them the surrounding land. Artisans and merchants could travel to markets without paying customs duties. Gradec (today part of Zagreb) received the greatest privileges. The Golden Bull of 1242 required the citizens to build city walls and organise their defence. They got their own judiciary, autonomy, privileges in crafts and trade, the right to organise fairs, and so on.

## The 13th and 14th centuries: Croatia flourishes again

The situation was different in the coastal cities. These were now faced with attempts at domination by both the Croatian king and Venice, and so developed their own political system. In the resulting social stratification the nobles tried to hold on to their power, and the newly-arrived and often rich commoners for their part tried to obtain the share of it to which they believed themselves entitled. Although the nobles yielded in time and admitted some of the commoners into their ranks, tension ran high for many more centuries. There was no feudalism in these communities. Peasants were tenants who enjoyed personal liberty, *colons* who could lease land at will and who by contract had the right to part of the harvest.

Between the twelfth and the fourteenth centuries the cities grew richer, capitalising on their excellent position on the eastern Adriatic maritime route and on their expanding trade with the hinterland. Bosnia developed in the mountainous interior, and Serbia became an increasingly important trading partner, even aspiring to dominate a part of the coast and Dubrovnik itself. There developed a variety of crafts in the cities, like shipbuilding and tanning, and traditional production in the surrounding areas, especially of wine, olive oil, salt and fish, both fresh and salted. Economic and commercial development was reflected in growth of the cities, such as Split where there was no longer room for everyone within the city walls and suburbs were created.

If the eleventh century was a time of monastery building, the thirteenth and later centuries left behind a different kind of structure. The newly-rich built splendid town houses in the developed Romanesque style, usually with three stories and a grand or un-adorned portal. Especially prominent in almost all the cities were the bishop's palace, town hall and loggia. Sculpture was closely linked to architecture and the most important sculptors were local men, Andrija Buvina of Split and Master Radovan. In 1214 Buvina carved the wooden door of Split cathedral with twenty-eight panels showing the life of Christ. Radovan built the magnificent portal of Trogir cathedral where the carving includes the nude figures of Adam and Eve, something exceptional and perhaps bold in contemporary European art.

In the 1220s and '30s the mendicant monastic orders came to coastal Croatia, the Franciscans and Dominicans, who unlike the earlier orders settled in the cities. Their monasteries and especially their churches changed the appearance of coastal cities because as a rule the orders built their houses at opposite ends of the city. They brought Gothic elements to Croatian architecture, sculp-ture and painting. Not to be outdone, the bishops built cathedrals in Trogir, Dubrovnik, Split and elsewhere. In Split the emperor-god Diocletian was replaced by another God when Diocletian's mausoleum (at the heart of the vast palace which he erected at the end of the third century) was turned into a cathedral and dedicated to the Virgin Mary, whose cult was already widespread, and later to the patron of Split, St Domnius.

The cities had to find a way to defend themselves, and their newly-acquired wealth allowed them to invest in town walls. These were built in Zagreb, for example, and in 1319 the con-struction of Minčeta, one of the strongest towers in Dubrovnik's walls, began.

The early thirteenth century brought a new atmosphere, and Croats began to gain first-hand experience of the Crusades. In

1202 knights of the Fourth Crusade levelled Zadar for the Venetian doge. In 1217 King Andrew II travelled across Croatia and embarked on his voyage to the Holy Land from Split, but did not have much success there. Finally, Dalmatian cities were the starting point for campaigns to quell the Bosnian 'Christians' (so-called Bogomils), a new dualistic heresy that found sympathisers within their walls as well. Although Dalmatian cities remained cosmopolitan, their clergy succumbed to the religious intolerance characteristic of Europe at the time.

In about 1170 some coastal communes began to employ notaries as public servants, which resulted in the appearance of the public document, and later the notarial or private document. In time the document became stronger proof than the living witness; thus a society founded on the written word was developing in coastal Croatian cities. Cities were given written statutes that codified common law, another step in the same direction. The first statute was written in the city of Korčula in 1214.

As the number of literate people increased, so did book production, at first in Latin. Although there are traces of annals and genealogies written in the old Benedictine scriptoria, it was only in the twelfth and early thirteenth centuries that the first hagiographies and chronicles appeared. These were the *Ljetopis popa Dukljanina* (Chronicles of the priest of Docleia) and the *Historia Salonitana* by Archdeacon Thomas of Split – the history of Split from antiquity up to the time of writing, and the best work of Croatian medieval historiography. The appearance of this excellent book, the first of its kind in Croatia, probably resulted from the great renown enjoyed by the Split church and its long-standing aspiration to educate its clergy. Thomas was born in the city about 1200 and probably studied canon and civil law in Bologna. He was not the only Croatian scholar to be educated abroad; many of these men returned home and helped build a new cultural atmosphere, while others remained in their places of study. One of the first to stay abroad and achieve fame was Herman from Dalmatia, born in Istria at the beginning of the twelfth century. He spent his youth in the south of France and Spain and became the most important translator of Arabic astronomical works in his time. His translations and his own writings greatly influenced the development of medieval European astronomy. He began too to translate the Koran into Latin.

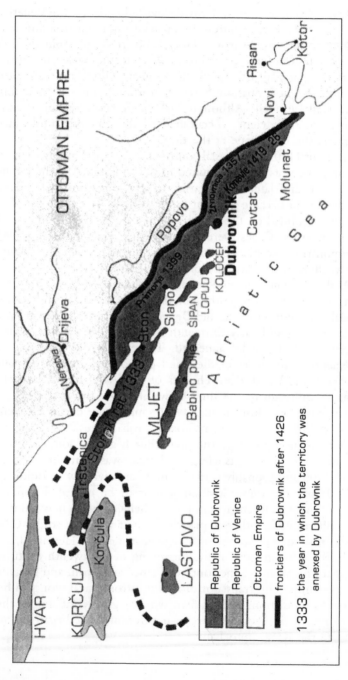

Republic of Dubrovnik

In 1301 the house of Arpad died out and a new dynasty acquired
the throne of Hungary-Croatia, the kings of Naples from the
French house of Anjou. The first Angevin king, who reigned till
1342, was Charles Robert. They were supported by the great
Croatian nobleman Pavao Šubić, count of Bribir, who thus displayed
the power of the Šubić of Bribir, ruler of the coastal cities of
Split, Trogir and Šibenik and of Bosnia in the interior. Pavao
Šubić became hereditary ban of Croatia and ruled like a king,
minting his own coins, trying nobles who offended, conferring
charters on cities and levying annual taxes on them. The other
Croatian nobles rose against him and his son Mladen and enlisted
the help of King Charles to remove them. After this the other
feudal families grew stronger, but they all had to submit before
the central authority of King Louis I, who managed to expel
Venice out of Dalmatia completely in 1358. After this for the
rest of the country the entire Croatian territory from the river
Drava in the north to the Adriatic in the south, and on the coast
from Istria in the north to Durres in today's Albania, was integrated
under one administration. As a result the economy in all of Croatia
flourished in the second half of the fourteenth century. A silver
coin, the *banovac*, began to be minted in Slavonia. New royal
towns were established on trade routes.

It seems that trans-Dinaric routes did not gain full affirmation
till then. Trade routes between the Adriatic and Hungary and
those to the west intersected in Zagreb. There were colonies of
Hungarian, German, Italian and French merchants in the city,
and Jews are also mentioned. At that time Gradec had more than
4,000 inhabitants, but after 1400 the population began to decrease
and did not regain that number till the end of the eighteenth
century.

New political and economic conditions brought the beginnings
of cultural integration between coastal and continental Croatia.
The vernacular Glagolitic script spread northward. The first literature written in the pure vernacular speech (with no admixtures
of Early Slavonic) dates from that time: prose describing the legend
of St Catherine and the *Životopisi svetih otaca* (Lives of the Holy
Fathers) and recasting pseudo-historical Western '*gesta*' like *Priče
o Troji* (The Tales of Troy) and *Aleksandar Makedonski* (Alexander
of Macedon). A copy of the latter was found in the late four-
teenth-century inventory of a Zadar merchant, and one of the

latter's peers possessed a text of Dante's *Divine Comedy*. All this shows that the written culture and the need for books were firmly rooted among laymen. What is more, they spread from the close urban communities to the interior. In 1368 in Lika Count Novak, a knight of the royal court, wrote a missal for the 'remembrance of my soul in prayer'. All this was no more than a pale reflection of literary life in the West, but in Croatia it was the peak of culture, especially that of chivalry, in that period.

## The independence of Dubrovnik: an encouragement of overall progress

Dubrovnik held a special place among Croatian cities, an instance of political independence being crucial for social, economic and cultural prosperity. It had been a city commune like the neighbouring cities but gradually developed into an independent republic during the twelfth and thirteenth centuries. In the mid-fourteenth century it was practically no longer under the jurisdiction of Hungarian-Croatian kings, and expanded its territory, mostly by purchasing land from Serbian and Bosnian rulers, along an extensive and important coastal belt. Immigrants from the interior and, later, refugees from the advancing Ottomans came there. At the end of the fifteenth century the republic may have had as many as 90,000 inhabitants, only a small number of whom lived inside the city. The economy relied heavily on trade; at first this was between the Balkan interior and the Mediterranean, but in the fifteenth century crafts developed and the republic began to export. Dubrovnik had small but influential colonies in Serbian and Bosnian towns, markets and mines. It surpassed all its competitors, even Venice, and became the leading intermediary between the Balkans and the West, its ships sailing to all the ports from the Levant throughout the Mediterranean and as far as Flanders and England. In this period Dubrovnik founded the first workshops in the Balkans for dying textiles, tanning leather, and manufacturing glass, wax and weapons.

Economic prosperity brought a public standard of living similar to that in Western Europe. In the fourteenth century the streets of Dubrovnik were paved, and it had sewerage and waterworks, the first system of quarantine in Europe for travellers to the city as a protection against epidemics, one of the first European orphanages, a hospital and a pharmacy. The following centuries brought the city even more glory and wealth.

## *The beginnings of crisis: a period of civil wars, Croatia between Venice and the Ottomans*

During Louis's reign the advantages of a unified state were fully apparent, but after his death in 1382 the forces of dissolution began to appear. Anarchy gradually set in, the logical consequence of the increasing might of feudal lords who for a time rallied around King Tvrtko I of Bosnia. Tvrtko rose successfully from being a Hungarian vassal to an independent sovereign, at the same time subjecting Croatia piece by piece to his direct rule until he became master of most of the Dalmatian cities. In 1390, when he added the title of king of Croatia and Dalmatia to his existing title, the power of Bosnia reached its peak. It became the focus around which many regions gathered, Serbian as well as Croatian, and its rule over the eastern-Adriatic coast brought it close to the goal of economic independence. However, Bosnia's rise was more the result of a set of propitious circumstances than of any particular military, political or economic strength, and when Tvrtko died in 1391 its strength was eroded by conflict between feudal lords and the resulting insecurity. For twenty-five years after 1382 Croatian lands were exposed to fighting between pretenders to the throne and powerful lords.

The crisis was comprehensive and felt by all social classes, because feudal clashes were joined by plague epidemics and fires that engulfed almost complete cities, most notably Zagreb. People criticised the ruling order. A Glagolitic poem from about 1400 accused the monastic orders and church prelates of serving their 'fat bellies' as if they were God, and said that the poor man who followed Christ's example was punished as a heretic. However, inclination towards heresy was probably real because of the feeling that the church could not offer any future. The number of Bogomils, members of the dualistic Bosnian church, grew in Croatian coastal cities. Even earlier an Englishman called Gvalterije (Walter), a follower of the reformer John Wycliff, headed a movement in Split against the church.

In 1408, while civil war raged in Croatia, one of the pretenders to the throne, Ladislas of Naples, sold all his rights in Dalmatia to Venice. After that Venice tore away one piece of Croatian territory after another and by 1420 held sway over Istria and cities and islands between the Kvarner gulf in the north-west and the border of the Dubrovnik republic in the south-east. Its power in the region lasted until the fall of the Venetian republic in 1797. The prosperity Dalmatia had enjoyed in the fourteenth century did not last; its cities had been of vital importance for Croatia as harbours and an outlet to the world, but for Venice it was merely strategically important for the control of maritime trading routes, and a potential competitor in trade and the production of very similar Mediterranean goods. The boundary between the Venetian republic and Hungary-Croatia, which ran through the immediate hinterland of the cities, long impeded trade and transit through Adriatic ports.

For several centuries from the late fourteenth onwards, the course of Croatian history was strongly affected by the coming of the Ottomans. The economy had to adapt to a new military and political reality; people had to move and became refugees. Catholicism waxed and waned as armies came and went. Fighting the Ottomans was an inexhaustible source of inspiration for Croatian poets and writers.

The Ottomans began their conquest of the Balkan peninsula in the mid-fourteenth century, appearing in Bosnia in 1386. The Croats probably confronted them for the first time in 1389 when a small Croatian unit fought on the Serbian side in the decisive battle of Kosovo between the Serbian army and the Ottomans. The businesslike Dubrovnik merchants tried to profit from the Ottoman presence and in 1396 were granted the right to trade in the empire. In that year, after defeating a great Christian army at Nicopolis, the Ottomans made their first appearance on Croatian territory, in Slavonia. In the 1420s their army appeared in Dalmatia. In the fifteenth century the kings of Hungary-Croatia tried to organise a line of defence, but every attempt ended in failure even though there was occasionally some initial success. When the Bosnian state finally fell to the Ottomans in 1463, conditions in Croatia deteriorated even further. Ottoman raids grew more frequent and ferocious: they were known as *akin*, and the raiders were *akindžije*. In early spring a group of Ottoman warriors – the size varied – would ride from the depths of Ottoman territory into the depths of Christian territory and burn and plunder the countryside, avoiding direct military conflict. In the autumn the raiders would return home loaded with rich booty. Several consecutive years of these raids emptied the country of peasants, who were completely ruined, and this left the small frontier castle garrisons without supplies. When the castles were finally surrounded by the Ottomans after several years of such treatment, they could offer no serious resistance. During one such Ottoman campaign in 1493 the Croatian nobility mustered an army and confronted the army of the Bosnian pasha in the Krbava Valley in Lika, but they were routed. The leader of the Croatian army, *Ban* Derenčin, was killed and a chronicler wrote that the 'flower of the Croatian nobility' was wiped out. After the battle the nobility were weak and impoverished and, under further Ottoman pressure, retreated into safer areas. Some of them did this in an organised way, taking their serfs with them. Waves of refugees moved to the north-west of Croatia, the coast and the islands, and also to areas outside the country. Large Croatian settlements were founded in Burgenland in eastern Austria, the west and south of Hungary and Slovakia, and others crossed from Dalmatia into Italian coastal areas. Later Croats also established villages in western Romania. Although most of the Croatian refugees were assimilated into the majority population, some communities still retained their identity at the end of the twentieth century. Many Croatian peasants fled to Slovenia and were completely assimilated; today the only clear proof of this migration is the large number of typically Croatian family names among the Slovenes. The early sixteenth-century migrations were the first stage of a process that lasted many centuries, in which Croatian ethnic territory underwent fundamental changes and finally lost its compactness. It took only thirty years from the battle of Krbava for the old nucleus of the Croatian state in the Dalmatian interior and the Dinaric mountains to be converted into Ottoman *sanjaks*, which triggered new immigration, some of it Serbian, from the interior of the Ottoman empire.

Ottoman conquest and Venetian conquest in Dalmatia, divided Croatia into three politically separate entities, among which hardly any links could be retained. This certainly had an extremely negative effect on the course of Croatian history because loss of territorial integrity led to a declining sense of economic and cultural integrity too. On the other hand, different parts of Croatia were exposed to different political, economic and cultural influences, which brought about the diverse and heterogeneous Croatian culture that exists today. Venetian rule meant influence from Italy, notably in language and culture. The European Renaissance attained its highest manifestation in Italy, and the flourishing of Renaissance art in the Croatian Adriatic region and the strong development of Croatian literature at that time were part of it.

Ottoman rule in south Slav countries in the seventeenth, eighteenth and nineteenth centuries, especially the nineteenth, was synonymous with oppression and a low level of development. However, although the Ottomans carved up the territory, caused migrations and brought misery to the Croats, in some parts of Croatia their rule functioned quite well until the end of the seventeenth century, and economy and trade were relatively well developed even on a European scale. Be that is it may, the Ottomans and the Venetians decided the future of the regions they ruled for many centuries to come. The strong regionalism that char-acterised Croatian history in the nineteenth and twentieth centuries is largely the outcome of events that took place at this time.

## *The other side of political breakdown: a thriving culture*

Despite political and military ruin, Croatian culture in the fifteenth century reached a high level. The first book in the Croatian language and the Glagolitic script was printed in 1483, the *Misal po zakonu rimskoga dvora* (Missal by the law of the Roman court). A new literacy developed under the influence of humanism and Italian Petrarchan and Renaissance poetry, first in Dubrovnik and then in Split, Hvar, Zadar and Šibenik, and at the end of the fifteenth century it had grown into a literature in the full sense. Although it never reached full maturity in Croatia's dismembered state, it did produce some works of lasting importance. In Dubrov-nik and other coastal and island communities, also in more northerly regions, writers of conventional love poetry were influenced by folk poetry, and these and other works have a stamp of originality, showing that their authors were closely tied to their native country. Because of this their poetry was never known outside Croatia, but Croatian poets gained European renown through their writing in Latin. No older Croatian writer approached the fame of Marko Marulić of Split, whose Christian morality texts were published all over Europe in their original Latin and in translation. However, even Marulić considered his epic poem in Croatian, *Istorija svete udovice Judite* (History of the saintly widow Judith), more important than any of those works.

In the art of the fifteenth century late Gothic elements remained mixed with those of the Renaissance. Byzantine influence was also felt, appearing via a roundabout route through its influence on Venetian art. Most building was done in Dubrovnik, and much of today's cityscape came into being at that time. The Rector's palace, the Divona customs house, the town fountains and parts of the town walls were built. Many buildings of that date were destroyed in the great earthquake of 1667. Šibenik's cathedral of St James represents a high point of late Gothic architecture and especially sculpture, but it also heralded the new Renaissance style. Much of it was designed and built in the 1440s by the outstanding Croatian master-builder of the time, Juraj Dalmatinac of Zadar. At the northern end of the Croatian coast line, in the small village of Beram in Istria in 1471 a local master painted a *Danse macabre*, reflecting late medieval sensibility on the foundation of 'folk theology'.

# 5

## THE 16TH – 18TH CENTURIES:
## CROATIA BETWEEN THE VENETIAN
## REPUBLIC AND THE OTTOMAN
## AND AUSTRIAN EMPIRES

In the 1510s and '20s Croatian humanists, aware of the catastrophe towards which Croatia was heading, addressed a number of West European potentates, including the Pope, in speeches and letters. In 1517 Pope Leo X called Croatia, as well as some other European countries, 'the ramparts of Christendom' (*antemurale christianitatis*). Two years later the humanist Tomo Crnić (Niger) described the country's desperate plight to the Pope and pleaded for help. If none came, said Crnić, Croatia would surrender to the Ottomans and thus open their way to the West. The idea of reaching an agreement with the Ottomans reappeared peripherally in later periods. Marulić's poem from that time, *Molitva suprotiv Turkom*, (Prayer against the Turks) was the first in a series of lamentations by Croatian poets over the fate of their homeland, a tradition which continued through the centuries.

Despite these efforts, the situation deteriorated from year to year: in 1521 the Ottomans conquered Belgrade, the 'golden key' to Europe, piercing the defence line at its most sensitive point. The way to Slavonia, the region between the rivers Sava and Drava, now lay open before them. Their victory in 1526 over the Hungarian army on the Field of Mohacs crushed the resistance of the Hungarian nobility, most of whom now sided with the newly-elected king and Ottoman protégé Ivan Zapolya; the Slavonian Sabor later did likewise. However, the Croatian nobility elected the Austrian Archduke Ferdinand Habsburg as king, who on his election pledged to 'honour, confirm and maintain' all the rights and laws of Croatia. Civil war broke out between Ferdinand's and Zapolya's supporters, which soon ended in an agreement to Ferdinand's benefit. Dynastic change did not result

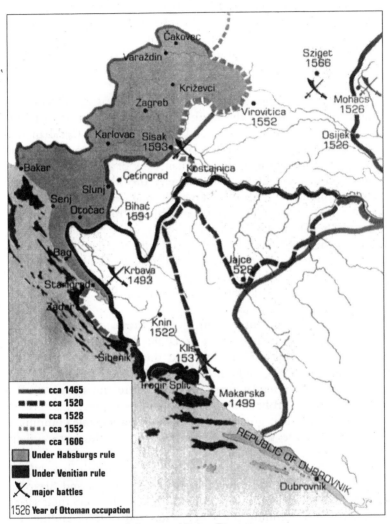

Advance of the Ottomans

in improved defences: Croatian cities fell to the Ottomans one after the other, and twenty-five years later Croatian territory under Habsburg rule had been reduced from 50,000 to about 20,000 km.[2]; it even began officially to call itself the 'remains of the remains of the formerly glorious kingdom'. For the Habsburgs it represented no more than a small cog in their great European policy.

One of the heroic episodes of these wars was the defence of Siget, a town today in the south of Hungary (Szigetvar in Hungarian). It is c. 30 km. west of Pécs. In 1566 the Croatian *ban* Nikola Šubić Zrinski held it with a small garrison in the face of an overwhelmingly superior Ottoman army of about 100,000 soldiers commanded by Sultan Suleiman the Magnificent, on his way to conquer Vienna. After a month-long siege all the defenders were killed, the last in a desperate attempt to break out of the town. The Ottomans had heavy losses too, which blunted their striking force. They also lost precious time and could no longer march on Vienna. Suleiman himself died under the walls of Siget. The heroism of Šubić immediately became a legend of heroism throughout Europe; he came to be known as the 'Slav Leonidas', and is still a Croatian national hero.

In the sixteenth century, during the Ottoman conquest, social stratification had reached a stage of stability in Croatia: the nobility had practically become a caste, and there were very few 'free men' who were not nobles. Many small nobles' communes disintegrated under feudal pressure. They were the remnant of a system of royal fortified cities whose members enjoyed administrative and judicial self-government based on considerable communal property. In places they built themselves 'tribal' castles to strengthen their defence.

At the time of the greatest weakness, when little was left of the formerly large kingdom but its name, Croatia and Slavonia finally united after many centuries of division. In 1558 their *sabors* united into a common body of 'estates and orders', ending the division into two administratively separate *banovinas*. This was connected with the long but irreversible process during which the centre of gravity of the Croatian state moved northward from coastal Dalmatia to the region along the Sava, and even further north. Zagreb gained in importance, as did nearby Varaždin, and because the north had a great need for safe sea harbours near at hand, the development of Rijeka and Senj in the northern Adriatic was encouraged. In this way Croatian territory lost compactness and Dalmatian towns were isolated from the more northerly regions. This was a difficult time for Dalmatia. Ottoman conquest narrowed Venetian territory to a thin coastal strip where the way life was different from that in northern Croatia. All the cities were under Venetian authority but they were nevertheless communes, each with different legislation and statutes and separate economic development. The economic and demographic crisis in Dalmatian cities was caused partly by the Ottoman presence and partly by the general European trend, whereby the Mediterranean was ceasing to be as important as the north of the continent and the Atlantic. Some Dalmatian communes fared better, particularly those on the islands that were far from areas of Ottoman domination, such as Hvar.

In this sombre environment Dubrovnik was a complete exception. Ridding itself of outside patronage of any kind such as it had had in earlier centuries, and underpinned by favourable contracts with the vast and prosperous Ottoman empire, it reached the peak of its development in the sixteenth century, mainly due to trade. Although Dubrovnik's business contacts reached distant lands, it had the special advantage that its merchants were the main mediators between the Balkans and Italian ports and cities. They had unquestionable advantages over Western merchants: an existing trading network developed in earlier centuries, knowledge of the language, and the fact that Dubrovnik presented no kind of military threat to the Ottomans or any other neighbouring country. However, by the end of the sixteenth century the first signs of crisis could already be felt. This came to a head in 1667 when Dubrovnik was levelled in a terrible earthquake and about half the population were killed. Only outstanding diplomatic skill managed to preserve the city's independence, but it never regained its old glory and wealth.

The parts of Croatia under Ottoman rule had a very different fate, and it certainly was not as black as folk tradition records. As one system of government and way of life disappeared, the Ottoman administrative system of *sanjaks* was immediately established and the land that had been left uncultivated was mostly settled by Christians from the interior. Some towns even had more inhabitants than during Hungarian-Croatian rule and became administrative or economic centres where markets were organised. Towns in Slavonia developed most quickly, especially Osijek, while small settlements in the barren Dinaric region lagged behind. Overall, conditions in the Ottoman empire were relatively favourable and this was reflected in Croatian lands under its rule, which lasted till the late sixteenth century and partly even into the seventeenth. The years of increasing crisis in the empire were also the last years of Ottoman rule in Croatian lands.

Some literary forms came to maturity at this time, confirming that the literary language was completely developed. For example, in the 1530s the first Croatian work in novel form appeared, *Planine* (Mountains) by Petar Zoranić of Zadar. Renaissance literature came to its fullest flowering in the comedies of Marin Držić of Dubrovnik. At the end of the century *Rječnik pet najuglednijih evropskih jezika* (Dictionary of five most prominent European languages) by Faust Vrančić of Šibenik was printed in Venice, in which 'Dalmatian' (by which the author meant Croatian) appeared alongside Latin, Italian, German and Hungarian. The choice of languages in the dictionary showed where Croatian cultural interests lay and indicated the future outline of 'Central Europe'. Vrančić was versatile, a true child of his time: diplomat, historian, philosopher and inventor, spending much of his life outside Croatia. His technical inventions included bridges, mills and even a parachute (*homo volans*). In Rome the Jesuit Bartol Kašić published the first grammar of the Croatian language a few years after Vrančić's *Dictionary*. Philologists and lexicographers continued to nurture the Croatian language, as they have done up to the present. Many other Croatian scholars and scientists were active at that time, but mainly abroad. Some became professors at Italian universities and in Vienna.

## The beginning of the military frontier and the turning-point in wars against the Ottomans

In the second half of the sixteenth century the Ottoman conquest slowed down; thus the reduction of Croatia's territory of 20,000 km.[2] did not go below 16,800. One of the factors in this was the beginning of efficient organised defence: Habsburg lands provided the money, and more numerous and better equipped mercenaries were drafted in to defend the frontier.

The entire defensive system was reconstructed with the establishment of a string of garrisoned castles along the Ottoman frontier. The system was centred at Karlovac, a new garrison town built on bare marshy land at a strategically important intersection of routes to nearby Zagreb and even nearer Slovenia. The fortress was shaped like a six-pointed star, and the town had a regular grid of streets and was surrounded by deep fosses. It was, and remains, an outstanding example of Renaissance town planning, a so-called ideal city.

However, in the 1580s and early '90s, when it seemed that their strength was waning, the Ottomans launched another offensive and pushed their frontier from the river Una to the river Kupa, thus increasing the pressure on Karlovac, with the danger that they would break through to the Slovenian border at that point and cut Croatia in half. However, the Ottomans did not move against Karlovac, which probably seemed impregnable, and the main blow had to be borne by Sisak at the confluence of the Kupa and the Sava, the last major fortress south-east of Zagreb. In 1593 the mighty Ottoman army was defeated under the walls of Sisak, and this marked the turning-point in many centuries of warfare on Croatian lands. In panic-stricken flight before the combined Croatian-Slovenian-Austrian army, many Ottoman soldiers drowned in the river Kupa, including their leader, the Bosnian Beglerbey Hasan Pasha Predojević. The 'year of dissolution', as it is known in Ottoman annals, broke the striking force of the Ottomans. The war that started then and continued till 1606 brought no great territorial gains to the Christian forces generally and thus to Croatia, but it showed that the initiative had passed to the other side. For the first time the post-war peace treaty was one between equals and the Austrian emperor did not have to pay tribute to the Ottomans.

An important role in the wars against the Ottomans was played by the Uskoks, descendants of Christians who had fled into Venetian Dalmatia before the Ottoman advance in the sixteenth century. Most of them quickly entered the service of Venice and, by order or on their own initiative, raided neighbouring Ottoman territory, plundering and attacking Ottoman soldiers and civilians. Later they and their families settled the northern Croatian littoral, especially around Senj. They were then already in Austrian service, and although the Ottomans were still their main enemies, they exploited political dissension between Austria and Venice and attacked Venetian ships, acting independently of major military campaigns. They were always in action, and their unexpected attacks exasperated the Ottomans on land and the Venetians at sea. They controlled the entire eastern Adriatic coast, as far as Dubrovnik. In 1573 five small Uskok boats captured the *Nava Contarina,* one of the largest and most modern Venetian ships carrying 300 soldiers and precious cargo, near Zadar. They towed the ship to Senj, and a small part of the cargo was returned. This and other attacks forced Venice to move against the Uskoks, and Senj was blockaded several times. Contemporaries compared this struggle with the impotent rage of a lion (the symbol of Venetian power) against the stings of a puny mosquito. A maritime super-power was resisted by a small number of daring sailors, 2,000 at most, who finally sailed right up to Venice itself and forced the republic to spend an astonishing 300,000 ducats a year on defence. The situation culminated in a war between Austria and Venice (1615-17), called the Uskok war. The result was that Austria had to agree to resettle the Uskoks in the interior, far from the coast, and burn their boats. In their last years on the coast the Uskoks were no longer just pursuing a struggle for liberation but had turned into looters; blockaded and pressed by poverty, they seized land from Croatian peasants or extorted tribute money from them as compensation.

The Uskok war between Venice and Austria was also fought in Istria. When it ended, the borders were unchanged but Istria was devastated, ravaged in addition by plague and malaria epidemics. The peninsula was divided between the two powers, and both governments began to encourage immigration – from Italy, from other parts of Croatia and from the Balkans. This brought Istria the ethnic diversity it has retained almost to the present.

Croatia's long-lasting and fierce wars against the Ottomans demanded the organisation of defence along new lines. Thus the frontier region was singled out and made into a separate unit directly under Austrian military administration. In the late sixteenth and seventeenth centuries, the depopulated land along the border was settled by the Vlachs, mountain inhabitants of both the Or-thodox and Catholic faiths (therefore, future Serbs and Croats) who came from the Ottoman side. They began to work the ruined and abandoned land and became frontier soldiers organised on the basis of a patriarchal-military order. In return they demanded independence from feudal overlordship, and the Orthodox frontiersmen also demanded religious freedom. The government had reason to give them such concessions because they proved themselves to be the best kind of defence. The Croatian nobility and clergy, on the other hand, waited too long to drop their demands to turn them into serfs and make them subject to church tithes. This inflexible stand enabled the government in Vienna more easily to remove the areas inhabited by the newcomers from the jurisdiction of the Croatian *sabor* and the *ban*. Among other things, The Vlach Statutes, enacted in 1630, granted the land to the Vlachs absolutely, enabling them to dispose of it at will. Almost at the same time the Military Frontier was organised as a separate Austrian province although technically it was still on Croatian territory. Its existence was a lasting threat to the survival of Croatia, whose area of some 10,600 square km. was only slightly greater than the *c.* 8,000 square km. of the Military Frontier.

## Reformation and Counter-Reformation

The great European social movement of the Reformation took strong root in Croatia's neighbour, Slovenia, but in Croatia itself it appeared only in fringe areas and was crushed by the onslaught of the Counter-Reformation in the early seventeenth century. The spread of the Reformation was not helped by the fact that some members of the greatest Croatian noble family, the Zrinskis, became Protestants. Matija Vlačić Ilirik, a Croat from Istria, was an important Protestant scholar who, in 1567, wrote and published in Basel the *Key to the Holy Scriptures*, a fundamental work of Protestant theology. He also encouraged the writing of the first systematic history of the church, consisting of thirteen large volumes (1559–74) in the typical manner of contemporary historical erudition. Each volume dealt with one century. Later the work was named the *Magdeburg Centuries* after the city in which the first volumes were printed.

The Jesuits played an important role in the Counter-Reformation. They arrived in Croatia in the mid-sixteenth century and, as in other parts of the world, took over education. Grammar schools were opened in several Croatian cities, and in 1669 the study of philosophy and theology was begun in Zagreb. This was followed

by the founding of the Royal Academy, from which emerged
the first university in south-eastern Europe. Many Jesuits played
important roles in Croatian culture and science in the seventeenth
and eighteenth centuries, their main purpose being to eradicate
the remains of the Reformation and Protestantism in Croatia. In
this they were very effective, receiving strong support from the
*Sabor.* At the beginning of the seventeenth century the *Sabor*
allowed the banishment of Protestants, and the Catholic faith was
proclaimed the only permitted religion, in contrast to the freedom
of religion in Hungary. In the northern town of Varaždin, for
example, a special commission was appointed which disbanded
the Protestant town council and rooted out Protestantism.

When the university was founded in Zagreb the centre of
cultural life definitively moved from the Dalmatian towns to the
north, primarily to Zagreb and Varaždin. Dalmatia, engulfed by
growing political and economic crisis, turned inwards, and artists
and scientists found themselves hampered in this constrained atmosphere. Dubrovnik was an exception because art could thrive
in the free and economically strong republic. The fact that Dalmatia
lagged behind Europe was reflected in architecture and the fine
arts. After the great heights reached in the fifteenth century, in
the seventeenth there were only a few periods of economic
prosperity in which patricians could build town mansions -- these
were few. The prominent artists and sculptors of southern Croatia
roamed through Europe and accomplished their best results in
other countries, far from the endangered and poverty-stricken
Dalmatian cities. Venetian Dalmatia was already peripheral in
European culture by the sixteenth century, and the trend continued
in the seventeenth and eighteenth centuries. The main reasons
were its position squeezed between Venice and the Ottoman
empire, which resulted in economic slowdown, and its loss of
the necessary hinterland in the Croatian interior.

Despite all the changes that gave a degree of cultural life, many
artists, scientists and scholars continued in the seventeenth century
to leave Croatia and go abroad. An outstanding figure was the
poet Ivan Gundulić of Dubrovnik, a classic of older Croatian
literature whose work showed faith in 'Slav' liberation from the
Ottomans, patriotism and the ideology of 'Catholic renewal'. The
progress of historiography was just as significant. The first historical
texts in the spirit of rationalism appeared in the sixteenth century,

and in the mid-seventeenth the first integral histories of the Croats were published: that by Juraj Rattkay in Vienna, and that by Ivan Lučić (Lucius), written in the then dominant erudite style of historiography, in Amsterdam (1667).

The Ottoman frontier became calmer, with the Ottomans engaged fighting in the east, and the Croatian nobles' light cavalry and their numerous armies fought on the side of the Habsburgs in the Thirty Years War. At this time Europe, especially Germany but also France, came to know Croatian soldiers (who were feared for their violent behaviour) and Croatian costume (from which the word 'cravat' originates).

## Eradicating Croatian consciousness: the Zrinski and Frankapan conspiracy

The seventeenth-century history of Croatia does not abound in memorable events, which gives even greater prominence to the conspiracy of the nobles Zrinski and Frankapan against the crown in 1670. Petar Zrinski was not only *ban* of Croatia; he was the most powerful grandee in the country, owning much of the land. The Zrinskis belonged to a branch of the Bribirski counts from the Šubić tribe, already mentioned in the twelfth century. They had to retreat to the north-west before the Ottomans leaving behind, among other things, silver mines and a mint in central Croatia. In the sixteenth century they acquired new properties mostly by purchase and through kinship. In size, number of inhabitants, and economic and military power their vast lands were like a regional kingdom, and tithes in money and in kind brought them great wealth and a host of serfs. The Zrinskis also developed a considerable economy raising cattle for the production of a special kind of cheese, and giving great attention to stock-breeding; they owned vineyards, a stud farm, saw-mills, a foundry and forge with 200 blacksmiths, flour mills, shops and inns. By exporting much of their produce, they were among the few who succeeded in including poverty-stricken and territorially reduced Croatia directly in European commercial currents. They made use of the best harbours, especially Bakar near Rijeka, where they warehoused leather, fabrics, wood, wheat, wine, iron products, salt, fish and olive oil.

Only Zrinskis and the last surviving branch of the formerly

large Frankapan family remained of the old Croatian higher nobility, but through owning vast estates in Hungary they played leading roles in the public life of both Croatia and Hungary. The brothers Petar and Nikola Zrinski were not only members of ancient families and exceedingly rich; they also wrote in Croatian and in Hungarian. For contemporary Croatian society they were both symbolic and actual bearers of the Croatian state tradition, and embodied the aspirations of its 'political class', i.e. the nobility and clergy, to increase their political independence. At the time this could only be expressed through the rights of estate-holders; and thus the struggle for political independence could not be separated from the immediate material and political interests of the nobility. However, in the second half of the seventeenth century Vienna was interested in centralising the administration of the state so that it could introduce a consistent economic policy of mercantilism, and so lay the foundations for an absolute monarchy. The main obstacle on this path was the independence of magnates.

Nikola and Petar Zrinski and their associate Fran Krsto Frankapan resisted Vienna's policy, and were additionally angered by its leniency toward the Ottomans. The Habsburgs were paying more attention to their greater-European goals, and less to freeing Croatia and Hungary from Ottoman occupation. The Zrinskis had fought against the Ottomans for generations. In the Habsburg-Ottoman war of 1663-4 they won many victories, and Nikola penetrated deep into their territory. When accounts of his bravery spread through Europe, Louis XIV of France sent him a gift of 10,000 thalers and created him a French peer; in 1664 Nikola was killed in a hunting accident. In the same year the Emperor signed a 'shameful peace treaty' with the Ottomans in the Hungarian town of Vasvar on the basis of *status quo ante*, although the war had been initiated by the Habsburg side. All this encouraged Petar to carry on with the plot, and he tried to develop the links with Louis XIV into a political alliance that would give the French king the throne of Hungary-Croatia and thus ensure continuation of the fight against the Ottomans. Although Louis XIV rejected this resolutely, he allowed Zrinski and some Hungarian nobles to believe that he might help them in their struggle against Vienna – until 1668, when Vienna sent Louis a favourable answer concerning the division of the Spanish inheritance. When hope for help from France failed, the conspirators turned to Poland and Venice, and finally even to the Sultan. They offered him too the crowns of Hungary and Croatia, and he refused. The conspirators then began to organise themselves. Petar Zrinski counted on help from the serfs, but the revolt was a complete failure. He and Fran Krsto Frankapan were arrested and finally executed in the suburbs of Vienna in 1671.

The plot largely reflected the contemporary mood in Croatia and met with a considerable response. Even some Orthodox Serbs sided with the conspirators, which made it the first occasion when members of the two religions fought together for the same political end. All the crucial problems of the Croatian people came to a head in the plot, which was the central event of Croatian history in the seventeenth century, with consequences that deeply affected the future. The Zrinskis and Frankapans were wiped out and soon no trace of them remained. Vienna could henceforth link Croatia more firmly with the central provinces of the empire.

At that time and for various reasons many people from all levels of Croatian society hated the Germans, and this hatred was expressed most notably in the work of Juraj Križanić, a priest and theologian. His ideal was to bring about a union of the churches, which Rome and Constantinople had tried to do without success for centuries. He believed that this might come about through closer relations between Slav Catholicism and the Russian Orthodox Church, and supported the idea that all Slavs had a common language and ethnic origin. However, he was not a pan-Slav if this meant seeking the political unity of all Slav peoples under Russian leadership. He considered that the only possible role for the Tsar to 'correct' or unify the orthography and script used in Slav-language books and awaken Slav consciousness through works conducive to education and logic. *In extremis* the South Slavs might join with the Russian tsar as a sovereign of the same language and people if the Catholic rulers supported his leadership in a war against the Ottomans. Although he had no direct followers, Križanić's work influenced many later South Slav thinkers who championed both reliance on Russia and South Slav cultural and political unification. After lengthy travels and fifteen years of exile in Siberia, Križanić died, misunderstood and disappointed, in battle during the Ottoman siege of Vienna in 1683.

*Croatian territory expands: towards a modern nation*

In 1683 the Ottomans began a war of conquest aimed at capturing Vienna, but their striking force was routed under the city walls and they retreated in apparent panic. In the next sixteen years much of northern Croatia was freed, from the town of Sisak eastward almost as far as Zemun which is today a suburb of Belgrade. This stabilised the border between Slavonia and Bosnia at Srijem, where it has remained almost unchanged ever since.

In the mid-seventeenth century Venice began to push the Ottomans out of the Adriatic coastal region. Late in the century it joined forces with Austria, and by 1718 they had gained territory and established the frontier with the Ottomans on what is today, with minimum changes, the state border between Croatia and Bosnia-Hercegovina. It was at this time that the territory called Dalmatia, which had often changed throughout history, finally got its present meaning. The Croatian historical provinces of Croatia and Dalmatia, separated by an Ottoman wedge for almost two centuries, now became contiguous again on Mount Velebit. Croatian lands enclosed the territory of Bosnia and Hercegovina on the north and south, acquiring their characteristic horseshoe shape.

The Muslim population in Ottoman-occupied parts of Croatia did not wait for the liberators but either fled or converted to Christianity. Soon the specific oriental features that had appeared in Croatian towns under Ottoman rule also disappeared as mosques and other structures were pulled down or put to different purposes. Today there are only negligible traces of the former Ottoman presence, mainly in the language and in place-names.

The liberation of considerable parts of Croatian territory brought new ideas, best expressed by Pavao Ritter Vitezović in his extensive and varied opus, especially the book *Croatia rediviva* (Zagreb, 1700), which he dedicated to 'all of Croatia'; he regarded Dalmatia as being part of Croatia. He assumed the words Illyrian, Slav and Croatian to be synonymous, and that all South Slavs were in fact Croats. His demands for the unity of all Croatian lands within the Habsburg empire were utopian for the time, but an important inspiration for Croatian revivalists a century and more later.

The great war of liberation at the end of the seventeenth century ended an important period in Croatian history. In the eighteenth century there were only two relatively minor wars.

In the first, in 1715-18, Venice and the Habsburgs fought the Ottomans and made minor territorial gains in Dalmatia and central Croatia. Then in 1737-9 the Habsburgs again campaigned against the Ottomans, but made no gains whatever; in fact, the Bosnian Muslims defeated the Habsburg army without help from the central provinces of the Ottoman empire. A time of frequent warfare, with a frontier that, fluctuated more or less constantly, was now succeeded by a time in which by economic and cultural contacts between Ottoman lands on one side and Austrian and Venetian lands on the other flourished. Croatia went through years of relative calm that fostered positive development. One of the more obvious results was an upsurge in Baroque art and architecture. In Slavonia fortresses and entire towns were built with a network of streets intersecting at right angles and a central main square, and the upper nobility built stately residences, often graced by gardens in the French style. Wealthy families built summer houses in Dalmatia, while old and dilapidated town houses, often wooden, were replaced by rows of Baroque mansions and citizens' house. This greatly changed the appearance of all Croatian towns.

In the eighteenth century Croatian artists, scientists and scholars continued to travel and reside abroad, but links with their homeland were now stronger. This was almost the last generation to live in an independent Dubrovnik, and its outstanding members were the composer Luka Sorkočević whose symphonies owed much to contemporary Italian composers, and especially Rudjer Josip Bošković, whose book *Theoria Philosophiae Naturalis*, printed in Latin in Vienna, achieved world renown, influencing not only contemporaries, but also scientists at the beginning of the twentieth century, especially in its interpretation of electronic motion. These cultural and scientific achievements reflected Dubrovnik's high level of development. It also developed socially despite economic difficulties; demographic transition, a change from high to low birth and death rates, began in Dubrovnik as early as the eighteenth century – ahead of other parts of Croatia where it did not occur till the end of the nineteenth century.

However, liberation from the Ottomans and the unification of Croatian lands under Christian rule did not bring the benefits that had been expected. The Croats had no great advantages from the spread of Venetian domination. Hopes that Austria would work to decrease the gap between newly-liberated lands and those it had ruled for almost two centuries were also dashed. Slavonia, which had in any case developed in its own way during about 150 years of Ottoman rule, now became attractive to foreigners who moved in and acquired – mostly through purchase – immense estates. Thus Slavonian society still differed from that of Croatia, in that it lacked a relatively numerous middle and lesser nobility, having only a few dozen large estate owners with many serfs stripped of all rights. Although the *županija* administrative system under the direct rule of the Croatian *Sabor* and *Ban* was introduced in 1745 in most of Slavonia, the nobility in the counties were financially subject to the Hungarian authorities. Six years later the joint Hungarian-Croatian *Sabor* decided, despite the protests of Croatian members, that the new Slavonian counties would also send representatives directly to the Hungarian Assembly as if they were Hungarian counties. After that, Slavonia lived a dual political life for almost a century and fell increasingly under Hungarian influence.

The former Zrinski and Frankapan estates around Rijeka were in a similar position. In 1670 the crown confiscated them because of the conspiracy, and after that they often changed owners. The most far-reaching consequence was the severing of economic and commercial ties between this region and its natural hinterland. Although the town and port of Rijeka became part of Croatia again at the end of the eighteenth century, it was still in a strange position because it became at the same time a special autonomous unit under the direct control of the Hungarian government. Thus a 'Hungarian Littoral' began to develop in Rijeka and its immediate vicinity, which came to be considered a Hungarian possession.

*Early modernisation attempts, revolts and Croatia's position in the monarchy*

Waves of capitalist development from Europe rolled into the Austrian empire, and in the eighteenth century the Habsburg rulers, especially Maria Theresa (1740-80) and her son Joseph II (1780-90), tried to reconstruct the society and state to meet the new needs. Vienna consciously initiated and exploited the new economic developments. It was natural that priority should be given to modernising the administration, finances, and the army which underpinned imperial power. From the beginning of the century various measures were introduced to encourage economic development, and internal customs were abolished. In 1717 free navigation along the Adriatic was proclaimed and ships sailing to ports under Habsburg rule were guaranteed safety. At the same time Rijeka and Trieste became free ports, which greatly advanced their development. Venetian domination over the Adriatic disappeared. In 1726 construction of the Caroline Road from Karlovac to Rijeka began, and was completed two years later: it was the first road linking the Pannonian plain with an Adriatic port, and enhanced the international importance of routes connecting the Danube basin with the Adriatic. Merchants from Rijeka and other parts of Croatia met strong competition from the Timisoara Company (from Timisoara in present-day Romania). There were fledgling attempts to establish industry in Croatia; at first this took the form of textile, silk and leather factories but most of them only worked for a few years before failing.. One of the greatest investments was the opening of a sugar refinery in Rijeka in 1751 with Dutch capital. It worked till 1828 using imported raw materials. A reason for the poor industrial development was that the government favoured the development of central parts of the empire; its fiscal policy and its bureaucracy encouraged industrialisation there, but in Croatia it was crippled by higher customs. Since, the owners of Croatian plants, and all their skilled workers were usually foreigners, the country felt little effect from this first, largely unsuccessful attempt to introduce capitalism.

Germans moved into Croatian towns in great numbers and brought with them some modernisation. In the 1760s the first books in German were printed there, and only a decade later German replaced Latin, first in schools and then in administration and the judiciary. The school system was reorganised. A Royal Academy of Science was founded in Zagreb in succession to the earlier Academy (dating from 1669), with three faculties: Philosophy and Theology, which had been founded earlier, and Law which began to function at that time. The former Jesuit library became the Academy library, and out of it later grew the present National and University library.

The Hungarian estate system was an obstacle to radical changes in Croatia, and thus Vienna's attempts at reform mostly came to realisation in the Military Frontier, which had expanded during the liberation of new territories at the end of the seventeenth century and was of almost the same area as Civil Croatia (see map, p. 35). The armed peasants had to be turned into regular soldiers, in accordance with current European military theory, and because the Ottoman frontier was now stable, the Military Frontier was slowly turned into great army barracks that provided most of the Habsburg military strength during the next century or so, until general military service was introduced in the second half of the nineteenth century. The frontiersmen fought throughout Europe, wherever Habsburg policy had need of them. These reforms completely changed life in the Military Frontier, in which the patriarchal community was extremely reluctant to renounce its privileges and resisted every innovation. Between 1730 and 1755, during the greatest changes, the frontiersmen in the broad area from the Pannonian plain to the Adriatic revolted seven times, fighting for their 'old rights', and managed also to arouse the serfs in neighbouring Civil Croatia. Though aware of the dissatisfaction of the frontiersmen those serfs wanted to become part of the Military Frontier because villeinage service and the constantly growing taxes were becoming increasingly difficult for them to bear. This was the motive behind the biggest revolt, in 1755, a chain of mostly spontaneous outbursts of rage in which, among other things, about thirty manor houses were burned. After that the nobles' army fell on the peasants, crushing the uprising and destroying their property. When the situation had calmed down, the government enabled Croatian peasants for the first time to air their complaints against the feudal lords before a special royal commission with extraordinary powers. The government intervened between the lords and the serfs and, wanting to preserve existing social relations and ensure the increase of state funds, it laid the foundations for the Croatian *urbar* (schedule of taxes and duties the serf had to pay to his master). This developed in the following years, and all the earlier private arrangements between feudal lords and serfs were replaced by common legal regulations for all the manors. The worst forms of feudal exploitation were abolished, and minimum holdings for serfs and maximum demands permissible for the lords were fixed.

When the Enlightenment swept through Europe, it was echoed in the Croatian lands. In 1762 the Slavonian Matija Antun Relković published *Satir ili divji čovik* (Satyr or the Wild Man), the first book in the region to gain wide popularity; it championed economic

progress and announced a struggle against backwardness, super-
stition, prejudice and bad Ottoman habits. The first edition was
printed in Dresden, the second in 1779 in Osijek. Six years earlier
the Dalmatian Andrija Kačić Miošić published *Razgovor ugodni
naroda slovinskog* (Pleasant Talks of the Slav People) in Venice, a
chronicle in verse and prose of events from the time of Alexander
the Great to the early eighteenth century. It was written in the
'folk language' and could be read by 'the poor, peasants and
shepherds'. This book gained unprecedented popularity, becoming
a folk 'song book' and for many the only source of knowledge.

The basic problem for Croatia, which would continue until
the monarchy's fall in 1918, emerged in the early eighteenth
century and grew more acute as time passed: how to preserve
independence in the infighting between Hungary and Vienna.
After Hungary liberated most of its territory from the Ottomans
at the end of the seventeenth century, the Hungarian nobility
tried to bring the laws of Croatia into conformity with those of
Hungary, and thus strike a blow at the strongest assurance of
Croatian independence. In 1712 the Croatian *Sabor* issued the
*Pragmatic Sanction.* The document confirmed that under certain
conditions it would recognise the female Habsburg line, but in
fact it emphasised that the Croatian *Sabor* made independent
decisions and that therefore the country was independent of Hungary. In the strife between the two Vienna tried to remain neutral
and please both sides: in 1715 it helped the Croats to ensure that
the common Hungarian-Croatian *Sabor* would have no jurisdiction
in internal Croatian affairs, but in its own dynastic interests it
agreed in 1723 to the Hungarian Assembly proclaiming Croatia
an indivisible part of Hungary. The 1715 settlement became one
of the most important arguments favouring the political and territorial independence of Croatia.

In the following decades relations changed. The reforms of
Vienna's 'enlightened absolutism' shook the foundations of the
state organised on the estate system and threatened the positions
of the Croatian nobility, who therefore sought security in links
with their Hungarian counterparts. In doing so they were primarily
striving to defend the interests of their order. However, they
were the Croatian 'political nation' (contrary to the commoners,
who were called the 'adjoined poor nation'): their estate privileges
included the 'municipal rights' which at that time expressed

Croatia's political individuality. Thus they did not accept even those measures initiated by Vienna that would in future contribute vitally to Croatia's position of independence. In 1767 the crown appointed a Croatian Royal Council as the central administration in northern Croatia to administer political, economic and military matters. It was headed by the *ban*, and executively independent of Hungary. But this made Croatia dependent on Vienna, which encouraged social and economic modernisation based on centralisation. The Croatian nobility were dissatisfied, and fiercely opposed many measures of the Viennese authorities, especially those designed to introduce a military regime in part of Civil Croatia which would have ended their privileges. All this made the government change its mind; the Croatian Royal Council was abolished in 1779, and Croatia was subjected to the royal Hungarian chancellery, as the result of which the Hungarians began to consider Croatia a 'subject' and not an 'allied' kingdom. This continued till 1848. The first seat of the royal council was the northern town of Varaždin, which at that time was in serious competition with Zagreb. But in 1776 it suffered a devastating fire, and administrative functions were moved to Zagreb, which has since been the undisputed capital not only of northern Croatia but of the whole country.

The crown's attempts at reform reached a peak in the reign of Joseph II, who tried to forge a new social order, abolishing serfdom and introducing general taxation. The emperor himself thought that the reform should begin in the Catholic church: he wished to subject it to the state and liberalise relations between different confessions. In 1781 he issued the 'patent on religious toleration', emphasising his wish to achieve 'brotherly accord' among his 'subjects of different religions'. Implementation of the decree in Croatia began in 1783, which meant that Protestants and Jews started to move there and into Slavonia; previously they had only been allowed temporary residence. They were also granted certain rights, e.g. to perform public services, and be educated at schools and at the university. In the following years Jewish communities were founded in northern Croatia, and in 1786 the Orthodox Serbs and Greeks also set up communities and parishes in Zagreb. The Emperor standardised church rites, holidays and fast days, and ruled that senior church dignitaries could not also perform state functions. He tried to improve the lives of the lower clergy and fixed their minimum pay. All these reforms demanded extensive financing, and in 1781 he followed the precedent of the Jesuit order: it was suppressed in 1773, and its land and property were transferred to a school endowment, and its schools came under state administration. In 1781 the Emperor abolished all the men's and women's orders not engaged in caring for the sick or teaching. In this way many important monasteries and convents were closed in Croatia.

At the same time Hungary was subjected to a new administrative division in an attempt to break up historical districts founded on an ethnic basis. In 1785 Croatia disappeared as a separate administrative entity and Croatian and Slavonian counties were joined with several others. As the result the districts of Zagreb and Pecs (a town in Hungary) were formed. The office of *ban* still existed in Croatia but was only nominal because he was at that time the Emperor's commissioner. All this was designed to unite the Habsburg lands, all so varied in ethnic composition and historical tradition, into a stable community which would be cemented by German as the official language.

In 1787 Austria and Russia went to war against the Ottomans, intending to seize as much Ottoman territory as possible. However, when the Austrian army encountered difficulties in 1789, more soldiers had to be mobilised and more money raised. Great dissatisfaction had been caused in Hungary and Croatia at that time by the reforms, and a new financial burden could have sparked a revolt. Joseph II promised to convene the *Sabor*, and then returned Hungary and Croatia to the political conditions that had existed on his accession. All that remained was the patent on toleration and the abolition of serfdom. There was great joy in Zagreb when the constitution was returned, and the current *ban*, Balassa, had to flee the town 'before the rage of the youth'. But in 1790 Joseph II died, and attempts at modernisation ended, at least for a time.

In spite of difficulties, the war against the Ottomans went well. In 1790 the Austrian army took some strategic points and villages in the Plitvice Lakes region of central Croatia, and when the war ended in 1791 the peace treaty fixed the line that separated the armies as the new frontier between Austria and the Ottoman empire. That line is today the frontier between Croatia and Bosnia-Hercegovina.

# 6

# 1790-1918: DEVELOPMENT OF
# THE MIDDLE CLASS

The period 1789-90 was crucial in the history of both Europe and Croatia. Processes that began then, such as the integration of the Croatian nation and the first breath of modernisation, were to affect the country's history throughout most of the nineteenth century.

This period of revolutionary and national movements in the whole of Europe found the Croats living on the southern and south-eastern fringes of the Austrian empire, although many of them also lived in the Ottoman empire in Bosnia-Hercegovina. Both empires possessed immense territory but were internally weak because the conditions that had led to their development and great power in past centuries had ceased to exist; yet neither was capable of changing its structure to meet the challenges of more modern political systems. As a result they were in permanent constitutional crisis right up till their disintegration early in the twentieth century. The growth of national movements intensified the crisis. That in Croatia was faced not only by the Hungarian national movement but also with attempts by both Vienna and Budapest to impose hegemony. From their position of weakness the Croats tried to gain whatever they could, often being forced suppress their logical ambition to create an independent state.

As we have seen, the death of Joseph II in 1790 put an end to his modernisation programme – this was largely due to the resistance of the upper classes – and the organisation of the state reverted to the *status quo ante*, which meant that Croatia again became administratively dependent on Hungary and lost its financial autonomy. Even so, in principle the Croatian nobility did not renounce their claim to the right to an independent government, and at the 1790-1 session of the joint Hungarian-Croatian parl-

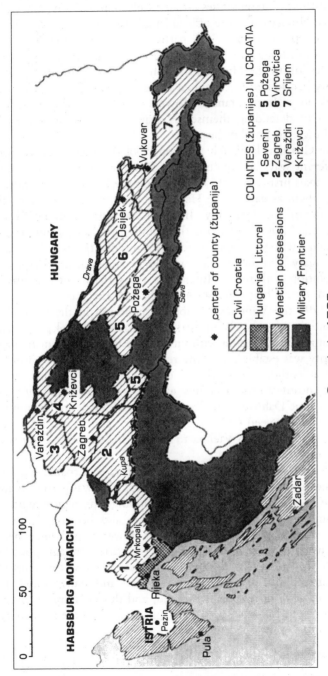

Croatia in 1785

COUNTIES (županijas) IN CROATIA

**1** Severin    **5** Požega
**2** Zagreb    **6** Virovitica
**3** Varaždin    **7** Srijem
**4** Križevci

✦ center of county (županija)

Civil Croatia
Hungarian Littoral
Venetian possessions
Military Frontier

iament their representatives emphatically opposed attempts to introduce Hungarian as the official language in Civil Croatia. Later, however, the Croatian *Sabor* partly gave in, allowing the introduction of Hungarian as an optional subject in schools. This was a concession to the Hungarian nobility with whom the Croatian nobility had joined forces when faced with the danger of revolutionary ideas from France. However, this was when the long process of defending themselves against nationalistic attacks by the Hungarian nobility began.

The Croatian lands felt the impact of the French Revolution in different ways, although there was never any mass movement. The Croats first came into contact with the French when fighting against them as part of the Habsburg army in northern Italy, the Netherlands and Germany. In 1794 an anonymous poem was published in Zagreb attacking the nobility and clergy, and praising the French who were fighting for the rights of citizens and peasants. In Hungary a former Franciscan, Ignjat von Martinović, plotted a revolution with some Hungarians and Croats, but this was an isolated case. They were soon caught and executed.

In 1797 the Venetian republic disappeared in the turmoil of war and its possessions in Istria, Dalmatia and Boka Kotorska were annexed to Austria without much difficulty. When Austrian authority was established in the region there were some disorders aimed at ending the privileges of the nobility, but the leaders were as hostile to the 'Jacobins' as they were to the nobility. For the first time Dalmatian intellectuals expressed a desire for political unification between Croatia and Dalmatia, and Dalmatian representatives travelled to Vienna to present this request. They were disappointed.

The coastal region, once the richest part of Croatia, was in a wretched state when Austria took it over. This was partly because Venice had had no interest in developing this region with an economy similar to its own, but partly also because, before it fell, Venice was no longer the great power it had once been. The Austrians were interested only in Dalmatia's strategic position, not in its economic development. Nevertheless, the Austrian government did establish free navigation and trade, which the Venetian government had restricted, and this encouraged overall development. But even in 1918 Dalmatia was still the Monarchy's most poorly developed province.

French victories against the Monarchy continued and in 1805 the Austrians ceded Istria and Dalmatia. In the following year the French army entered Dubrovnik and soon that long-lived republic formally ceased to exist. Finally, in 1809 the French established their rule in all the Croatian lands south of the Sava and formed the Illyrian provinces with their capital in Ljubljana, which once more closed Austria's outlet to the sea. The French did not hide their ambition to expand eastward and weaken their major enemies, the British (in their trading and maybe their strategic routes) and the Russians. In 1805 the Russians occupied the southernmost part of Dalmatia, Boka Kotorska, and did not withdraw until two years later, after which the British navy sailed into the Adriatic. The exchange of British goods from India for Central European goods began in the Adriatic on a large scale despite French attempts to prevent it by introducing a blockade and the death penalty for smuggling. The British responded by a counter-blockade from Trieste south to Corfu, occupied the farthest outlying Croatian island of Vis, and in the next year and a half requisitioned as many as 218 Austrian ships.

The French government initiated widespread social reforms. They abolished differences between the 'estates', making all people equal in rights and obligations to the state; introduced a modern administration and judicial system; and improved the economy and education. Chambers of the different economic interests were founded and universities and high schools opened in Dalmatian cities. Roads were built linking the interior with the nearest points on the Adriatic coast, and for the first time the sea depth in the Adriatic was systematically measured. The Venetian democrat Vicenzo (Vicko) Dandolo became governor of Dalmatia, and his goal was to Italianise the region by introducing the fruits of the Enlightenment. However, when he allowed the *Kraljski Dalmatin* (King's Dalmatian, 1806-10) to be published in Croatian as well as Italian, he helped to awaken Croatian national consciousness. This first Croatian-language newspaper had a circulation of between 500 and 1,000. In 1809 the former military commander of Dalmatia, Marshal Auguste-Frédéric-Louis Marmont, became governor of the newly-founded Illyrian provinces. He wanted to give public life in the region a strong national character, but Croatian society was not mature enough to turn those beneficent intentions to its advantage. There was no class able to benefit from the freedom

of crafts he introduced, nor was national consciousness sufficiently
developed for people to consider the opening of schools in Croatian
a great step forward. In any case, the ideas of the Revolution
were by that time seriously tarnished, and hence these broad
reforms seemed out of place. The power of Napoleon had begun
to decline, leading to increased taxation and military recruitment,
and this, together with commercial stagnation, rapidly brought
the country to ruin. Such a state of affairs made it easier for
people to return to things as they had been. After Napoleon's
fall and French withdrawal, Austrian rule over the Croatian lands
was resumed. The memory of radical reforms quickly faded after
the Austrian authorities declared all laws of the earlier state null
and void.

Croatia again faced the fragmentation of its territory. Those
parts previously under the Venetian republic, the Dubrovnik
republic and the bay of Boka Kotorska now became part of the
province of Dalmatia and directly subject to Vienna. On the
other hand, the Croatian nobility had come, during the reform
attempts of Joseph II, to rely completely on the Hungarians. This
led to concessions, one of which was to change Hungarian from
an optional to a compulsory subject in secondary schools.

Life became very difficult. In 1811 the state went bankrupt.
In 1812 the Hungarian parliament was dissolved and Emperor
Francis I introduced absolute rule – the regime of Metternich. A
period of crop failure and famine followed after 1815, but according
to some statistics overall conditions were improving. A larger
amount of European trade began to pass through Croatia, and
the first factories were built. Demographic statistics reflected the
changes: from 1785 to 1805 the population increased by 3.4 per
cent, and between 1805 and 1840 by as much as 30 per cent.

*Towards a modern nation: the Revival Movement*

Ideas of modernisation and revival came to Croatia slowly but
steadily in the late eighteenth century. At first their focus was
Maksimilijan Vrhovac, bishop of Zagreb, whose many and varied
activities included the purchase of a printing press in 1794 on
which, during the next thirty years, he printed many literary,
scientific and religious works at his own expense. He also helped
to found the first civilian general hospital in Zagreb modelled on

that in Vienna. When French administration ended in 1813, it was Vrhovac who demanded a new administrative framework for the unification of 'Croats south of the Sava' with northern Croatia; Vienna considered this a 'possible source of disorder'. Vrhovac also took a key role in opening the Academy library (later the National and University library) to the public in 1819. He donated several thousand volumes and instructed the clergy to collect popular lore, old books and 'Illyrian' words, proverbs and songs.

The work of Josip Šipuš was also important. In 1796 he wrote the pamphlet *Temelji žitne trgovine* (Bases of the Wheat Trade), the first work of economics published in Croatia. In the spirit of the French Revolution, Šipuš supported the development of trade and emphasised linguistic unity as one of the conditions for progress. After many important publications in the eighteenth century, in 1801 Joakim Stulli, a Franciscan from Dubrovnik, published a major three-language Latin-Italian-Illyrian (i.e. Croatian) dictionary of almost 5,000 pages. In contemporary European national revival movements, language was considered an essential feature, and hence extensive work was done on researching and promoting vernacular speech. At that time Croatia was politically and culturally disunited and regionalism ran high. Of the three dialects – Štokavski (in central Croatia, Slavonia and Bosnia), Čakavski (mostly on the coast) and Kajkavski (in the north-west around Zagreb) – each had its own norms, but it was gradually accepted that a standard language and orthography might be a way to overcome territorial fragmentation and lay the foundations for Croatian national integration. It was believed that a common standard language would be a basis for introducing the Croatian language into public life; at that time the official language in northern Croatia and Slavonia was Latin.

After 1810 there were many suggestions for how to achieve a standard language for all Croatian regions, but no important results were achieved till the late 1820s. In 1829 a group of very young people in Zagreb, under the capable leadership and organisation of Ljudevit Gaj, championed the idea of linguistic unity and in time others joined them. Not all were Croats; there were Slovenes (Stanko Vraz), Greeks (Dimitrije Demeter) and Serbs, and Gaj's own family roots were in Burgundy and Slovakia. Although some nobles joined the group, most of the members were commoners: merchants, intellectuals and professionals – members of the fledgling bourgeois class that had begun to develop in the lap of the traditional 'feudal' society. This was where the foundations were laid for Croatian national integration. It was a movement of the prosperous, because only merchants and the owners of large estates could acquire significant amounts of capital. In 1830 Gaj wrote *Kratka osnova hrvatskog pravopisa* (Foundations of Croatian orthography) in which he proposed the development of a single orthography for all South Slavs, especially those who used the Latin alphabet. Language unification would provide a foundation for resisting the Hungarian nobility; in Hungary the national movement was growing in importance and attempts had begun to create a national Hungarian state from the Carpathians to the sea. The 'Foundations' provided the basis for a common orthography for all Croatian lands, and marked the first step in introducing contemporary ideologies of national integration into the early stages of the Croatian national movement.

Later the Illyrians chose the Štokavski dialect as the foundation for the standard language. This dialect was most widespread among Croats, but was also spoken by Serbs, and by choosing it the Illyrian leaders made plain their wish to incorporate the broader South Slav language community in the movement right from the beginning. Its leaders tried to give it breadth by calling it Illyrian, a name that had already been used in administration (e.g. by the French) and in literature. In the eighteenth country it was considered by scholars that the name of the Illyrians, the ancient inhabitants of the Roman provinces Dalmatia and Pannonia, might be a suitable umbrella for all the South Slavs, including the Macedonians and the Bulgarians, that would cover all regional and vernacular names. At that time Slavists regarded all the Slavs as one people speaking a single language with four dialects: Russian, Polish, Czech and Illyrian. Since scholars believed language to be the basic attribute of nationhood, the Illyrians wanted to introduce one 'Illyrian' standard language. This gave birth to the idea of a single 'Illyrian' nation including all the South Slavs, allegedly the descendants of the ancient Illyrians. The name 'Illyrian', however artificial, was the most suitable way of combating regional antagonism since it encouraged the belief that the Slav population was indigenous in south-eastern Europe. This feeling of strength was necessary as a counterweight to Hungarian and other external pressure.

All the Illyrian dreams and attempts to spread their ideas to Slovene and Serbian national territory (they hoped above all to establish links with the Serbs in Vojvodina, which was part of the Habsburg Monarchy) proved fruitless, although some enthusiasm for Illyrism was manifested. Slovene and Serbian feelings of national consciousness also began to develop at that time; the Slovenes had long been working on their own standard language, and the existence of the principality of Serbia strongly boosted the Serbian national movement. Thus the Illyrian movement remained as it had begun – a Croatian national movement. It did, however, lay the foundations for Croatian national consciousness and for the idea of South Slav solidarity, and the name 'Illyrian' was successfully used to combat Croatian regionalism. The innate difficulty of regional partisanship that the process of national integration encountered is summed up in Ljudevit Gaj's advertisement for his newspaper in 1834, in which he cited 'Croats, Slavonians, Dalmatians, Dubrovchani, Istrians, Bosnians.'

The Illyrian resistance to Hungarianism was not confined to language but included language-related issues in Hungarian-Croatian relations, and in relations between the Croats and Vienna. In 1825 the Emperor convoked the Hungarian and Croatian parliaments after a time-lapse of almost fifteen years, a sign that absolutism was weakening. The Croatian *Sabor* in Zagreb instructed its deputies in the joint parliament to place on the agenda the unification of Civil Croatia, Istria (which by imperial decree had become a single administrative and political entity), the Military Frontier and Dalmatia. In the following year, however, the Chancellery (*Staatsrat*) in Vienna opposed the wishes of the *Sabor*, and at the same session Croatian deputies came into conflict with the Hungarian nobility, who demanded the introduction of Hungarian as the language of instruction in all lands subject to the Crown of St Stephen. The Croats fiercely opposed this and supported the use of Latin. Already in 1830, at the next session of the joint Hungarian-Croatian parliament, Croatian deputies were attacked anew by Hungarian nationalists. Although the Croatian *Sabor* had agreed to accept the introduction of Hungarian as a compulsory subject in Croatian schools, the unexpectedly strong Hungarian pressure made them temporise. The official language remained Latin. The basic strategy employed by Hungarian deputies was to deny Croatia's individuality as a state, which was expressed in its municipal rights; they claimed that Hungary and Croatia were not allied kingdoms but that Croatian lands were parts of Hungary and subject to it. The Croatian *Sabor*, in order to find arguments to support its contentions, organised the collection and transcription of documents underpinning Croatian rights. In 1830 Josip Kušević published *O municipalnim pravima i statutima kraljevina Dalmacije, Hrvatske i Slavonije* (On the Municipal rights and statutes of the kingdoms of Dalmatia, Croatia and Slavonia), presenting the Croatian nobles' interpretation of Croatian state law. He expounded the origins of the Croatian state and the link between it and the Hungarian state, which was based on a contract in 1102 between the Croatian nobility and the Hungarian king. This ensured the state's continuity. As time passed this interpretation of Croatian state law changed somewhat, but it remained an important part of Croatian national integration ideologies and political activities right up till the end of the twentieth century.

On their return to Zagreb Croatian deputies reported to the *Sabor*: 'The Hungarians attacked the municipal rights of Croatia with great ferocity; this time we managed to defend our laws, but we are seriously afraid that we will not be able to do so at the next session.' These clashes were the beginning of a struggle between Croats and Hungarians that culminated in 1848-9; however, the problem remained unresolved till 1918.

Preparations for the next parliamentary session were much sounder. In 1832 Count Janko Drašković (1770-1856), closely allied to the younger generation, wrote the first political pamphlet in Croatian: *Disertacija ili razgovor darovan gospodi poklisarom* (Dissertation or conversation presented to our Gentlemen Deputies). It provided the political and social programme that the deputies of the Croatian nobility were to put forward at the session of the joint parliament. The 'Dissertation' advocated some reforms of the feudal system and an economic policy which would encourage a degree of capitalist development. It demanded an independent Croatian government and the introduction of Štokavski as the official language. It also upheld the idea of establishing an Illyrian kingdom uniting all Croatian and Slovenian lands on the basis of Croatian state law (in the case of Croatia, Slavonia and Dalmatia), language similarity (in the case of Slovenia) and the principle of Croatia's historic territory (in the case of Bosnia). The kingdom would be part of the Habsburg empire and have close political links with Hungary. The economic and social demands in the 'Dissertation' were moderate, but its tone was nationally and politically resolute: 'We do not wish any other nation to consider us just as a mass to increase their number. [Nor do we wish], or others to abuse us, rebuke us and be suspicious of us while we are supposed not even to open our mouths or say a word.'

The Croatian *Sabor* passed Drašković's programme, and it was acclaimed by the small but increasingly influential middle class, thus becoming the programme of the Croatian political élite. This moment marked the end of the Croats' defensive policy in the face of nationalistic Hungarian encroachment.

The Illyrian movement developed into what became known as the Croatian National Revival, and accelerated the development of a modern nation that had begun at the end of the eighteenth century. But integrating the Croatian nation was to prove by no means easy. Split between different administrative units, both in the Habsburg monarchy and in the Ottoman empire, the Croats had weak economic and political ties. The upper classes were traditionally more closely identified with their own regions (central Croatia, Dalmatia and Slavonia), and their interests rather than, as later, with Croatian lands as a whole.

In 1832 Ljudevit Gaj wrote the poem '*Horvatov sloga i zjedinjenje*' (Croatian Concord and Unity) or, as it was later known (after its first line), *Još Hrvatska ni propata* (Croatia is not finished yet). It became very popular and was called the 'Croatian Marseillaise'. Patriotic songs of this kind were a good means of mobilising the masses. Like many others written at the time, it symbolised the basic strivings of the Croatian Illyrians: to unite all Croatian regions into one entity and forge links with other Slav peoples.

The real beginning of the Croatian National Revival came in 1835 with the first number of Gaj's *Novine Horvatske* (Croatian News). Contributions in the literary supplement *Danica Horvatska, Slavonska i Dalmatinska* (Croatian, Slavonian and Dalmatian Morning Star) – fiction and poetry, letters and political commentary – were printed in the new standard language and orthography. Poems, most of them in a patriotic vein and of no great literary value, were the most popular and were important in creating a revival atmosphere.

The Illyrians based their policy on the tradition of Croatian state right. They also promoted the idea of South Slav cultural and even national unity. Their 'political Croatism' was a programme designed to keep Hungary at bay, achieve a high degree of autonomy for Croatia and Slavonia, and unify Dalmatia with them. In all these attempts the Illyrians counted on the support of the imperial court, which had approved the publication of the *Novine* and *Danica* and, somewhat later, the opening of a printing press. The court's main interest was in keeping down its chief adversary the Hungarian government, and in line with this it supported the Illyrians and their resistance to the Magyarisation of Croatia.

The Illyrian movement spread and became dominant among the Croatian nobility, who saw it as a way of defending their municipal rights against the Hungarian nobility. However, opposition came from some of the aristocracy and the 'peasant nobles' of north-western Croatia (the surroundings of Zagreb) who demanded the use of the specific dialect of that region (*Kajkavski*), the introduction of Hungarian as the official language, and a close alliance with Hungary leading to a uniform Hungarian state that would include Croatian ethnic territory. Their political position was extremely conservative. In 1841 these *Madjaroni* (*Magyarones*) founded the Croatian-Hungarian Party. The Illyrian Party was founded in the same year, supporting Hungarian constitutionality as a common political framework within which a unified Croatian state would enjoy a special status. These were the first political parties in Croatia.

Pressure from the Hungarian nobility grew, threatening to lead to a more serious state crisis, and in 1843 Vienna banned the word 'Illyrian' in Croatia. At the same time the imperial government gave its approval to cultural activities, the most important being work on advancing the Croatian language, and promised to protect Croatian municipal rights. This meant that the crown did not want to break the Illyrian movement, considering it a lesser danger than the activities of the Hungarian nobility. However, no prohibition could seriously impede the Illyrian movement, which had put down strong roots in the seven years of its existence; it had been adopted by the highest classes and achieved organisational status. In any case, it had become obvious that the name 'Illyrian' had lost its justification – less because of the unconvincing scholarly arguments on which it was based than because the Slovenes and Serbs had clearly refused to join it. The banning of the word

'Illyrian' was even useful because it thus became logical for the Illyrian Party to be renamed the National Party, and for 'Illyrian' gradually to be replaced by 'Croatian'. Two years later the crown lifted the prohibition on the word in literature, wishing to exploit Croatian resistance to the Hungarians and considering that Hungary was in a state bordering on revolution.

Meanwhile, in 1842, the *Matica Ilirska* (Illyrian Bee), a fund intended for the publication of books, was founded in Zagreb. When that name was banned, it was re-named the *Matica Hrvatska* (Croatian Bee). In the following decades it became the central cultural institution for the Croats.

During all these fluctuations the Illyrians still focused mainly on the struggle for the Croatian language. In 1840 the Croatian *Sabor* demanded that the Emperor establish a chair for Croatian at the Zagreb Academy, and introduce the language into secondary schools. In 1843 a young member of the nobility, Ivan Kukuljević Sakcinski, addressed the *Sabor* in Croatian for the first time (before that discussions were only held in Latin). He said: 'We are Latins a little, Germans a little, Italians a little, Hungarians a little, Slavs a little, and when it is all added up, to be honest, we are nothing at all! A dead Roman language and the living Hungarian and Italian languages, these are our masters; the living ones threaten us, the dead one is clutching at our throats.' This speech was a turning point, if not immediately then certainly in the long run. The language struggle against the Hungarians entered its final and even more irreconcilable stage. In 1844 the Croatian representatives left the session of the joint Hungarian-Croatian parliament in protest at not being allowed to speak Latin instead of Hungarian. The Hungarian parliament remained adamant and passed a ruling that Hungarian should be introduced as the official language in most counties in Croatia within six years. The Emperor did not confirm this ruling but secured that Croatian representatives in the Hungarian-Croatian parliament should begin to speak Hungarian within six years.

Emperor Ferdinand (1835-48) benefited the Croats in other ways. In 1845 he helped the National Party to win a majority in the Croatian *Sabor*, which then voted the restoration of an independent government like the one Croatia had in 1767-9, the reinstatement of all the *ban*'s prerogatives, and the unification of Dalmatia and Civil Croatia. It also demanded that the Zagreb

Academy be raised to the status of a university and that the Zagreb diocese become an archdiocese. This would administratively separate the Catholic church in Croatia from that in Hungary. The *Sabor* session of 1847 continued this policy and decided, among other things, that Croatian should be the official language in public life. This was the *Sabor's* last session as a feudal institution.

In the political struggles of the 1840s the *Magyarones* were initially successful, but in 1845 the National Party decisively defeated them and neutralised their attempts to endanger the results of the revival movement in the *Sabor*. This was not an easy or a smooth process. In July 1845, during elections in the county of Zagreb, the army had to restore order after violence broke out between the *Magyarones* and Nationals: twenty-two people were killed. The 'July Victims', in addition to embittering political relations, became part of national historical memory.

The period in which the national revival movement was reaching maturity was also one of economic advance which saw the development of a class of merchants with a diversified trade in cereals, wood, leather and foreign-made industrial products: fashion clothes, manufactured goods and 'colonial' goods. The first important industries were founded. In 1841 the enthusiastic Illyrians initiated the Croatian-Slavonian Economic Society to advance modern methods of agriculture, and soon the first specialised paper on husbandry appeared. The first steamship sailed up the Sava to Sisak in 1838, and in the same year the state subsidised a shipping line along the Adriatic coast from Trieste to Kotor. Increased road traffic used improved roads connecting the Pannonian plain with the sea. In 1832 the first road was built connecting Zadar in Dalmatia to Zagreb across Mount Velebit. In the 1820s the golden age of development began for Senj, which became the strongest economic centre on the Croatian littoral and an important port which traded throughout the Mediterranean. However, by mid-century Senj had been outstripped by the nearby ports of Pula and Rijeka. This economic advance reached its highest expression in the mid-1840s when Pula began to develop into the main port of the Habsburg navy, and a large shipyard was built there. Rijeka was strategically important for both Croatia and Hungary, and obtained its first major quays in that decade. Railways came late to Croatia because Vienna's priority was the Vienna-Ljubljana-Trieste route (the line reached Ljubljana in 1849 and

Trieste in 1857). Although plans had existed earlier, the first train reached Zagreb in 1862 and Rijeka in 1873. Croatia, with little capital available, had to shoulder most investments of this kind.

National awakening was much slower and more difficult in other Croatian lands. Dalmatia had Italian schools and it was only in 1844, under the influence of the Illyrians, that papers in Croatian began to be published again. This was after a long interval since those published under French rule early in the century had closed down. The revival movement did not gain momentum till about twenty years later when it clashed with the movement for Dalmatian autonomy.

## The revolutionary solution of 1848-9

Revolutionary currents spread throughout Europe after the revolution that broke out in Paris in February 1848. Inevitably they reached the heart of the Austrian empire in Vienna and the Chancellor, Metternich, had to resign. Revolution flared up in Hungary with demands for democratisation and maximum independence from Austria. However, in their national enthusiasm the Hungarians offered extremely unsatisfactory solution for the status of non-Hungarians in their own country and for the status of Croatia. Their parliament drew up a new administrative division for Croatia that reduced its territory, deprived it of an outlet to the sea, and reinstated Latin as the official language. The course and outcome of revolution and war in 1848-9 were to keep Hungarian attempts of this kind in check until the 1860s.

Disturbances throughout Europe had political repercussions in Zagreb. Croatian politicians sent a committee to Vienna calling on the Emperor to convoke the Croatian *Sabor*, and demanding preservation of the territorial integrity of Croatia and its closer links with Austrian crown lands. At the same time preparations began in Zagreb for a great national assembly to replace the *Sabor*. Many prominent people from Croatia proposed that the imperial court should appoint Colonel Josip Jelačić, a loyal Austrian officer and a Croat who embraced the ideas of Illyrism, as Croatian *ban*. Vienna readily agreed, and Jelačić was nominated at the end of March. Jelačić sincerely believed that he could reconcile the great responsibilities he accepted by becoming *ban* of Croatia at such a crucial moment with the duties of his military career.

At the end of March the 'National Assembly' in Zagreb adopted the 'Demands of the People' (*Narodna zahtijevanja*), the programme of the national movement in Croatia in 1848-9. The 'Demands' emphasised that the 'Slav people of the Triune Kingdom' (Dalmatia, Croatia and Slavonia) wished to remain loyal to the Habsburg dynasty and to continue living within the framework of Hungary, but that they desired autonomy. Their call for the preservation of the Habsburg monarchy was in opposition to the new Hungarian constitution that laid down the division of the state and allowed only that the monarchy should be held in common with Austria. They also demanded the unification of Croatia, Slavonia and Dalmatia, an independent government answerable to the Croatian *Sabor*, which that would no longer be an assembly of estates; financial independence from Hungary; and the abolition of estate privileges. This primarily meant statutory and fiscal equality for all citizens, the abolition of villeinage service and serfdom, and general democratic and civil freedom (universal suffrage and freedom of the press, speech and confession). They demanded that Croatian soldiers should be recalled from frontier duties in Italy so that they should no longer have to fight against Italian revolutionaries as part of the Austrian army. Another reason for their recall was the increasing danger of war against Hungary. These demands were the first consistent democratic programme of the middle class in Croatia, underpinned by ideals inherited from the 1789 French Revolution. They were accompanied by proposals for economic measures, which included the foundation of a modern bank. Thus the atmosphere of general enthusiasm brought about by the National Revival was combined with the prosperity of the merchant class which had emerged during the 1840s.

When Jelačić came from Vienna he issued a proclamation abolishing serfdom. Even earlier, some serfs had managed to make use of commercial development and the rise of capitalism to trade, lend money and buy land. However, the great majority were tied down by poverty and obligatory labour on the feudal estates. They spent almost half of their time, and during seed-time and harvest as much and two-thirds, working for the lord. This made the abolition of serfdom and villeinage service the most important and obvious benefit of these revolutionary events to Croatian society as a whole. In the summer of 1848 the Croatian *Sabor* made the classes that had previously been privileged – the nobility and the clergy – liable to taxation.

The Croats and other nations under the Habsburg monarchy showed great enthusiasm for these revolutionary changes, but their leader did not want to sacrifice their newly-acquired freedoms to German (for Slovenes, Czechs and Italians) or Hungarian (for the Croats, Serbs, Slovaks, Romanians and Ukrainians) domination. The imperial court made use of this resistance to crush the Hungarian revolution. Parallel developments took place in Croatia. On the same day as he proclaimed the abolition of serfdom, Jelačić also announced that he was breaking off relations with the Hungarian revolutionary government. He called on all local authorities in Croatia to deal only with him, and two days later proclaimed martial law. His targets were not only the declared 'bandits, robbers and arsonists', but *Magyarones*, the movement's political opponents who continued to rule in Zagreb county for several more days and had important strongholds in Slavonia. The Hungarian government immediately deposed Jelačić, of which he took no notice. A day or two later, on 18 May, he founded in Zagreb the *Bansko vijeće* (ban council), an independent Croatian government with six departments. Relations between Croatia and Hungary became even more tense.

At that time the imperial court still wanted to mediate in the Croatian-Hungarian conflict, and in June the Emperor confirmed the Hungarian deposition of Jelačić. However, since even Vienna realised that things he could not be settled without force, this decision was revoked after only fifteen days. In the mean time the Croatian *Sabor*, convened for the first time according to the new electoral law that turned it from a feudal assembly of estates into a modern parliament, began its session. It was to have members from Civil Croatia and from the Military Frontier, Dalmatia, Rijeka and Medjimurje. Since Jelačić had already been installed as *ban*, the main issue was Croatia's state-law position in relation to Austria and Hungary. The *Sabor* demanded the transformation of the Habsburg monarchy into a constitutional federation that would guarantee civil liberties, with a central parliament for joint affairs. In it Croatia, together with Slovenian lands and parts of Hungary (today's Vojvodina in Serbia, where Serbs were in the relative majority and Croats a significant minority), would be one of the federal units. This was part of the broad concept of Austro-Slavism

– especially favoured by the Czechs – for transforming the monarchy: it required federalisation and more freedom for Slav peoples
on the basis of natural right. Austro-Slavism was the prevailing
option of Croatian politicians in the stormy years 1848-9.

At the beginning of July the *Sabor* session ended, and because
of peasant revolts and tension with the Hungarians the deputies
voted Jelačić dictatorial powers. The *Sabor* also addressed to the
European public its *Manifest naroda hrvatsko-slavonskoga* (Manifesto
of the Croatian-Slavonian People). This explained the policy of
Austro-Slavism, presented the genesis of the Croatian-Hungarian
conflict and, using arguments of natural and historic law, backed
Croatian demands to be a 'free nation in the free Austrian empire'.
In accordance with the *Sabor's* recommendation, Jelačić tried to
improve relations with Hungary, but the two nations were by
now far apart, and the Hungarian parliament would not accept
the conditions for negotiation. Croatian-Hungarian relations continued to deteriorate. In June the Serbs from Vojvodina rose
against the Hungarians because the Hungarian government would
not fulfill their modest national demands. Jelačić strengthened his
ties with the Vojvodina Serbs – the first more or less organised
and conscious movement for close cooperation between Croatian
and Serbian political leaders. Jelačić's installation ceremony as *ban*
was one of strong symbolism. In the absence of the bishop of
Zagreb, he took the oath before Josip Rajačić, the Serbian patriarch
in the Habsburg monarchy. But things were not always so idyllic:
bands of Serbian armed men from Vojvodina sometimes raided
the easternmost parts of Croatia.

In July and August 1848, after negotiations had failed, people
in Croatia increasingly realised that conflict with the Hungarians
could not be avoided. Preparations for war intensified, and money
and other donations were collected for the army. Jelačić wrote
to Archduke Francis Charles in Vienna: 'Is everyone to gain freedom
but us? Are we Croats and Slavonians alone to be left to the
arbitrary will of the Hungarian ministry? Things have come to a
head and only a resolute step by Your Highness can save the
Habsburg monarchy from total disintegration....'

Revolutionary ferment in Hungary did not abate, and at the
beginning of September Jelačić took 40,000 second-call conscripts
(Croatian élite troops were fighting in Lombardy as part of the
Habsburg army), marched them across the river Drava, annexed

the border region of Medjimurje (with its absolute Croatian majority) to Croatia, and entered Hungary. The first battles were indecisive, and it became clear that the Croatian army alone (even with the possible help of the Serbs) could not break Hungarian resistance. Jelačić was appointed commissary and commander-in-chief of the imperial forces in Hungary, but he and his army were only part of the Austrian war machine that entered Pest at the beginning of 1849. By that summer the combined armies finally broke Hungarian resistance.

In the mean time, the forces opposing the Hungarian and other revolutionary movements were growing stronger. In March 1849 they disrupted the Austrian parliament that had sat for four months in the Moravian town of Kremsier (Kroměříž) and had voted a democratic constitution recognising the rights of all the peoples under the Habsburg monarchy to nurture their national identity and language. Following this the Emperor imposed a constitution that denied the wishes of those peoples and revoked all revolutionary democratic changes, except the abolition of feudalism and the changes necessary for the administration and judiciary to function properly. Although the imperial court freed Croatia of all state links with Hungary, it imposed a constitution that organised the monarchy as a centralist state under Austrian domination. The *Sabor* sent a petition to the Emperor protesting at the abolition of Croatian autonomy that had been proclaimed a year earlier and requesting the unification of Croatian lands. These requests were refused, and even Jelačić's influence at court could not save Austro-Slavism. Dissatisfaction with him and the moderate Serbian patriarch Rajačić grew in democratic circles, and there were even some attempts to create links with Hungarian revolutionaries, but it was in vain. It was said at the time that what the Hungarians had got as 'punishment' was the same as what the Croats had got as a 'reward', namely absolutism.

## *1849-67: beginnings of modernisation and the rapid integration of the Croatian nation*

A ten-year-long period of Habsburg rule now began, named the 'Bach system' after the minister of internal affairs, Alexander Bach, the main proponent of imperial absolutist and centralist policy. The authorities, who considered themselves 'civilised', allowed

the small peoples in the monarchy a degree of autonomy, but it
was their aim ultimately to assimilate them into the larger nation
with a 'higher' level of culture.

This policy had a twofold impact on social change in the
1850s. On the one hand, Croatian state institutions were abolished
(in 1850 the *Sabor* was dissolved and the self-governing counties
ceased to exist), the opposition press was stifled, the Croatian flag
was banned, and German began to be introduced as the official
language and as the medium of instruction in high schools. Reading
rooms, which had been centres of cultural and political activity,
were closed. On the other hand, Vienna introduced a comprehensive reform programme throughout the empire designed to provide
the foundations for a modern society based on free enterprise
and capitalism. This marked the beginning of the fragmentary
and hesitant modernisation that marked Croatia's development to
the end of the nineteenth century.

The process can be divided into three stages: the first from
1848 to the beginning of the 1870s, when relics of the feudal
system were still in place; the second to the beginning of the
1890s, when a modest foundation was laid for radical economic,
social and cultural transformation; and the third from the 1890s
to 1918, when economic growth and social change were speeded
up but were still at a comparatively low level.

A modern bureaucracy began to be formed, the gendarmerie
was introduced, and the judiciary was reorganised. The two largest
cities, Zagreb and Osijek, were given a modern administration.
In the following years environmental plans were made for Croatia
and Slavonia, and Zagreb got its first town plan. A state administration for the construction and maintenance of roads and
for water regulation was founded, and preparations began for the
building of a railway line to Zagreb and Sisak. The first telegram
was sent from Vienna to Zagreb. By the mid-1850s, the telegraph
network covered every part of Croatia. In 1851 the Habsburg
monarchy became a single market and all internal customs were
abolished. The fiscal system was also reorganised, with direct and
indirect taxation on modern principles. The postal service was
modernised and postage stamps were introduced. All these reforms
and innovations, at least to start with, were adapted to those parts
of the monarchy where the industrial revolution had already started,
and with the exception of Istria and the city of Rijeka, Croatia

and Dalmatia were the least developed. Even with the best will, modernisation that came 'from the outside' found no social forces 'on the inside' that could respond. There was almost no bourgeoisie whose capital might have played a supporting role. Most of the people were still peasants and very poor, with 90 per cent of households paying the lowest house tax because their houses were built of wood and had thatched roofs. There were six times more wooden than iron ploughs, and peasant families were ragged and went barefoot. Most peasants were quite unprepared for the new social relations, which resulted in many of their families falling apart. Only a small number managed to integrate into the market economy, most being too poor to have anything to sell. In the 1850s laws were passed abolishing the last traces of feudalism, and church tithes were abolished. Nevertheless, the process encountered great difficulties up to and beyond the end of the decade, because of conflicting interests between the former serfs and masters.

In 1851 Jelačić tried to liberalise crafts and trade. He did not immediately abolish the guilds, on which artisans and small merchants relied heavily, but they gradually disappeared during the following years. Landowners felt deprived because the state had abolished serfdom without helping them to overcome the protracted crisis of change from feudal to capitalist production. Furthermore, they were in danger of tax exhaustion and could not acquire mortgage loans. The backward economic structure and chronic lack of capital held back the more prosperous merchants and entrepreneurs. The 'national' intelligentsia felt rejected because the surge of Germanisation halted the first stages of modern civic culture that had developed in the 1830s and '40s.

One of the good results of modernisation was the network of four-year elementary schools, although some villages still did not have them and many peasant children never attended school. They had to help on the farm and the roads leading to the schools were bad and in winter sometimes impassable. Even in the 1860s illiteracy ran at almost 80 per cent. As for high schools, the government's main purpose was to make them places for learning German, and furthermore to turn young people away from their national culture. They adopted a neo-absolutist stand that all non-German languages, with the exception of Italian, were inferior where the education of the intelligentsia was concerned. Statements

of the type that only the 'higher' German culture could mediate
new scientific findings dismayed Croatian intellectuals and slowed
down cultural development in the 1850s. *Ban* Jelačić and his
government only managed to translate and publish a few elementary
and high school textbooks by Croatian authors in Croatian.

In 1852 Pope Pius IX issued a bull, with the Emperor's approval,
that elevated the diocese of Zagreb to the status of an archdiocese,
thus continuing the tendency to separate Croatia from Hungary
wherever possible. Zagreb became the metropolitan centre of the
newly-founded archdiocese, which embraced three dioceses. In
1855 the Pope and Emperor Franz Joseph signed a concordat
regulating the position of the Catholic church: the monarchy
pledged not to obstruct papal authority in church matters, while
the church placed itself under imperial protection. The clergy
were charged with educating the Catholic youth.

On the last day of 1851 the Emperor proclaimed the so-called
Sylvester Patent which abolished the hated constitution but also
constitutional order as such. A time of open absolutism began,
based on a military-bureaucratic centralist system. The authorities
supported economic modernisation but prevented political activities. The new general civil code for Croatia and Slavonia gave
all citizens equality before the law, although Jews still did not
enjoy it fully.

The system allowed a degree of civic development. Various
measures prevented, limited or controlled social, economic and
national emancipation. The ruling system still relied on the remnants
of patriarchal relations, with permissiveness at one moment and
increased social coercion at another, and on absolutism cloaked
in parliamentary forms (only 2 per cent of the male population
were entitled to vote, with suffrage based on a property census).
The Press Act of 1852 banned street vending and increased cen-
sorship. The district police authorities could ban newspapers, and
trials concerning newspaper infringements had no juries.

The modernisation of the 1850s was only the first step in
transforming a feudal society of large estates into an industrial
middle-class society. Regardless of the widespread hatred of the
reforms and of the methods used to implement them, they remained
in force even after the fall of Bach's absolutist system.

The burst of creativity that had occurred during the time of
National Revival also died away under the pressure of Germanisa-

tion and absolutist rule. Disappointment following the collapse of the aspirations of 1848 gradually gave way to a greater realism and a mustering of new energy. The specific conditions of the 1850s gave birth to two basic political currents. These were both Croatian ideologies of national identity, and the dilemma they created lasted right to the end of the twentieth century. One was Yugoslavism – a Yugoslav orientation – and the other was exclusive Croatian nationalism.

Yugoslavism, south-Slavism, grew on the foundations of Illyrism (though expressly distancing itself from the name 'Illyrian' and what it signified). It continued the programme that had started in the 1848-9 revolution – of forging links between South Slavs in the monarchy. It connected Croatian national consciousness to feelings that the Croats belonged to the broader family of Slavs, primarily in the cultural sense, and that Yugoslavism was the best framework, even a condition of survival, for the small and weak Croatian nation. The Yugoslav ideology was to have many interpreters in Croatia, who perceived the relationship between Croatian and Yugoslav feelings in different ways. Their attitude depended on many factors, including contemporary events in the monarchy and in the Balkans, the relationship with Serbia, and the development of the Serbian ideology of national integration.

On the other hand, Croatian nationalism was growing too: Ante Starčević and Eugen Kvaternik were already attacking Austria as the 'sworn historic enemy' of the Croats. They condemned Illyrism as a tragic error, rejected a Yugoslav framework for Croatia, and attempted to proclaim all South Slavs Croats. They considered that no future Croatian state could function without the basic postulates of the French Revolution. When, in 1857, Kvaternik was banned from practising law, he went to Russia where he planned to lead a struggle for Croatia's complete liberation. Disappointed there, he then pinned all his hopes on the France of Napoleon III. In connection with the war against Austria he wrote the book *La Croatie et la confédération italienne* (Paris, 1859) in which he presented the programme of the future Croatian Party of State Right (*Hrvatska stranka prava*). He denied the claim of the Habsburg dynasty to the Croatian crown and demanded the unification of Croatian lands.

In the 1850s, wishing to create a modern civic culture, educated individuals began to rally around the idea of Yugoslavism as a

Croatian ideology of national integration. The entwined Croatian and Yugoslav feelings of Yugoslavism left a mark on literature and on the struggle for a standard language and historiography. People raised every cultural activity to the level of a 'national science' in an attempt to create an original but modern Croatian culture as part of the overall Yugoslav culture. In their wish to express the soul of the people creatively, Croatian scholars and artists had to resist the inclination merely to imitate German culture. The feeling of 'awakening', already very evident in Illyrian times, continued on a higher level. Invoking Yugoslavism, these unassuming cultural activities, limited to a narrow group of people, formed a bridge between Illyrism and the impetus that would come in the 1860s.

In 1859 war broke out between the Habsburg monarchy on one side and France and Piedmont on the other, and the main campaigns were fought in northern Italy. Many Croatian soldiers fought and died there, and it took the greater horrors of the First World War to overshadow the terrible memories of these battles in the minds of the people. The French fleet entered the Adriatic and sailed as far north as the island of Lošinj without encountering any major resistance, and did not withdraw till the armistice.

The war against France and Piedmont eroded the Empire's already catastrophic finances, and when the Habsburg army was defeated at Magenta and Solferino the imperial court was forced into making great concessions. At the beginning of 1860, to prevent financial collapse, Emperor Franz Joseph convened his advisory body, the *Reichsrat*, and it met in its broader form that included representatives of all the crowns, which showed that open absolutist rule was no longer possible. Josip Juraj Strossmayer (1815-1905), bishop of Djakovo and one of the most important Croatian figures in the second half of the nineteenth century, who was present at the meeting as representative of Slavonia, advocated the unification of Croatian lands and a federal organisation of the empire. The representative of Dalmatia, Count Frane Borelli, was opposed to this and proclaimed the 'Slavo-Dalmatian' nation, laying the foundations of the movement for Dalmatian autonomy. Matters developed quickly: Vienna was forced to reinstate Croatian as the official language in Croatia and Slavonia, and in October 1860 the Emperor issued the 'October Diploma' introducing in Hungary and Croatia a combination of absolutism and constitutionality, of federalist and centralist elements, of liberal principles and imperial autocracy. The Habsburg monarchy acquired a new common legislative body, the *Reichsrat*. The military, foreign relations and foreign trade, and their financing were dealt with centrally, but everything else was left to land parliaments. The Emperor's 'Diploma' was designed to make peace with the Hungarians, and the demand of the Croatian *Sabor* for autonomy made in 1848 was ignored.

The following week the *ban* conference met in Zagreb and in principle rejected these documents. Representatives of Croatia and Slavonia submitted a request to the Emperor formulating the basic elements of Croatian state ideology. It assumed that the triune kingdom of Dalmatia, Croatia and Slavonia was independent of any other, and demanded the unification of Dalmatia and parts of Istria with Croatia and Slavonia. It also demanded the establishment of a Croatian court chancellery as a body of executive government independent of Hungary. The crown agreed to this in 1861.

In the spring of 1861 the Croatian *Sabor* met to discuss the problem of Croatia's legal status within the unresolved internal conditions in the monarchy. The *Sabor* began with the installation ceremony for the *ban*, the first since 1848. Despite efforts to encourage the participation of all Croatian lands at the *Sabor*, some were missing. The majority in the Dalmatian *Sabor* supported Dalmatian autonomy and refused to send a delegation for talks about unification; elections had not even been called in the Military Frontier. The Emperor demanded that the *Sabor* should only discuss issues he considered important (the relationship between Croatia-Slavonia and Hungary, the election of delegates for the *Reichsrat* and for his coronation as king of Hungary and of the triune kingdom, and discussion of how deputies should be elected for the central parliament), but the *Sabor* members would not accept these restrictions, and sent the Emperor a document demanding the unification of the triune kingdom. Besides the reintegration of the Military Frontier, they demanded a 'large portion of Istria' and some border areas of Slovenia. They emphasised that 'Turkish Croatia', as they called the westernmost part of Bosnia (then still part of the Ottoman empire), was in principle part of Croatia also. The document outlined Croatian state-law ideology in detail and gave arguments for a new delimitation. The *Sabor* unanimously demanded the unification of Croatia and Dalmatia, but this was unrealistic considering the opposition of both Austria and Hungary. After this Croatia was buffeted by the conflicting interests of, and power-play between, Vienna and Budapest even more than before, fearing the hegemony first of one and then of the other.

The Emperor finally allowed elections for *Sabor* deputies in the Military Frontier and their participation in discussions on Croatia's state position. Six prominent Dalmatians, three of them members of the Dalmatian *Sabor*, were co-opted to the Croatian *Sabor*, with only an 'informative vote'.

The central issue discussed at the *Sabor* was loyalty to Hungary. The deputies submitted three proposals. One – for an alliance with Hungary without precondition – was proposed by a group of deputies headed by Mirko Bogović, who in the following years, with their supporters, formed the Unionist Party. Eugen Kvaternik submitted the second proposal, which was for personal union with Hungary and Austria with the proviso that they recognise the entirety of Croatian lands. Only Ante Starčević seconded this proposal, and even he rejected the idea of Croatia and Austria having any common affairs.

The *Osrednji odbor* (moderate committee), headed by the poet and politician Ivan Mažuranić, deemed that all state links between Croatia and Hungary had been dissolved in 1848 except in the person of the monarch. It expressed readiness to enter into a new alliance with Hungary after the latter recognised the 'independence and autonomy' and the 'real and virtual territory' of the triune kingdom. This proposal included the stand that minimum autonomy in politics, the judiciary, education and religion should be conceded without discussion in any new alliance. It was adopted by a majority of 120 votes, with three abstentions and forty-seven absent deputies. The Emperor sanctioned the proposal, which made it a law. It was the only conclusion of the *Sabor* which obtained imperial confirmation and was of vital importance in later negotiations on the working out of Croatia's autonomy within Hungary and the terms of the agreement known as the Hungarian-Croatian *Nagodba*.

In further discussions the *Sabor* refused to choose delegates for the *Reichsrat*, asserting that the body had not been formed con-stitutionally. Starting from the position that the *Sabor* was competent to discuss these issues in the first place, the deputies were convinced that they had effectively proclaimed Croatia's statehood in relation to Hungary and Austria.

They also discussed what to call the standard language used in Croatia and Slavonia: of four proposals (vernacular, Croatian-Slavonian, Croatian or Serbian, Yugoslav) the name 'Yugoslav' was accepted by majority vote. The next year, the Croatian court chancellery annulled this decision and settled on the name 'Croatian' for the language. As political conditions at the end of the nineteenth and during the twentieth century changed, so did the official name of the language ('Croatian-Serbian', 'Croatian' or 'Serbian'), but in everyday life only the name 'Croatian' was used. In the second half of the nineteenth century scholars completed the standardisation of the Croatian language. The Illyrians had done a lot of the work and it was no longer an issue that the Štokavski variant had been chosen as the official dialect. There were still some nuances and details to be decided, and a group under the influence of the Serbian philologists Vuk Stefanović Karadžić (1787–1864) and Djuro Daničić (1825–82) carried out the final standardisation. This made the Croatian and Serbian standard languages very similar, and in the twentieth century this solution was a source of controversy.

The *Sabor* also adopted a law about the 'Yugoslav theatre' in Croatia, which was to be the legal foundation for Croatian theatrical activities, and placed the theatre under the permanent care of the state. In the 1850s most performances had been in German and only a small number in Croatian, but in the 1860s all performances were in Croatian. Despite the small size of the theatre company, plays by Shakespeare, Schiller, Goethe, Molière and Goldoni had all been staged for the first time by 1865. The law called for guest performances outside Zagreb, and these were given not only in many Croatian towns but even in Vojvodina where there were large proportions of Serbs. In 1862 the theatre performed in Belgrade. The *Sabor* also supported Strossmayer's proposals for founding a Yugoslav academy of sciences and arts and a modern university. However, it took respectively five and thirteen years for these institutions to materialise because of the strong resistance and bureaucratic obstacles that needed to be overcome.

In 1861 a number of crucial developments for Croatian national integration took place in other Croatian lands in the Habsburg monarchy. Istria became especially important for the monarchy after 1846 when the main naval port was transferred to Pula on the tip of the peninsula because Venice was no longer safe. In the mid-century 59 per cent of the Istrian population were Croats, 26 per cent Italians and 14 per cent Slovenes (all in the northernmost part), and fewer than 1 per cent were Germans and other nationalities. Tension between the predominantly Italian coastal towns and predominantly Slav inland villages grew with modernisation. In 1861 the Istrian *Sabor* was founded in Poreč, but it had only one Croat deputy and of the three bishops who were nominated members, two were Croats and the third was a Slovene. Italian was the official language.

The central figure of the Croatian National Revival in Istria was Juraj Dobrila, a friend of Strossmayer who shared his opinions. In 1857 he became bishop of Pula-Poreč, the first Croat to hold the position, and subsequently wrote his pastoral letters in Croatian. Although he did not directly participate in revival activities, he inspired much of their development. He became Istrian deputy in the *Reichsrat* in 1863, and always encouraged the use of the 'Slav' language in the Istrian *Sabor*.

In 1861 the National Party was founded in Dalmatia under the leadership of Miho Klaić and Mihovil Pavlinović. Both championed the Croatian national revival in the region and gave political support to the annexation of Dalmatia to Civil Croatia. However, in the same year the Autonomists (supporters of an autonomous Dalmatia) won twenty-seven seats at the elections, and the National Party won fourteen. Pavlinović spoke Croatian at the first session of the Dalmatian *Sabor*, despite protests form the majority, which led to later turmoil. In 1862 the National Party paper *Il Nazionale* began publication in Zadar. It was printed in Italian and mostly addressed to the intelligentsia and to city people in general, although it had a weekly supplement in Croatian for the rural population. Not till the 1870s did the paper begin to be printed entirely in Croatian. In its first year its editor was the historian Natko Nodilo, one of the leaders of the National Revival, who endorsed the unification of Dalmatia and Croatia and other national and liberal policy aims. His opponent was the most prominent Autonomist in Dalmatia, the writer and politician Nikola Tommaseo of Šibenik. Tommaseo and his supporters were not Italian nationalists but were great lovers of Italy; most had been educated there. They thought that Dalmatia should remain outside the Croatian National

Revival, and supported instead the idea of a 'Slav-Dalmatian' nation. For this reason the Croats rejected Tommaseo, as did the Italians.

In 1862 the *Matica Dalmatinska* (literally the Bee of Dalmatia) was founded and started the paper *Narodni Koledar* (Folk Carols) with texts designed to awaken national consciousness. The first two 'Slav' reading rooms were also opened in that year, and soon they opened in all the major Dalmatian communities.

The 1860s were notable in Croatia for railway construction. In 1862 the first line linking two towns was built between Zagreb and Sisak, and a branch connected it to the country's other railway line. The supporters of Croatian autonomy wanted a railway network that would advance the country's economic development, but in the following years most new lines were built in the Hungarian interest. Although there were disputes over railway construction, regions that could be reached by train developed more quickly. Industrialisation was strongest in Zagreb where the first Dalmatian-Croatian-Slavonian exhibition was organised in 1864, although much goods traffic still plied along the Sava, Drava and Danube rivers.

By 1865-6, largely because of unsuccessful wars against Prussia and Italy, Vienna had to change its policy of applying pressure to Croatia, Hungary and Bohemia. To save the state the crown had to negotiate with its strongest opponent, Hungary. At that time some Croats abroad called on the international community to break Austria up and establish an independent Croatia, which would include Slovenian lands. This was an offshoot of the French-Polish policy to reconstitute Poland as a state (and hence possibly other Slavic nations). Others wanted an independent Croatia in the framework of a South Slav community centred on Serbia. However, all this was unrealistic. When Croatian politicians realised that Austro-Hungarian negotiations were leading to a dualistic state in which they would be completely at Hungary's mercy, they made yet another attempt to approach Austria. It was unsuccessful.

## 1867-90: a failed attempt to solve the national question and rapid economic development

The Austro-Hungarian agreement of 1867 gave the state a new

name, the Austro-Hungarian monarchy, and divided it into two parts with a common foreign policy, army and finances (for common affairs). Croatia and Slavonia came under Hungary; Dalmatia and Istria under Austria. The 'Basic Laws' came into force in the Austrian part of the monarchy at the same time as the agreement. These laws included the liberal advances of 1848: general civil rights, the equal rights of all peoples to their own nationality and language, and language equality in communities with a nationally mixed population.

The new situation also called for negotiations between Hungary and Croatia. The starting positions were known because the representatives of both sides had clearly expressed them a year earlier in Budapest. The Hungarians upheld the totality of the kingdom of Hungary with only insignificant regional autonomy for the Croats; the Croats, headed by Strossmayer, demanded broad autonomy with aspects of statehood. In 1867 Croatian representatives did not attend the coronation of Franz Joseph as king of Hungary because they considered that in the formal and legal sense it was none of their business.

The Croatian representatives, members of the National Party, entered into negotiations with Hungary in a pragmatic state of mind, wishing to reach a compromise as soon as possible. Their demands were minimal, but even these were dashed against the rigid Hungarian position. It was in this situation, at the end of 1867, that the new *ban*, Levin Rauch, imposed elections with the full support of the imperial court. The Unionists won fifty-two seats (the Nationals won fourteen), accepted the dualistic organisation of the Habsburg monarchy, and proclaimed 'national unity'. The Nationals withdrew from the *Sabor*, and in 1868 the Unionists and the Hungarians signed the Croatian-Hungarian *nagodba* (agreement) which defined Croatia's legal position as a state for the next fifty years. Croatia and Slavonia remained in control of what had been in their competence since 1861 (internal affairs, judiciary, education and religion). The Croats attained the status of a political nation in Hungary, with which they formed a single state. The Hungarians promised to support the unification of the Military Frontier and Dalmatia with Croatia and Slavonia. Croatia had to contribute a fixed sum for the expenses of the common state (Hungary) and a quota for the common expenses of all Austria-Hungary. Dependence on Hungary was also expressed in the fact that the Emperor would only nominate as *ban* a candidate whom the Hungarian prime minister had proposed and approved. The central government in Vienna had a minister for Croatia-Slavonia-Dalmatia who was responsible to the Hungarian, not the Croatian, parliament. Croatia obtained the right to five delegates in the Hungarian delegation for solving problems that arose in common affairs with Austria, but they were elected by the Hungarian parliament. The status of the port of Rijeka remained unresolved in later negotiations: legally it remained part of Croatia, but was actually under the competence of the Hungarian government.

Although the *nagodba* included some indisputable benefits (recognition of territorial integrity), it made Croatia completely dependent in financial matters on Hungary, and subordinated the Croatian *ban* to the Hungarian prime minister. This meant that all economic and financial affairs, from taxes to trade, and including banking and the railway, were common. There was great dissatisfaction in Croatia, and Emperor Franz Joseph visited Zagreb at the beginning of 1869 in the hope of lessening tension. He approved the founding of a modern university and proclaimed the abolition of the Military Frontier. In this way he wished to show that academic, cultural and political progress was possible even within the framework of *nagodba* autonomy. On the tide of the general dissatisfaction the National Party, helped by Austrian army circles in the Military Frontier, exerted pressure on the authorities because of the provisions in the *nagodba*. When the National Party roundly defeated the Unionists at elections in 1871, winning 51 seats compared to the Unionists' 13, it proclaimed the *nagodba* illegal.

About twenty days later Eugen Kvaternik, one of the leaders of the Party of State Right, raised a rebellion of Serbian and Croatian peasants in the Military Frontier village of Rakovica. He founded a 'provisional national government', with ministries of the interior, defence and finance, which issued a proclamation setting forth the goals of the rebellion, namely 'to free the people from German and Hungarian masters' and to integrate the Military Frontier completely into Croatia. The Austro-Hungarian authorities introduced martial law, and after only three days the army surrounded the rebels and crushed them. Some were killed in the battle; others were condemned to death and executed. The Party of State Right also suffered. Although Ante Starčević had nothing to do with the rebellion, the authorities imprisoned him and banned the party's organ *Hrvatska*. This isolated revolutionary act, ill-prepared, unrealistic and without dramatic consequences for Croatia as it may have been, left a strong mark in the national consciousness and inspired later generations.

When the National Party resumed power, popular dissatisfaction continued, but at the same time government pressure increased. Antun Vakanović was appointed acting *ban*, and demanded a signed undertaking from civil servants that they would vote for the Unionists. They used forged documents to accuse the National Party of treasonable cooperation with the Czechs, Russians and Serbs, and even with the Hungarian exiles around Lajos Kossuth. In spite of this, at the 1872 elections the National Party again won a majority of seats. Negotiations began about revising the Croatian-Hungarian *nagodba*, and after lengthy bargaining the modified *nagodba* was signed in the autumn of 1873. Croatia managed to have its fixed contribution to state funds according to the 1868 agreement annulled, and instead 55 per cent of all Croatian and Slavonian revenues were to go to the state treasury, while the remaining 45 per cent were allowed to finance autonomous affairs. It was widely felt that Croatia had shown insufficient resolution and settled for too little; this was the view of Bishop Strossmayer, who retired from political life (while continuing his patronage of the arts). One consequence of the revised *Nagodba* was the election of Ivan Mažuranić as the first *ban* who was a commoner and not a noble.

The revival of Croation national consciousness came to Dalmatia more slowly than to northern Croatia, was partly because of the strong autonomy movement, but in the 1870s it was well under way. A crucial year was 1870, when the National Party defeated the Autonomists at elections for the Dalmatian *Sabor* (25 versus 16 seats). However, it took much longer to break the tendency towards autonomy. At the local level the Nationals took forty-two of the seventy-nine municipalities existing at that time (the strongest were in Split and Dubrovnik and their surroundings), but in 1882 the Autonomists still controlled thirteen municipalities. In 1872 Croatian was given equality with Italian in the business of administration and the courts that did not have an external dimension. Bilingual instruction in schools was abolished and municipalities could decide on the language of instruction. Not till 1876 did the *Narodni list* (National News), the paper of the National Party, begin to be published in Croatian only; it had previously appeared completely or partly in Italian, which Dalmatian citizens then understood better than Croatian. The 1882 the Nationals' victory over the Autonomists at municipal elections in Split marked the final victory of the Croatian national revival in Dalmatia. Only Zadar, the administrative centre of Dalmatia, remained outside the Nationals' reach. In 1883 the Dalmatian *Sabor* adopted the 'vernacular Croatian or Serbian language' instead of Italian, but deputies were free to choose whether they would speak Croatian or Italian. However, none of this led to major changes because after 1885 the National Party in Dalmatia adopted a programme designed to appease the government. Nothing more was said about unifying Dalmatia and Croatia since this would have threatened the party's existence. In later years it did no more than pledge that it would request the Emperor to unite the two countries at a suitable moment. This tactic led to contention and an upsurge of the state-right movement in Dalmatia.

Almost at the same time, the national revival was gaining strength in Istria. The first political paper of the Istrian Croats, *Naša Sloga* (Our concord), was started in 1870 in Trieste. In the 1880s the national movement reached a more mature stage under the leadership of the young generation of 'Rightists'. The attorney and writer Matko Laginja (1852-1930) became a member of the Istrian *Sabor*. Although the *Sabor* voted for language equality in the judiciary, the official language in the *Sabor* itself was still Italian. In 1883 Laginja attempted to make the first speech in Croatian but Italian members prevented him. However, at the elections in 1886-7 and later the National Party gradually took over in all the municipalities of central and south-eastern Istria.

In the 1870s the national revival also started among a relatively isolated group of Croats, the Bunjevci and Šokci, who were concentrated in northern Bačka (the western part of Vojvodina) and in the south of Hungary. This area was centred on the town of Subotica. The ancestors of these two groups had moved there from Croatian ethnic regions during wars against the Ottomans, but their integration into the Croatian national corpus was hampered by the fact that they often called themselves Bunjevci and Šokci rather than Croats. In addition, northern Vojvodina was inhabited by many Hungarians and Serbs, both of whom placed great pressure on the Bunjevci and Šokci in the attempt to assimilate them.

This came about through kinship of language in the case of the Serbs and through Catholicism in the case of the Hungarians. The first Croatian newspapers in the region appeared in 1870, after which followed a reading room, a literary magazine and historical writings on the Croatian origin of this population. But it was not till just before the First World War that the Bunjevačka Party issued a proclamation emphasising that the Bunjevci and the Šokci were a 'branch of the Croatian people, and our language is pure Croatian', adding that they 'confess national unity with the Serbs, whose language they also consider their own'.

Ivan Mažuranić's term as *ban* (1873-80) was marked by liberal reforms and economic and cultural efforts to create a middle-class society. The *Sabor* separated administration from the judiciary at all levels, and voted to introduce relatively liberal laws on the press and on the right of assembly. It legally abolished the last remains of feudalism. Modern health and veterinary services were introduced, and new laws made it easier to dissolve *zadrugas* (extended families) on a voluntary basis and gradually adapt them to civil law. It introduced compulsory four-year schooling and both the Catholic and Orthodox churches lost the right to supervise education. Reorganisation covered all institutions, even prisons. In 1874 the decimal system for measuring weights and measures was introduced in Croatia and Slavonia.

The founding of the Yugoslav Academy of Sciences and Arts in 1867 gave science and culture an important boost. The first president was the prominent historian Franjo Rački, but it was Strossmayer who inspired its birth. More books were published generally, and by 1900 the Academy had published 144 numbers of its collected *Rad JAZU* (Academy Papers), and started nine other fundamental series of collections or printed sources. The founders named it the Yugoslav Academy because of their desire for it to play an enlightening role in the entire Slav south. However, both at the time of its foundation and later, in membership and in interests, it was first and foremost a Croatian academy. The name was changed to Croatian Academy in 1941-5, and this has also been its name since 1991.

The main scholarly and cultural event in this period was the establishment of a modern university in Zagreb in 1874. Tuition began immediately at the faculties of philosophy, law and theology, but the medical faculty did not open till 1918 although its foundation had already been approved in the 1860s. In addition to these three faculties, tuition also took place in the newly-founded laboratories and demonstration rooms in physics, botany, zoology, mathematics and chemistry. The following years saw the beginnings of the study of world languages and geography. Prominent scholars and scientists, mostly of the younger generation, came to Zagreb from other parts of the monarchy – mostly from Bohemia because of the linguistic affinity. This improved the level of tuition, and in some cases was the only means of making it possible.

Various new associations were founded at this time, and societies that already existed began to work systematically. These were mainly professional associations such as the Croatian Pedagogical -Literary Assembly for teachers and the Natural History Society. Doctors, lawyers and members of other professions organised themselves. Sports societies were formed, and some sports, notably gymnastics, developed strongly. The less affluent classes mostly assembled in fire-fighting and choral societies.

Romantic nationalism captivated the public interest and for the first time people began to give mass support to important national anniversaries. In 1866 they celebrated the tercentenary of the battle of Siget, and in 1871 Kvaternik was inspired by the bicentenary of the Zrinski and Frankapan sacrifice. He considered them anti-Austrian heroes and contrasted them to the 'servitude' of Nikola Šubić Zrinski who 'died not for Croatia but for the goals of Austria'. In 1874 there were celebrations for the 800th anniversary of King Zvonimir's coronation. The most popular and versatile Croatian writer at this time was August Šenoa (1838-81), who wrote historical novels in a realistic style inspired by romanticism. These contributed to the growth of a Croatian reading public and aided the acceptance of the Štokavski dialect. The historical canvases of the painter Ferdo Quiquerez, and by the end of the century also of Oton Iveković (who painted scenes of epic events in Croatian history), reflected the prevalent artistic currents of the time. Musical life also flourished in the 1870s. After the composer Ivan Zajc returned to Zagreb from Vienna, musical education took a great step forward; organised musical life came into being and, with it, improvement in the quality of performers and in public taste. Zagreb now had its first permanent opera company and its first orchestras.

Economic growth followed this swing towards modernisation,

but it took place unevenly because of the great world depressions after 1873. In the mean time agrarian production and village life as a whole went through a great crisis. However, the end of the 1880s brought visible changes in the economic strength of the ruling class and in the average growth of the national product per person. In the long run this decreased the death rate and increased the birth rate. The following decades saw the greatest natural population increase ever recorded in Croatia, although in the first half of the twentieth century it began to decrease again. By 1873 railway lines linked Zagreb and its surroundings with other parts of the monarchy and particularly with the port of Rijeka, and intense railway construction continued, especially in Slavonia. Peasants began to move into the burgeoning cities. In 1843 Zagreb had less than 15,000 inhabitants, in 1857 just under 28,000, in 1880 41,000, and in 1910 100,274. Relatively prosperous town centres developed surrounded by poor suburbs, which fundamentally changed the appearance of towns. Workers were very badly paid and did not have a limited working day; they had to work Saturdays and Sundays as the factory owners strove to remain competitive with foreign goods. This was a time of fledgling workers' organisations; the first trade union was founded in 1869 and the first workers' helps paper appeared in 1874. No public welfare programmes yet existed because of the belief of employers and the government that 'Christian charity' would suffice to solve the problems of poverty.

As the Eastern Question and the future of Bosnia-Hercegovina grew in importance, Croatian politicians increasingly addressed the question of that land and its position. Croatia had two reasons for its interest: national, because in the 1870s about 18 per cent of the Bosnian population were Catholics, i.e. Croats; and territorial, because until the coming of the Ottomans the Croatian state had incorporated the westernmost parts of Bosnian territory, down to the Vrbas river basin. Croatian politicians and ideologues called that area 'Turkish Croatia' and used historical arguments to prove that it was part of Croatia.

In the nineteenth century the Ottoman empire was in deep political and economic disarray. There was almost no industry, and the quality of life was inferior to that in neighbouring Croatia in all aspects. Because of this the process of national integration among Bosnian Croats was late in developing. The Ottoman government's liberal reforms played an important role. In 1839 the *Hatt-i Serif* of Gülhane was issued. This was a decree of equal taxation for all, but it did not greatly improve conditions because the influence of the central authorities in this fringe region was weak. The Sultan's *Hatt-i Humayun* (imperial decree) of 1856 extended the reforms, guaranteeing religious freedom and equality of opportunity in public service for all the peoples and confessions in the Empire. This improved the position of Croats somewhat, but great social and economic inequality remained. Under the influence of the revival and accompanying changes taking place in Croatia, the first movement among Bosnian Croats began in the 1850s. As in earlier centuries, it was the Franciscans who initiated this modernisation. In 1850 Father Ivan Franjo Jukić began to publish the periodical *Bosanski prijatelj* (Bosnian Friend) in Zagreb, which appeared with interruptions in Zagreb and Sisak till 1870. This first periodical for the people of Bosnia-Hercegovina had 'necessary, useful and amusing articles'. The following year Jukić published his *Zemljopis i povjesnica Bosne* (Geography and History of Bosnia) in Zagreb. He also composed a petition that was sent by the Christians of Bosnia, both Catholic and Orthodox, to the Sultan. It was the first attempt to achieve a modern approach to the functioning of the state, and in it they demanded to be treated as Ottoman subjects and not as *raya* (the Sultan's non-Muslim subjects, then almost without rights in the empire), an equal number of Christian and Muslim judges, and abolition of the poll-tax or *harač*.

In June 1875 an uprising began near Gabela in Hercegovina, a region largely settled by Croats. It soon spread to the mainly Serb-settled eastern Hercegovina, and in about two months to the rest of Bosnia-Hercegovina. Already in July committees to aid the rebels were being organised in Zagreb (and Belgrade) and in towns along the Bosnian and Hercegovinian frontier. An international committee was formed in Paris, headed by the Serbian Metropolitan Mihajlo and Bishop Strossmayer. About 100,000 refugees from Bosnia-Hercegovina (almost 10% of the population, which in 1879 stood at 1,160,000) found refuge in Croatia, and many volunteers went to Bosnia-Hercegovina to fight the Ottomans.

For three years the rebels resisted the Ottoman army, at times even taking the initiative, which led to extensive diplomatic activity

concerning the future of Bosnia-Hercegovina. In 1876 Serbia and
Montenegro declared war on the Ottoman empire, partly in the
hope of conquering parts of Bosnia-Hercegovina for themselves,
but the Serbian army was defeated. Austria-Hungary and Russia
decided that in order to prevent Bosnia-Hercegovina from being
annexed by Serbia it was necessary to divide Ottoman territory.
Hence they agreed that the monarchy should occupy Bosnia-
Hercegovina; in August 1878 the Austro-Hungarian army moved
in from the south and north from several points in Croatia and
within about two months had conquered it completely.

This event directly benefited Croatia because it wiped out its
long frontier belt with Bosnia-Hercegovina, always a potential
crisis zone. Also, the Habsburg monarchy wanted to integrate its
new acquisition culturally and economically, and all moves and
contacts necessarily went through Croatia. In 1879 the first railway
bridge across the Sava was built at Slavonski Brod, thus beginning
the construction of the first Bosnian railway line.

The occupation of Bosnia-Hercegovina speeded up the national
movement of the Croats there. The Austro-Hungarian authorities
thought it best to promote the development of a single Bosnian-
Hercegovinian nation that would incorporate members of all the
three religions. Benjamin Kallay, who was in charge of Bosnia-
Hercegovina as minister of finance, would implement this policy,
but neither he nor his staff realised to what extent Croatian and
Serbian national consciousness had already developed in Bosnia.
They unsuccessfully tried to win the Croats over to their idea
with the help of the Catholic hierarchy and the first Archbishop
of Sarajevo, Josip Stadler. But the Franciscan Frano Miličević had
already founded a Croatian printing press in Mostar in 1873 and
published an orthography (*pravopis*) for Catholic primary school
children. In the 1880s he began to publish newspapers, and he
and his followers opposed Kallay and worked to build up a Croatian
consciousness.

The economic and social development of Croatian lands was
greatly impeded by the impossibility of their political unification.
Dalmatia and Istria were in the Austrian part of the monarchy,
and it was impossible in practice to identify and realise interests
common to the entire Croatian territory. It was also a lengthy
process making the demilitarised Military Frontier part of provincial
Croatia because of conflicting Austro-German and Hungarian

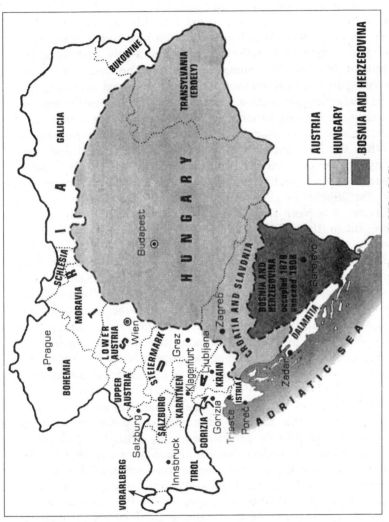

Austro-Hungarian Empire (1878-1918)

economic interests and because the Hungarian government wanted
to suppress Croatian political activities throughout northern Croatia.
The frequent Hungarian infringement of the *nagodba* was also a
great problem, and in 1880 it led Ivan Mažuranić to resign as
*ban*. A new round of difficult and often interrupted Hungarian-
Croatian negotiations followed, leading to a new financial arrangement but leaving unresolved the most important questions
relating to Croatian autonomy. Croatia remained dependent on
the Hungarian government. Hungary agreed to endorse the unification of the Military Frontier with Croatia if Croatia would agree
to decrease the number of its deputies in the joint parliament.
When the Croatian Committee of the Realm agreed that their
fifty-five deputies (in conformity with the 1868 *nagodba*) should
be reduced to forty, Emperor Franz Joseph finally issued a manifesto
in the summer of 1881 annexing the Military Frontier to Civil
Croatia; complete administrative unification was finally implemented in 1886. The territory of the former Military Frontier
was now administratively part of Croatia and Slavonia, but the
deep differences in social life and economic development were
not overcome till 1918 and some can still be felt today.

It seemed that Croatian-Hungarian relations might become relatively stable and even greatly improve after the revision of the
*nagodba*, but this did not happen. The Hungarians infringed the
*nagodba's* terms by making Hungarian the operative language on
Croatian railways and opening language schools for instructing
civil servants concerned with finance in Hungarian. In the summer
of 1883 the Hungarian Minister of Finance, Antal David, ordered
bilingual coats of arms (Croatian and Hungarian) to be placed on
the building of the financial administration in Zagreb, although
the *nagodba* called for the Croatian arms only. This led to demonstrations, and in a few days disorder spread from Zagreb to other
towns and even for the first time to some villages. The peasants
and the population at large expressed political dissatisfaction, partly
too because of their hard life. However, the Party of State Right
played an important role in fomenting the disorders, channelling
popular anger at the increasing gap between the wealth of the
middle class and the poverty in both towns and villages into
resistance to Hungarian domination, and singling out representatives
of the Hungarian government as targets. Their receptivity to
propaganda based on national arguments clearly showed that

politically the Croatian nation had matured. The demonstrations developed into a national movement; a state of emergency was declared and the Emperor appointed a commissioner to help reach a compromise. As a result Hungarian inscriptions were removed from buildings in Croatia, but the Hungarian and Croatian arms remained, which still infringed the *nagodba*. In Hungarian eyes the moment was ripe for imposing a Hungarian as *ban* to bring the situation under control. The appointee was Count Károly Khuen Héderváry (1849- 1918), a landowner from Slavonia, who ruled Croatia for the next twenty years, till 1903. It was a time of great economic progress, but the negative effects of false moves made by his regime were more significant.

## The Croats and the Serbs: cooperation and conflict

With the integration of the Croatian nation, and that of the Serbian nation which took place almost in parallel to it, a special group of issues concerning Croatian-Serbian relations necessarily emerged. The ethnic foundations from which these two nations had developed were very similar; in much of Croatia, Bosnia-Hercegovina and Vojvodina, Croats and Serbs live mixed together, and the similarity is reflected in the Croatian and Serbian standard languages. In their nationalistic enthusiasm some ideologues on both sides, like Ante Starčević and Vuk Stefanović Karadžić, tried to incorporate in their own nation as much as they could of the ethnic corpus that finally became part of the other nation, using to this end a variety of arguments from history, ethnology and philology.

During the nineteenth century, however, the almost concurrent development of Croatian and Serbian national integration increasingly showed that the nations were delimited according to religion: with negligible exceptions, the Catholics became Croats and the Orthodox became Serbs. As their national identity matured, the relations between Croats and Serbs developed on two levels: those of the common people and of politicians. Despite the fact that the ordinary people intermarried and had many other contacts, differences among them always smouldered. The reasons for this were religious intolerance, xenophobia, and the habit of people to use national instead of economic or other reasons to explain conflicts. As a minority in Croatia, the Serbs felt threatened by assimilation into the Croatian majority, and in time this feeling developed mythological dimensions; the integration of the Serbian nation in Serbia made them feel that they were part of a larger nation whose mother-state was Serbia. The Croats, on the other hand, accused the Serbs of not thinking of Croatia as their homeland. In cities these differences were minor, but in the villages they remained strong. Croatia was a predominantly rural country, and as people moved into towns, every new rural generation brought its intolerance with it. Croatian-Serbian political relations veered from pitched fights and polemics to reconciliation. The idea of a friendly life in common, and even of cultural and political unity, was aired but it was interpreted in different ways. The Croats took refuge in the Yugoslav option, fearing that they could not survive as an independent entity between such large nations as the Germans and the Hungarians, but they counted on entering such a community on an equal footing and being treated accordingly. In general, few people thought before 1914 that the Austro-Hungarian empire could ever cease to exist. Nevertheless, the 'Piedmont effect' was important in Croatian polities on the ideological level; for example, Ante Starčević was full of praise for the medieval Serbian Nemanjić dynasty, particularly because it was able to form an independent state. The very fact of the Serbian state's existence in itself motivated the Croats. On the other hand, most of the Serbs and their politicians viewed the actual everyday implementation of the Yugoslav idea as the extension of the Serbian state that had been established in the nineteenth century. It is clear from many documents that the Serbs often considered the concepts of Serbianism and Yugoslavism to be synonymous.

Periods of understanding and conflict alternated. The close cooperation between Croats and Vojvodina Serbs in the 1848-9 revolutions was followed by a heated dispute at the 1861 *Sabor* session over the name of the language. At the 1866 session Serbian deputies demanded that the name 'Serbian' should be recognised as 'diplomatic', i.e. that the Serbs should be recognised as a 'political nation' in the triune kingdom on an equal footing with the Croats. Croatian deputies opposed this, and Croatian-Serbian relations deteriorated. For the first time polemics on the subject appeared in newspapers. In the following year already the *Sabor* accepted the style 'Croatian or Serbian' for the official language in Croatia and Slavonia, and the equal status of the Latin and Cyrillic scripts.

It unanimously accepted the statement that 'the Triune Kingdom recognises the Serbian nation, which lives in it, as a nation identical to and equal to the Croatian nation.'

However, the celebration of St Sava was organised in 1869 at Knin, marking the beginning of the Serbian national movement in Dalmatia as well. Although both Croatian and Serbian politicians at that time considered the movement for Dalmatian autonomy to be their main opponent, rivalry between them was already apparent.

Relations grew more strained in the 1870s under *Ban* Ivan Mažuranic. He laicised primary education, which also affected Serbian confessional schools and thus developed into a national problem. The uprising in Bosnia–Hercegovina against Ottoman rule, which started in 1875 and was primarily led by local Serbs, and later the war of Serbia and Montenegro against the Ottomans, reverberated strongly among the Serbs in Croatian lands. Under pressure from Vienna, the Croatian government forcibly suppressed some activities organised to help the rebels, which made the situation even worse. The question of where Bosnia–Hercegovina belonged politically began to poison relations between the Croats and Serbs. Strossmayer and Rački, from their Yugoslav point of view, and Starčević as an anti-Austrian decisively condemned Austria's occupation of Bosnia–Hercegovina, forecasting that it would be fatal for the future of the Monarchy (their prescience became apparent in 1914). Despite the Emperor's frequent threats after 1875 that he would put off the *Sabor* session or dissolve the assembly altogether if it discussed Bosnia–Hercegovina, in 1878 it supported the occupation and expressed the hope that the territory would in time be joined to the united Croatian lands. On the proposal of the Hungarian ministerial council, the imperial court ruled that the *Sabor* had overstepped its competence.

Differing attitudes to the occupation of Bosnia–Hercegovina additionally complicated Serbian–Croatian relations and led to a rift in the National Party in Dalmatia: in 1879 the Serbs in inland Dalmatia voted for the Autonomist candidate against the Croatian one. Soon the Serbian Party was founded, which acted in coalition with the Autonomists and opposed the unification of Dalmatia and Croatia.

The 1880s and '90s brought new complications. When the Military Frontier became part of Croatia in 1881, the Serbian question came to the fore because Serbs in Croatia now accounted for 26.3 per cent of the population instead of, as previously, 7 per cent (the population of Dalmatia contained 20 per cent of Serbs). This was much higher than the population in 1991 (12.2 per cent). However, this statistic included Srijem, which already had a Serbian majority at that time, but not Istria, where Croats dominated and there were no Serbs at all. The policy of Serbia, which was formally under the influence of the monarchy, also greatly affected the Serbs in Croatia, who considered it opportune to side with Héderváry's regime, which the Croats hated. In time Serbian capitalists organised themselves into one political organisation, the Serbian Independent Party, and through the ramifications of their economic and political connections the party leaders gained a firm foothold in all the regions inhabited by Serbs. They systematically influenced the development of crafts and trade, spread culture and strengthened national solidarity. Croatian capitalists never formed such a strong organisation because of the tension in society, and their banks and firms were thus often identified with the narrow interests of political groups or local cliques.

Héderváry's skill at playing the Croatian and Serbian middle classes off against each other helped him to remain in power. In 1887 the regime-imposed majority in the Croatian *Sabor* legalised Serbian national-church autonomy in Croatia and Slavonia. Since executive power was vested in the Hungarian prime minister, not in the Croatian *ban*, this decision infringed the autonomy that the 1868 *nagodba* had guaranteed to Croatia.

## Immigrants and emigrants

The economic boom brought immigrants from other parts of the monarchy to Croatia – Czechs, Slovaks, Italians, Hungarians, Germans. Most of the former three nationalities were factory workers and ambitious peasants, but many of the Hungarians and Germans bought large estates (of over 100 hectares).

Jewish immigration was especially important. It had begun in north Croatia in the late eighteenth century and intensified in the second half of the nineteenth and the early twentieth. Like the others immigrants, most Jews came from elsewhere the Habsburg lands. At first they were peddlers, small-scale grocers and artisans, but as Croatia grew richer so did the Jews and their communities. Jewish capital helped to found the first important financial institutions and was invested in major economic projects. The percentage of Jews among intellectuals was much higher than in the population at large (in Zagreb they accounted for around 5 per cent). Jewish doctors, lawyers and other professionals made an important contribution to social development. As Jews grew wealthier, anti-Semitism – which was present among both the Croats and the Serbs in Croatia – became stronger, but it never dominated relations between Jews and the other members of Croatian society, Croat or Serb. It was stimulated by the usual factors of religious intolerance, xenophobia and economic competition, but the fact that most first-generation Jewish immigrants spoke German or Hungarian played a part too: this was not to the liking of either Croatian or Serbian patriots.

As foreigners moved into parts of Croatia, so Croats emigrated from their homeland. In the first decade of the twentieth century alone, 6 per cent of the population left northern Croatia. The process had started in Dalmatia in the 1870s and '80s and was even stronger there. The reasons were mainly economic. In the 1870s steamships began to replace sailing ships, a change to which Dalmatian shipowners were unable to adapt. In 1891 Austria-Hungary and Italy signed a commercial treaty that included the so-called wine clause that allowed Italy to export wine to the Habsburg monarchy with minimum custom duties. This made Italian and especially Sicilian wines cheap and thus dealt a hard blow to the Dalmatian wine industry. When the treaty expired in 1901 the clause was not renewed, but ten years of hardship had sent many Dalmatians abroad. The traditional orientation to seafaring and distant lands also contributed to emigration. In the first years of the twentieth century the central Dalmatian island of Brač alone lost 8,063 (over 32 per cent) of its inhabitants. This was the first great wave of emigration, which became so great that Croatia as a whole, but especially Dalmatia and some other parts, became one of Europe's principal emigration regions. This tendency lasted right to the end of the twentieth century.

*New economic developments, new political and national events*

The twenty years of Héderváry's rule witnessed ceaseless political tension in which the opposition was thwarted and could do nothing that might endanger the government. The *ban* controlled the *Sabor*, and the new electoral law of 1887 allowed only a strictly limited franchise: most of the voters were civil servants in institutions of the Hungarian and autonomous Croatian governments. There was much gerrymandering to ensure that the opposition had no chance of success. Elections were no longer held every third year, but every fifth.

The first years of Héderváry's rule were marked by scandal. The *ban* organised the secret transfer of documents from the Zagreb archives to Budapest, which led to an outcry in the *Sabor* in 1885. In the discussion that ensued he expressed his doubts as to Zagreb's 'legal ownership' of the documents, which provoked a rightist to kick him in the behind. The following year another rightist, the attorney Erazmo Barčić, delivered his notorious 'treason' speech, one of the nineteenth-century *Sabor*'s more notable performances. In it he expressed the hope that Russia would break Austria-Hungary and so open up the possibility of Croatian independence: 'There will be no peace', he said, 'until the Cossack hoof resounds through Vienna.'

Because of the regime's determined efforts to block all political initiative, the great economic exhibition held in 1890 in Zagreb turned into a political demonstration. Many Croatian delegations from Dalmatia and Istria attended. The leader of the Istrian delegation, Vjekoslav Spinčić, said that Istria belonged to Croatia, and was dismissed from the civil service.

Convinced that radical changes were impossible, the Party of State Right began in the 1880s to change its political goals. It advocated maximum Croatian self-rule within the monarchy and unification with Bosnia-Hercegovina. In the early 1890s, when Ante Starčević became infirm, his successors Fran Folnegović and, even more, Josip Frank completely abandoned the idea of an independent state. Ante Kovačić vividly showed the disappointment of those years in the realistic novel *U registraturti* (In the Registry Office). This story of the tragic fate of a peasant boy who goes to school in the city is a parable of the conflict between straightforward peasants and corrupt townspeople, and was a remarkable clearest example of Starčević's rightist ideology applied to literature. The most important poet of this period, Silvije Strahimir Kranjčević, also found inspiration in collective Croatian suffering, although his message is universal: his poem about Moses was a reference to Ante Starčević who was to lead the Croatian people out of 'terrible slavery'.

The political lethargy of the late 1880s and '90s was suddenly interrupted in 1895 when Emperor Franz Joseph came to Zagreb to open the new Croatian national theatre, one of the city's finest buildings. Political circles in Zagreb interpreted this as his approval of *Ban* Hédervary pro-Hungarian policy, and students burned the Hungarian flag in the main city square to show the Emperor the reality of the anti-Hungarian mood. There had been similar incidents in earlier years but this gesture marked an important turning-point in Croatia's political and spiritual life. The young people who emerged at that time were pronounced anti-traditionalists and critical of earlier models. The movement spread to literature, art and culture, and life in general. Right from the beginning, two currents were apparent, one progressive, nationally-oriented and strongly influenced by circles in Prague, and the other political and cosmopolitan, interested in art for art's sake.

The movement occurred simultaneously with similar movements in Europe and got the name *'Moderna'*. One of the basic demands was freedom: freedom of creativity, freedom to write on the subjects of one's choice, and freedom to be in contact with, and accept influence from, whom one pleased. Some circles were obviously growing wealthier and this made it possible to travel more widely and to live abroad. Young people made use of this to broaden their horizons and study and train in Prague, Munich and Paris. Their Paris days left an indelible mark on the work of the painters Josip Račić (1885-1908) and Miroslav Kraljević (1885-1913), the sculptor Ivan Meštrović (1883-1962), and the prolific and diverse writer Antun Gustav Matoš (1873-1914). People in Croatia became much more familiar with contemporary European art and literature, and constant comparison with the great centres of European culture gave birth to critical thought that had earlier usually been apologetic and formal. Nevertheless, all this involved only a small number of people: in 1910 northern Croatia still had 56 per cent illiteracy, and the whole county could only claim about 2 per cent intellectuals (excluding the clergy). However, in the long term modernisation and modernistic movements increased the number of literate people and the spread of middle-class culture.

After 1895 new ideological and political options came into

being in Croatia. In 1894 the Social Democratic Party was founded as a response to the working-class consciousness that was developing, especially among urban craft workers such as printers. Industrial workers were unskilled and most of the peasants were tied to their tiny holdings and had no class-consciousness. After the foundation of the Second International (1889) organised socialist movements were formed under the influence of socialist ideology, first in Zagreb and Osijek, and then in other towns. May Day was celebrated in Zagreb for the first time in 1890, and two years later the social-democratic paper *Sloboda* (Freedom) was inaugurated.

The new liberal currents in Croatia brought about a reaction. The political movement within the Catholic Church aimed at re-Christianisation of all sections of society: Roman Catholicism was the only authentic form of Christianity, and religious/ ecclesiastical and national interests were closely linked. But this 'Catholic Croatism' never became a relevant political force.

When the charismatic Ante Starčević died at the beginning of 1896, the earlier ferment in the ranks of the Croatian Party of state Right grew in intensity. Different rightist currents offered very different solutions, although all of them invoked Starčević's name. Since it was impossible for Croatia to gain full independence, some rightists saw a solution in close links with Vienna and, along with this, took a radical stance towards the Serbs in Croatia. Others saw Austria-Hungary as the greatest enemy and sought links with other South Slavs. Dispute was the rule and agreement an exception. In 1911 representatives of all rightist currents in Civil Croatia, Dalmatia, Istria and Bosnia-Hercegovina united and held the First All-Rightist Conference, as it was called. They demanded a Croatian *Sabor* with representatives of all Croatian lands and Bosnia-Hercegovina, which would decide, together with the Emperor, on the future relationship between Croatia and the Habsburg monarchy. In the following year, conflict between the currents was renewed, mainly due to differences in their positions concerning Serbia and the monarchy.

One of the men who (at the age of twenty-four) organised the burning of the Hungarian flag in 1895 was Stjepan Radić. After spending six months in prison he continued his political work, studied abroad and in 1904 with his brother Antun founded the Croatian Popular Peasants Party (*Hrvatska pučka seljačka stranka*).

He headed the party until his death in 1928, and in the 1920s was the leading Croatian politician. Although at first the party was small, in the '20s its influence rocketed because the peasants, still by far the most numerous class in Croatia, became conscious of their economic interests and national identity.

At the turn of the century very important events took place for the relationship between Croats and Serbs. Many years of strained relations culminated in the incendiary article by the Serbian nationalist Nikola Stojanović 'Do istrebljenja vašeg ili našeg – Srbi i Hrvati' (Until our Last Man or Yours – Serbs and Croats), published in 1901 in Belgrade and reprinted the next year by the Zagreb Serbian paper *Srbobran* (Defender of the Serbs). The article denied the existence of the Croatian nation and language and announced the victory of the Serbs over Croatian 'servitude'. This was because 'the Serbian national idea means progress'. This incited anti-Serbian demonstrations in Zagreb in which private property was destroyed and barricades were built. Some members of the Party of State Right took part in the disorders and Stjepan Radić and the Social Democrats spoke out against them. The Zagreb Serbs later distanced themselves from Stojanović's views.

In Croatia opposition to Héderváry's regime grew, especially the struggle for Croatian financial independence from Hungary. In March 1903 the Hungarian Committee of the Realm refused demands to rectify the financial terms to Croatia's benefit. A rally was then organised in Zagreb, at which, before a crowd of over 5,000, speakers demanded financial independence and political freedom for Croatia. Fifty similar rallies were organised in other Croatian towns but Héderváry banned them, which set off demonstrations in Zagreb, Osijek and elsewhere. In Zaprešić, a village west of Zagreb, the army fired at peasants taking the Hungarian flag down from the railway station, and this led to new disorders through almost all of Civil Croatia. Peasants went on the rampage and broke the windows of hated *Magyarones*, threw Hungarian officials out of their offices, and burned portraits of Héderváry and Hungarian flags. The authorities introduced martial law, and insurgents filled the prisons. Some fled the country and notified the foreign press, which took note of conditions in Croatia for the first time and ceased regarding them merely as an internal affair of the monarchy. The movement broadened and extended to all social classes, and this was echoed in other Croatian lands;

Croatian national integration was thus shown to be almost complete, not only in Croatian lands but also among the Croats of Bosnia-Hercegovina and Vojvodina. Dalmatia enthusiastically supported her 'sister', Croatia. Protest assemblies were held, telegrams of protest were sent to the Emperor, and there were appeals for money for the victims of persecution. It was similar in Istria, and anti-Austrian demonstrations broke out in Slovenia too, thus showing a measure of South Slav solidarity. When Franz Joseph refused to receive Dalmatian and Istrian deputies, they addressed a manifesto to the European public. After three months of turmoil Héderváry had to leave Croatia, though not in disgrace: he became prime minister of Hungary.

The movement of 1903 was mostly a Croatian affair but the younger generation of Serbian politicians viewed it sympathetically. The engagement of Dalmatian politicians, who saw the German *Drang nach Osten* as a danger for the development of all the small nations in the region, was crucial. In time many political parties and forces rallied around these views; their leaders were Fran Supilo (1870-1917) and Ante Trumbić (1864-1938). At a meeting in 1905 most Croatian opposition parties and politicians from Croatia and Dalmatia adopted the so-called Resolution of Rijeka. Exploiting the clash between the Hungarian opposition and the imperial court, they opted to help the Hungarians on condition that, when they came to power, the Hungarians would abolish repression and Hungarian hegemony in Croatia and help to bring about the unification of Croatian lands. This was the beginning of the so-called 'New Course' policy. Two weeks later Serbian politicians from Civil Croatia and Dalmatia adopted the Resolution of Zadar at a meeting in that town. They accepted the Rijeka Resolution and pledged to help the Hungarians and Croats if they recognised the equality of Serbs and Croats in Croatia.

The Croat-Serb Coalition which began at this time survived for several years despite the complicated and difficult political circumstances. At the end of 1905 it issued an electoral proclamation emphasising support for democratic freedoms, labour legislation and the protection of peasant holdings, and the gradual realisation of national demands (improvement of *nagodba* terms, financial independence, unification of Croatia and Dalmatia). In the spring of 1906, though unable to agree with the programme of the

Croat-Serb Coalition that threatened its hegemony, the Hungarian government allowed elections to be held for the Croatian *Sabor*. The regime did not exert the pressure that had marked earlier elections, and the Croat-Serb Coalition won. However, it did not manage to realise its key economic demands because the Hungarian government refused to extend the state support it provided for Hungarian industry to Croatian areas, or to allow a broadening of the franchise. The Coalition was constantly under attack. In the autumn of 1906 the Italians organised anti-Croatian demonstrations in Rijeka that put an end to cooperation between Croatian parties in Dalmatia and the Italian Party. The Austrian government intervened, promising economic aid to Dalmatia if it would abandon the 'new course' and implement a policy acceptable to Vienna. With these actions, and informal pressure from the police and its secret service, Vienna did indeed manage to break the 'New Course' in Dalmatia. Something similar soon happened in Civil Croatia with the help of the Hungarians. At around the same time, some rightist deputies paralysed the work of the *Sabor* in protest against the Serbian name used by deputies representing the Croat-Serb Coalition. To retain power in Civil Croatia, the latter obstructed the work of the Hungarian parliament for a month, and this only ended through a parliamentary coup. In the summer of 1907, after just over a year, the government of the Croat-Serb Coalition under *Ban* Teodor Pejačević fell. It had managed to pass some liberal laws, including one guaranteeing freedom of the press.

The turn of the years 1907-8 brought new complications when Austria-Hungary decided formally to annex Bosnia-Hercegovina. Pavao Rauch, a supporter of the regime, became *ban* with the task of creating favourable political conditions in Civil Croatia to implement the annexation. He was greeted by demonstrations. The authorities tried to secure legitimacy and called elections in which they relied on the resurrected *Magyarones*, the Rightists of Josip Frank and a Serbian party. This policy was a complete failure and the pro-regime parties did not win a single seat. Absolute rule was then proclaimed.

In the summer of 1908, fifty-three Serbs were arrested. Most were members of the Serbian Independent Party (which belonged to the Croat-Serb Coalition), and the government took this action in order to be able to present the forthcoming annexation of

Bosnia-Hercegovina as a defence against the imperialistic plans of the kingdom of Serbia. In October the Austro-Hungarian government proclaimed the annexation. It did so without consulting the other European powers and a crisis was provoked in which war almost broke out between Austria-Hungary and Serbia. This moment was used to publish the charges against the arrested Serbs, and at the beginning of March 1909 their trial for 'treason' began. They were accused of promoting the 'Greater Serbian' national programme in Croatia, Dalmatia and Bosnia-Hercegovina, and of engaging in subversive anti-government activities for the annexation of those lands to Serbia. At the end of March the Russian government recognised the annexation of Bosnia-Hercegovina and forced the Serbian government to do the same. Although the international reasons for pursuing the trial no longer existed, and the accusations were refuted and it was proved that the trial had been arranged so as to justify the annexation, all the accused were sentenced. However, in 1910, in the changed circumstances when the danger of war had passed, the trial and the convictions were annulled.

On the same day as Russia and Serbia recognised the annexation of Bosnia-Hercegovina, the Austrian historian Heinrich Friedjung began to publish a series of articles in the *Reichspost* of Vienna. On the basis of forged documents received from the ministry of foreign affairs, Friedjung accused some members of the Croat-Serb Coalition, most notably Fran Supilo, of treasonable cooperation with Serbia. The slandered deputies sued Friedjung and the *Reichspost*, and at the trial proved that the documents had been forged. The foreign minister, Aerenthal, and Crown Prince Franz Ferdinand intervened and a compromise was reached: the charges were withdrawn and the hated Rauch regime would be removed.

Several months later Khuen Héderváry became Hungarian prime minister again, and Nikola Tomašić, formerly a prominent figure in his National Party, was appointed *ban*. Tomašić's task was to reach an agreement with the Croat-Serb Coalition, but he did not succeed in doing so, and the authorities dissolved the *Sabor* with its Coalition majority. For Supilo the unscrupulous and unsuccessful negotiations conducted by Tomašić were the last straw and he retired from political life. Thus the man who had placed the problem of Croatia at the centre of the monarchy's South Slav policy disappeared, to be replaced by Svetozar Pribičević.

Pribičević nurtured close relations with Serbia, which began to show greater interest in events on its immediate western flank after the beginning of the century, especially in relation to the Serbian minority there. Pribičević's policy ran on the lines of Yugoslav unitarism, and this became crucial in the stormy events of 1918.

On the eve of the outbreak of war in 1914, the atmosphere and political conditions became even more menacing. New forms of repression were widespread and it became impossible for the opposition to fight for its political goals or even to express them. When Tomašić's following did not win a majority of seats in the 1911 *Sabor* elections, he resigned and was succeeded as *ban* by Slavko Cuvaj, who believed in solving all problems by force. He impounded newspapers and announced the dissolution of the *Sabor*, which had not even had time to assemble after the elections. Demonstrations by students and secondary school pupils immediately followed, and then a general secondary school strike, resulting in all the schools being closed. The Hungarian government abolished the constitution and nominated Cuvaj commissary. He stifled the press, rescinded the law on freedom of assembly, and appointed police commissioners in towns. Dalmatian and Slovene representatives in the *Reichsrat* protested, and the Austrian Prime Minister Karl Stürgkh was forced to condemn the commissary's actions. This caused a stormy reaction from the Hungarian government because of the alleged interference of the Austrian government in the affairs of the Hungarian part of the monarchy.

Cuvaj's repression provoked the Bosnian Croat Luka Jukić, inspired by Kvaternik's revolt in 1871, to attempt his assassination, but he killed the wrong man, was caught and condemned to death (the sentence was commuted to life imprisonment). Several months later the schoolboy Ivan Planinšćak also attempted to assassinate Cuvaj and, failing in his object, committed suicide. To calm the situation the Hungarian government sent Cuvaj 'on leave' at the end of 1912, but it did not abolish the commissariat. Political activities thus died down, and in the autumn of 1912 the shadow of war loomed in the east, with the outbreak of the First Balkan War; the second followed in 1913.

At the turn of the century, the wealth of bankers and industrialists initiated a degree of economic and social development, but even then the results were poorer than they might have been. While more than half of the population in Austria and Bohemia lived from jobs in industry, crafts, trade and rail, river and maritime traffic, in Croatian lands this number hardly exceeded one-fifth. The political framework and the inherited social structure did not allow changes of this kind to take place because of the extent of regional differences. When the modernisation process began, Civil Croatia had an estate feudal system, the Military Frontier a military system with elements of feudalism, Dalmatia a society of the Mediterranean type, and Istria a partly feudal and partly Mediterranean society. These systems became converted into peasant-middle-class societies, each in many ways specific and all retaining some elements of traditional pre-capitalist forms of production and way of life. Statistics from 1910 show that 68 per cent of all firms were engaged in crafts without hired workers (i.e. with only the master craftsman and possibly members of his family); that another 30 per cent had between one and five workers and were the employers of almost half the workers in the country; and that only 0.54 per cent of firms had more than twenty workers. At the beginning of the twentieth century Croatian society was fundamentally different from what it had been before the first modernisation in 1848, but it had not developed beyond the 'pre-industrial' level. For example, it was only now that the transformation took place from large to small family sizes, a characteristic of industrialisation. The peasants and lower middle classes still lived in traditional families that acted as economic units and made up a large part of economic life – the remainder consisting of the richest and poorest families. In the richest the father could support the entire family, and in the poorest adults and children had to seek work outside the household. Women always played an important role in the economy, primarily because of the general poverty and low level of development. In the subsequent decades women in Croatia did not have the chance to become housewives, the role middle-class society intended for them; industrial expansion in the second half of the twentieth century and mass immigration into cities forced them to find jobs.

In the early twentieth century Rijeka led the way in economic development. Its six largest firms – shipyard, oil refinery, torpedo factory, and tobacco, paper and rice-husking plants – employed as many as 54,000 workers. The length of railway track in northern Croatia increased from 430 km. in 1873 to 1,200 km. in 1890 and 2,100 km. in 1910. But the great majority of banks and savings banks still did not have significant amounts of capital at their disposal, but relied on counterparts in the more developed parts of the monarchy. However, their number alone indicates economic growth: from thirty-eight banks in 1875, to 130 in 1905, and over 200 banks in 1913.

Economic expansion brought much construction, and the centres of most towns throughout Croatia acquired their characteristic neo-classical or Secession stamp, which they have more or less preserved up to the present. Some of the finest buildings were in Osijek, but most of the building by far was done in Zagreb.

These were the conditions in Croatia when, on 28 June 1914, Gavrilo Princip, a member of the Serbian-organised and -directed terrorist organisation Young Bosnia (*Mlada Bosna*), assassinated the heir to the Habsburg throne, Franz Ferdinand, and his wife Sophie Chotek in Sarajevo. Austria–Hungary thereupon demanded that its inspectors be allowed to investigate the assassination on Serbian territory, Serbia refused and Austria–Hungary declared war. Russia declared war on Austria–Hungary, and within the next few days the whole of Europe had been plunged into war.

Everything thus began (and a lot happened) in a country where Croatia had national and economic interests, but where its direct influence and interests could not find expression. It had no say in the starting of the war, or later in the way it was waged. Thus Croatian soldiers became involved in the great European war with neither any real motivation nor any clear goal. They were expected to fight for a state with which Croatia had been in conflict, either open or hidden, for decades.

# 7

# 1918-1941: CROATIA IN YUGOSLAVIA

## 1918-29: democracy or dictatorship? An equal community or a Greater Serbia?

There was not much fighting on Croatian territory in the First World War, but many Croats fought in the Austro-Hungarian army on the eastern, Serbian and Italian fronts, and especially in the navy. At the beginning of the war 13-14 per cent of the Austro-Hungarian army's conscripts were from Croatia and Bosnia-Hercegovina, which did not account for as much as 10 per cent of the empire's total population. Many were killed; it was never established exactly how many. Tragic memories of those war years lasted a long time and only the even greater horror of the Second World War relegated them into the background. Miroslav Krleža (1893-1981) wrote impressively about Croatia's fruitless pre-war existence in Austria-Hungary and the absurdity of the Croats fighting for interests that were completely alien to them.

The war reached Croatian territory when French ships sailed to the island of Vis at the end of 1914 and set fire to several army stores before retreating. The forces of the Entente blockaded the Adriatic to stop Austro-Hungarian ships from sailing out of it. When Italy joined the war in 1915, parts of Istria were near the front line, especially the surroundings of the main Austro-Hungarian naval base, Pula. Many civilians were evacuated from those areas into camps in Austria, Bohemia and Moravia. In 1916 conditions deteriorated rapidly throughout Croatia. The economy was a shambles. The war economy that had been introduced meant requisitioning in the villages, and many impoverished people were exploited by money-lenders. Undernourishment was widespread. Urban life was devastated as many newspapers ceased publication and businesses were forced to close down. Apathy was everywhere. As the end of the war approached, the 'green cadre', consisting mainly of deserters from the Austro-Hungarian army, but also including impoverished peasants, appeared in villages in northern Croatia and in regions outside the gendarmerie's control. They mostly attacked and robbed landowners, merchants and money-lenders. The 'green cadre' survived the end of the war, and in late 1918 martial law was introduced to deal with it. There was famine in some parts of Croatia and Bosnia-Hercegovina at the end of the war, and about 17,000 children from Hercegovina were relocated to more prosperous Croatian families in Slavonia and Srijem.

As the war progressed, world politicians increasingly accepted that Austria-Hungary would not survive the war. More or less from the beginning, Entente members energetically discussed possible territorial gains after their victory at the expense of Austro-Hungarian lands, including Croatia. Both Serbia and Italy were interested in acquiring large portions of Croatia. In the secret Treaty of London of April 1915, the Entente powers promised Italy large parts of the eastern Adriatic coast and islands, and even Croatian territories deeper inland, as a reward for breaking off its alliance with the Central Powers and joining the Entente. On the other hand, Serbia knew that it too would obtain much Austro-Hungarian territory to its west and north if it emerged on the winning side in the war.

Croatian politicians seem to have been aware of the games that were being played with Croatian territory, but they were wrong in imagining that they would have any serious say in postwar decision-making. Some of them turned east because they thought that Croatia would have a better future in a common state with Serbia and Montenegro than if it remained part of Austria-Hungary. To implement this idea, the *Jugoslavenski Odbor* (Yugoslav Committee) was formed in Paris in April 1915. Its members considered themselves representatives of the western part of the future state – that is, the present states of Croatia, Slovenia and Bosnia-Hercegovina and the Serbian (Yugoslav) region of Vojvodina. The Serbian government, wishing to retain its dominance at every stage in the creation of the new state, never wanted the *Jugoslavenski Odbor* treated as a significant power, nor did it ever treat it as such. It was pursuing a hypocritical policy. On the one hand, the Serbian government stated at the end of 1914 that 'Serbia's fight was a struggle for the liberation and unification of all our enslaved brothers, the Serbs, Croats and

Slovenes'. It later issued many similar proclamations. On the other hand, the Serbian prime minister Nikola Pašić (1845-1926) did all he could to annex for Serbia only lands whose annexation would not endanger the emergence of a Serbian majority in the future state. In April 1916 he recognised Italy's right to the eastern Adriatic coast in some Russian papers, saying that Serbia would be content with an outlet to the sea and some parts of Croatia. This gave rise to great disputes between Pašić and the *Jugoslavenski Odbor*, exacerbated by disagreement over the manner of unification and the organisation of the future state. Pašić rigidly supported a centralist monarchy. The *Jugoslavenski Odbor*, and especially its most prominent Croatian politician Frano Supilo and others, upheld unification in a federal state based on the consent and equality of all its nations. Because of the Serbian stand and the benevolent attitude of Britain and Russia towards the plans of Italy and Serbia, Supilo quarrelled with Trumbić and the other members and in the spring of 1916 resigned from the *Jugoslavenski Odbor*.

In July 1917 representatives of that body met members of the Serbian government on the Greek Adriatic island of Corfu, and adopted the Corfu Declaration that formulated the basic principles for unification and the structure of the future state. It was to be a constitutional, parliamentary and democratic monarchy ruled by the Serbian Karadjordjević dynasty, and founded on general civil liberties. The declaration especially guaranteed equality for all the three flags (Serbian, Slovenian and Croatian), all the three names, all the three religions (Orthodoxy, Roman Catholicism and Islam), and the Cyrillic and Latin scripts.

In May 1917 the Yugoslav Club of deputies in the imperial council in Vienna issued the May Declaration demanding the unification of all Austro-Hungarian lands inhabited by the Slovenes, Croats and Serbs 'into a single autonomous state, free from the mastery of any foreign nation and democratically based, under the sceptre of the Habsburg-Lorraine dynasty'. This was an option that left Austria-Hungary alive, but later events showed it to be an idea bereft of vital force. At the beginning of 1918 the Yugoslav Club presented other initiatives and, together with most Croatian and Bosnian-Hercegovinian opposition parties, issued the Zagreb Declaration. On the basis of the principles of US President Woodrow Wilson concerning national self-determination, the declaration presented the Draft of Basic Principles for the Concentration of Slovenes, Croats and Serbs and demanded a completely independent state. The idea of dissolving Austria-Hungary and creating national states was gaining increasing support. In April a congress of the subject peoples of the Habsburg empire was held in Rome (Italy was Austria-Hungary's enemy in the war) at which they demanded the abolition of the empire and recognition by its enemies in the war of themselves as allies, of their voluntary units as allied belligerent forces, and of their national committees as legitimate representative bodies.

At the end of the war it became clear that Austria-Hungary would not survive and that its peoples wanted to proclaim independent states. At the beginning of October 1918 delegates of the Slovenes, Croats and Serbs from Austria-Hungary met in Zagreb and founded the *Narodno Vijeće* (National Council), a body to represent them politically, with a programme of uniting their nations within the empire into an independent and democratic state. About ten days later, the *Narodno Vijeće* proclaimed that all the 'national parties and groups' had agreed to it representing them. They would not listen to Vienna's calls for compromise, demanded a completely sovereign state of Slovenes, Croats and Serbs, and participation in the peace conference that would follow the end of the war. On 28 October the Czechs proclaimed that they were breaking off all state links with Austria, and the next day the Croatian *Sabor* did the same; as well as severing links with Austria and Hungary, it proclaimed Dalmatia, Croatia and Slavonia a single independent state. After that the *Sabor* recognised that supreme power was vested in the National Council of Slovenes, Croats and Serbs, and in this way the state of that name came into being. It included Slovenia, Croatia, Bosnia-Hercegovina and Vojvodina – all the South Slav lands in the former Austria-Hungary. In theory the new state could opt for any possibility – to remain independent or to ally itself with other states – but in practice there was almost no choice. No allied government, including that of the United States, would recognise it; on the other hand, in the next few days the Italian army occupied the towns of Pula, Rijeka, Zadar and Šibenik and many islands, and penetrated deep inland, taking Knin. It claimed certain territories under the Treaty of London, but it grabbed much more and brushed all protests aside. Most of the occupied areas had a considerable Croatian majority.

During the thirty-odd days of its existence, there was an urgent need to resolve all the dilemmas facing the state of Slovenes, Croats and Serbs: many matters that would remain important for decades to come had to be decided in that short time. At the beginning of November representatives of Serbia, the *Narodno Vijeće*, and the *Jugoslavenski Odbor* met in Geneva and arranged to create a common state, which they would invite Montenegro to join. However, they did not conclude any agreement on how the state would be organised and other key issues. The Serbian side gave no guarantees. Unrecognised by the world, frightened by Italian military advances, exposed to manipulation, speculation and diplomatic games, the state was forced to react quickly. In principle it accepted common sovereignty with Serbia, but there was fierce debate over whether this should be a confederation-federation with preconditions and guarantees for unification firmly laid down (the stand of Stjepan Radić), or whether there would be agreement on rapid unification in which unitary and centralist ideas would predominate (the stand of Svetozar Pribičević). The 'Conclusions and Instructions of the Central Committee of the National Council about Unification with the Kingdom of Serbia', which were voted at that time, left the organisation of the future state to the Constituent Assembly, and in the mean time King Alexander of Serbia was to rule as Regent. A delegation of the National Council went to Belgrade: Stjepan Radić's call for them 'not to go like geese into the fog' went unneeded, which was hardly surprising in the circumstances. There they presented an address to Alexander in words that did not completely conform to the 'Instructions'. Alexander then formally proclaimed the existence of the Kingdom of Serbs, Croats and Slovenes (*Kraljevstvo Slovenaca, Hrvata i Srba* – SHS), and on 1 December 1918 the delegation signed the act of unification with the kingdom of Serbia. Ante Trumbić, who signed in Cyrillic in the name of the *Narodno Vijeće*, became foreign minister in the first government of the newly-created state, but this was only formally an important position. Svetozar Pribičević, minister of the interior, was much more powerful and he now had a chance to put his ideas about creating a unitary and centralist state into practice.

As soon as it was signed, and for decades later, this document was interpreted in different ways, which caused misunderstanding and fundamental disagreement. While the Serbs considered that the new state was an extension of Serbia on the basis of its having been victorious in the 1914–18 war, the others – primarily (and at that moment almost exclusively) the Croats and the Slovenes – considered it the unification of several nations on an entirely equal foundation and without anyone having a specially privileged status. The Serbs and the Croats were by far the most populous nations of Yugoslavia, both after the First World War and after the Second, and in many regions lived mixed together. This made it clear that Croat-Serb relations and the Croatian national question would present the Yugoslav state with its greatest problem in the coming decades.

The new state stretched from the Alps almost to the Aegean, and covered an area that had never been under a single administration since the fourth century. It certainly brought a number of benefits to Croatia. First, the act of unification brought it on to the winning side in the war, and thus meant that Italy could not completely realise its pretensions to Croatian territory. Of places with a Croatian majority, only Istria, Zadar and some islands came under Italian rule. Had Yugoslavia not been created, Italy would certainly have acquired much more Croatian territory, possibly all of Dalmatia.

In a manifesto at the beginning of 1919, Regent Alexander proclaimed constitutional and parliamentary rule, universal suffrage, free elections for the Constituent Assembly, land reform, state borders that would conform to ethnic boundaries, and a programme of care for soldiers and others who had suffered in the war. In the following months the government abolished serfdom and other relations of subjection where they still existed. It expropriated the great estates and started implementing land reform, allowing people to lease land until the process was complete. There were many beneficiaries, but there was an undercurrent of nationally-based favouritism and Serbian peasants usually fared best.

The new state faced an external problem because its border with Italy in the territory of west Istria and Rijeka was under dispute. To put stronger pressure on Yugoslavia, Italy continued to hold the parts of Dalmatia it had occupied at the end of 1918 although it clearly would not be able to keep them. Italy still did not recognise the SHS kingdom, although every great power had done so by the summer of 1919. Furthermore, it demanded that others should not recognise the new state, and President

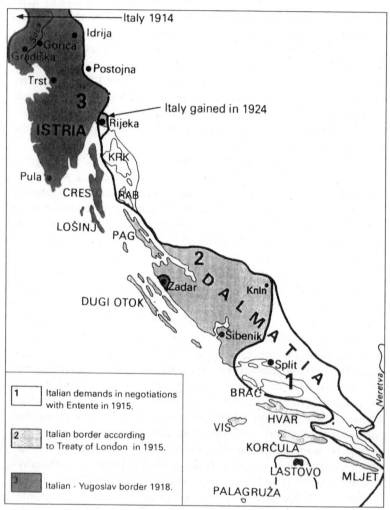

Yugoslav - Italian territorial dispute 1914 -1941

Woodrow Wilson's expressed intention to force territorial concessions from it caused a wave of displeasure in the country. Borne on this tide, the Italian poet and Fascist sympathiser Gabriele d'Annunzio entered Rijeka with his legionaries, in the autumn of 1919 and in 1920 proclaimed a separate state, the Italian Regency of the Kvarner (the bay on which Rijeka is situated), and foiled the plans of the major powers to establish the 'Free State of Rijeka' under League of Nations trusteeship. Under pressure of these events, the SHS kingdom and Italy signed the Treaty of Rapallo in November 1921, whereby Italy got all the territory west of Rijeka, some Kvarner islands, Zadar and the two southernmost Dalmatian islands. A compromise solution was found for Rijeka, which was to become the Free State of Rijeka (it was called Fiume by the Italians), but in an agreement signed in Rome in 1924 the two states agreed that the 'Free State', which had never actually been founded, should become part of Italy. In 1921 d'Annunzio and his men withdrew from it, and members of the Italian minority began to move out of areas which Italy had to cede by the Treaty of Rapallo. This led to a temporary respite in relations with Italy, which improved further with the Nettuno conventions of 1925 which solved practical (border) issues between the two states. Nevertheless, Italy was the main threat to Yugoslavia during the entire inter-war period, primarily because of its openly expressed territorial designs on Croatian territory.

In 1920 Yugoslavia signed the Treaty of Trianon with Hungary, a territorial compromise that left several tens of thousands of Croats as a minority in Hungary, mostly along the Drava and around the town of Pecs, and about 400,000 Hungarians in Yugoslavia, mostly in Serbian Vojvodina, and some in Slavonia.

Right from the start people doubted whether the new state would bring them a better life. When the currency was changed, the Serbian dinar was overvalued in relation to the Austro-Hungarian forint, and then every banknote was devalued by 20 per cent. Soon a new incident took place. On 5 December spontaneous demonstrations broke out in the centre of Zagreb opposing the establishment of the new state and protesting at bad social conditions. In the clash between units of the former *Domobran* (home guard) – these were disbanded in December 1918 – and the police several people were killed and wounded.

Almost all the pre-war political parties in Croatia disappeared.

Some kept their old names, but they now faced completely new issues that demanded new answers and a change in their ideologies. The central issue was whether the country should be a republic or a monarchy and how this could be resolved democratically. Another dilemma was whether the new state would be centralist and unitary, or whether special national features would be taken into account. As it addressed these and less pressing national problems, Stjepan Radić's opposition Croatian Republican Peasant Party grew increasingly popular. In the 1920 elections it showed itself to be the strongest party in Croatia, winning fifty out of the total of ninety-three seats, and the fourth-strongest in the whole of Yugoslavia.

Some individuals who were dissatisfied with the regime gathered around parties with a national profile, while others thought that a radical social change was needed. The socialist and social democrat parties merged and a quite strong Communist Party developed in the whole of Yugoslavia. Until June 1920 it was called the Socialist Workers' Party of Yugoslavia (of Communists), but then the revolutionary faction defeated the others and it changed its name to the Communist Party of Yugoslavia. In Croatia the Communists were stronger than in other parts of the country, but they participated in only one election, at the end of 1920, and with fifty-eight seats took third place in the Constituent Assembly. Their programme rejected reform and supported class struggle and a socialist revolution.

The SHS kingdom had a relatively free parliamentary life, but there was nevertheless a tendency to eliminate undesirable programmes and ideologies by undemocratic means. At the municipal elections of April 1920 the Communists obtained most votes in many Croatian towns (Osijek, Zagreb). In Zagreb they won 39 per cent of the vote, and the moderate Croatian Union won 31 per cent. Since the Communist deputies did not want to swear an oath of allegiance to the King, the government annulled their mandate, broke up the town assembly and ousted the town mayor who held office for only two days. Almost at the same time there was a general railway strike (about 50,000 people stopped work throughout Yugoslavia) in response to a reduction in the rights which railway employees had previously enjoyed. Communications were completely paralysed and the government called up all the railway workers to a military exercise and introduced martial law.

The railway strike was broken, as were all the strikes which had been called in sympathy.

Even before that, in 1919, Croatia had been engulfed by a great wave of strikes to ensure collective work agreements, recognition of labour union representatives and an eight-hour working day. The workers also managed to force the state to introduce elements of modern social insurance. Health insurance and, in the 1920s, social security generally were expanded.

## Despite all, rapid economic development

Although Croatia's very important links with Central Europe, especially with Vienna and Budapest, deteriorated as time passed, the economy found its feet in the new community. Like other parts of the country, Croatia was predominantly agricultural (not till the 1920s did the proportion of people dependent on agriculture fall below 70 per cent), but it had more industry than the more poorly developed regions further east. This opened up the market for Croatian products. Many industries, especially timber, had a secure internal market, and as mechanisation increased, crafts also flourished. Trade developed, and Zagreb became a centre for commerce and banking. Croatia, like the rest of Yugoslavia, was now a place of great developmental and business possibilities where quick profits might be made. This favoured foreign capital investment – more in Croatia than in other parts of Yugoslavia. Up till 1926 Croatia's economy was on an upward curve and even in 1930 conditions were still tolerable, but in spite of these favourable circumstances and great capital growth, workers' purchasing power in the 1920s was below its 1914 level. Urban development in Zagreb and other towns was similar to the rest of Europe. Zagreb radio began to broadcast, a Zagreb-Belgrade airline was opened, and the prosperous middle class supported the growing artistic production that was partly influenced by the post-war European avant-garde. Tourism developed on the coast, and Dalmatian ports, especially Split, received a boost in 1925 with the opening of the Zagreb-Split railway line via Gospić and Knin.

## New political pressure and the murder of Stjepan Radić

The constitution was voted in on *Vidovdan* (St Vitus' Day – 28

June) 1921, the anniversary of the famous battle of Kosovo in 1389 and thus a great holiday for the Orthodox Serbs – something which the other Yugoslav nations might have seen as a provocation. The constitution was voted in with a simple majority (over half), contrary to the terms of the Corfu Declaration and to decisions of the *Narodno Vijeće* that demanded a qualified majority (235 deputies voted for, 35 against, and 161 were absent). It guaranteed citizens personal and political rights, legalised monarchy as the form of government, introduced a limited parliamentary system (the separation of powers was only formally guaranteed), and promoted the principles of unitarism and state centralism. Over time, regulations were passed that enabled people to be brought to trial because of their political ideas and activities; one such was an enactment called the *Obznana* (1920), which banned all Communist activities.

In July 1921 Alija Alijagić, a member of the Communist organisation Crvena Pravda (Red Justice), which advocated individual terrorism, killed the minister of the interior. The authorities responded by introducing a Law for the Protection of the State which annulled the mandates of all Communist deputies and placed the Communist Party outside the law. Unlike the *Obznana*, which had specified twenty days in prison for Communist activity, the punishment was now draconian. The influence of the Party weakened when it went underground (although this could not be tested in elections), but the Communist spirit remained firmly alive in some intellectual circles. Writers, philosophers and artists who promoted interest in social themes made a great contribution to Croatian thinking and artistic production between the World Wars. In time even more severe laws were passed.

In the early 1920s Stjepan Radić and his party steadfastly opposed the regime and supported a republic. In 1920 they changed the party's name from Croatian Popular Peasant Party to Croatian Republican Peasants Party (HRSS). Before the *Vidovdan* constitution was enacted, HRSS members refused to swear an oath of allegiance to the King and participate in the work of the Constituent Assembly. They presented him with an Address on Unfulfilled Conditions for Unification, stating that there was no freedom to consider the organisation of the state. They then adopted the constitution of the Neutral Peasants' Republic of Croatia that called for confederation with Serbia, Slovenia and Bosnia-

Hercegovina. Just before the *Vidovdan* constitution was voted in, the Croatian parties in the Constituent Assembly founded the Croatian Block under Radić's leadership, which opposed the dominant unitary-centralist policy and challenged the Assembly's right to vote on a constitution for Croatia. The next year, 1922, the Croatian National Representation, comprising sixty-three deputies of the Croatian Block, adopted a memorandum for an international conference in Geneva. They repudiated the way in which the SHS kingdom had been formed and spoke of the 'internationally recognised territory of Serbs, Croats and Slovenes'. Almost at the same time a congress of public figures in Zagreb turned into an anti-centralist manifestation which demanded a revision of the *Vidovdan* constitution. At the 1923 elections for the National Assembly the HRSS took second place, with seventy seats, to the Radicals (107). In northern Croatia the party won fifty-two out of sixty-eight seats, in Dalmatia seven out of fifteen. They began negotiations with the strongest party of Bosnian Muslims, the Yugoslav Muslim Organisation (JMO), and the strongest party of Slovenes, the Slovenian People's Party (SLS), on forming a common front against centralism and for the reorganisation of the state. They also signed an agreement with the Radicals, whereby they agreed to vote in an exclusively Radical government in the Assembly, in return for which the Radicals would put off the decision to divide the state administratively on unitary principles. However, the Radicals did not honour the agreement.

Radić then went on a long European tour ending in Moscow, where he enrolled the HRSS in the Peasants' International. In 1924 political conditions in the state deteriorated because of the chronic parliamentary crisis, and only three days before parliamentary elections in February 1925 Radić was arrested and charged, with the entire leadership of the HRSS, under the Law for the Protection of the State – above all because the HRSS had joined the Peasants' International. While Radić was in prison the government block won a convincing victory in the elections, but the HRSS just as convincingly came second. The HRSS and other opposition parties, including the predominantly Serb Democratic Party, demanded an internal reorganisation of the state on the basis of the agreement between the Serbs, Croats and Slovenes. At the same time political games were being played over the verification of the HRSS's seats.

Then within only a few days there was a complete change. At the end of March, Stjepan's brother Pavle read a statement in the Assembly saying that the HRSS recognised the Karadjordjević dynasty and the *Vidovdan* constitution. The word 'Republican' was dropped from the party's name, which now became the Croatian Peasants' Party (HSS). The seats of HSS deputies were now verified, and a Radical-Radić government was formed with four HSS members. Radić himself became minister of education and held the post for several months. There were large and ever-increasing policy differences among the Croatian political parties at this time. In 1926 the Croatian opposition, gathered around the Croatian Union that grew into the Croatian Federalist Peasants' Party (HFSS), condemned the HSS's political turn-around and demanded an uncompromising policy in relation to Belgrade. The HFSS and the right-wing Croatian Party of State Right created the Croatian Block. In 1927 Ante Pavelić, the future leader of the Independent State of Croatia, gave his first political speech that attracted attention in the Zagreb District Assembly as representative of the Croatian Block. He demanded that all the deputies representing Croatian lands in the District Assembly should unite to work for the establishment of Croatian independence.

Despite the agreement with Radić, Belgrade still not only insisted on a centralised state but even tried to strengthen centralisation. It was thus logical for the HSS to step out of the government and join the opposition, which it did at the beginning of 1927. Sharp controversies continued in the Belgrade Assembly. These developments brought the HSS a new and unexpected ally when Svetozar Pribičević, leader of the Independent Democratic Party (SDS) that represented most of the Serbs in Croatia, completely changed his policy and accepted coalition with the HSS. At the end of 1927 the HSS and the SDS formed the Peasant-Democratic Coalition, with the goal of transforming the state and enhancing parliamentary life, democracy and the legal equality of religious faiths, languages etc.

In June 1928, acting in connivance with government inner circles, Puniša Račić, a deputy of the Serbian Radical Party, shot at HSS deputies in the Belgrade Assembly, killing two and wounding three, including Stjepan Radić. The attacker was placed under house arrest but was never tried. When news of the attack broke, there were demonstrations in Zagreb, and in the next ten days at least five people were killed and many more were wounded in clashes with the police. Deputies of the Peasant-Democratic Coalition withdrew from the Assembly. The situation grew worse when Stjepan Radić died from his wounds two months later. His funeral turned into a great political manifestation against the hegemony of Belgrade. The alliance between the HSS and the Serbs in Croatia (the Peasant-Democratic Coalition) had been strengthened by a proclamation that demanded a new constitution and reconstruction of the state in such a way that individual nations would be recognised. The entire Croatian opposition had rallied to the Coalition. However, the assassination of Radić and his co-workers so shocked people in Croatia that much of the desire and ambition for alliance with Serbia and association in Yugoslavia disappeared.

## 1929-41: unitary Yugoslavia and open dictatorship

*Proclamation of dictatorship and eliminating its opponents.* For months the situation did not settle down, and on the tenth anniversary of the proclamation of the Kingdom of Serbs, Croats and Slovenes (1 December 1928) clashes with the police in Zagreb claimed new casualties. Because of these developments King Alexander abolished the constitution on 6 January 1929 (the new regime thus became known as the 'sixth-of-January dictatorship'), dissolved the National Assembly, banned all political parties whose name had a national, religious or regional meaning, and founded the regime-supported Yugoslav National Party. General Petar Živković became prime minister. The Law on Royal Rule and Supreme State Administration legalised the King's absolute authority as the supreme organ of state rule.

Then the elimination of political opponents began. Ante Pavelić fled from Zagreb and did not return till 1941. The authorities accused Vladko Maček, head of the HSS since the death of Stjepan Radić, of aiding terrorist activities but after he had spent five months in jail the charges against him were withdrawn and he was released. Some prominent HSS members travelled abroad in order to inform the international public of conditions in Yugoslavia, especially in Croatia, and two of them, Juraj Krnjević and August Košutić, handed a memorandum to the League of Nations.

The Communists went through an especially hard time. Much of the leadership and about 1,000 members were subjected to police persecution; some were imprisoned and about ten were killed. The Communist Party virtually ceased its activities and the leaders fled abroad. Even Svetozar Pribičević, the former great believer in Yugoslavia, fared no better. He was interned in the small southern Serbian town of Brus, and then went abroad where he championed greater independence for Croatia till his death in 1936.

*New administrative division and new economic conditions.* In 1929 also, the name of the state was changed to the Kingdom of Yugoslavia. It was administratively divided into *banovine* named after rivers. This factor gave no consideration to ethnic, economic or geographic boundaries, its only purpose being to annul the continuity of historical and national regions and their boundaries, and to impose Yugoslav national unity under the leadership of ruling Serbian circles. Most Croatian territory was in the Sava *banovina*, based in Zagreb, and the Primorska (Maritime) *banovina*, based in Split, which included the predominantly Croatian areas of western Hercegovina. However, the Danube *banovina*, based in Novi Sad, included the eastern Croatian towns of Vinkovci, Vukovar and Ilok and the Baranja area. The Zeta *banovina*, with its seat in the Montenegrin town of Cetinje, included Dubrovnik, the Pelješac peninsula and the islands of Mljet and Korčula. This openly revealed plans to amputate areas that were completely Croatian or in which the Croats were the great majority (at that time the number of Serbs in eastern Slavonia was well below 20 per cent, and in and around Dubrovnik it was negligible).

State-controlled banks grew stronger, and new private ones were founded, with strong links to the government, which led to a great concentration of financial capital and power. The government founded a joint stock company to export agricultural produce so that it could control prices and monopolise the import and export of wheat. This was the beginning of the end for economic prosperity in Croatian regions. Centralisation grew, and since it was administered from a less developed region, pressure was put on the more developed regions to comply with the models and mode of operation of a weaker economy. In these conditions businesses could not be run according to normal economic rules.

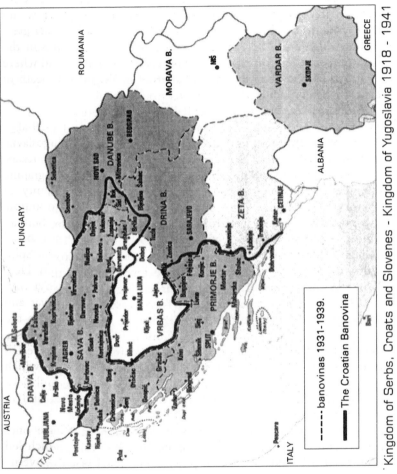

Kingdom of Serbs, Croats and Slovenes - Kingdom of Yugoslavia 1918 - 1941

In 1930 the situation became especially bad, mostly because of the World Depression. Foreign capital was withdrawn from Croatia, which did not receive the financial aid from Belgrade that it needed. In 1931 Croatia suffered a catastrophic financial crash after more than eighty years of almost unbroken economic growth and development. After this the unorganised private credit market became dependent on the state or on favoured credit institutions in Belgrade. The first bank to go bankrupt in Yugoslavia was the First Croatian Savings Bank, Croatia's oldest bank.

The Croats in Istria, then under Italian control, were also exposed to violence in those years. Bloody disorders occurred in 1921 when miners from Labin (who called their movement the 'Labin republic') and peasants from the region surrounding Pula rebelled unsuccessfully, demanding more national freedom and better living conditions. When the Fascists became the rulers of Italy in 1922, conditions worsened. They immediately closed Croatian classes in schools; they ousted the Croatian language from the administration in 1923 and from the judiciary in 1925. Also in 1925 they banned Croatian societies and dissolved co-operatives. Croats were indirectly put under pressure to take Italian forenames and surnames. Many Istrians emigrated into neighbouring Yugoslavia or overseas. In 1929 the last Croatian paper in Istria ceased publication. In the same year Vladimir Gortan, member of the revolutionary organisation TIGR (Trieste, Istria, Gorica, Rijeka), fired at an Italian demonstration-cum-procession marching to vote in the elections, for which he was tried and shot. Consequently, he became an Istrian symbol of the struggle against Italianisation and Fascism. Many Croats and Slovenes were arrested and tried on various political charges.

Political repression and economic depression in Yugoslavia caused frustration among the population, and this indirectly threatened the stability of royal power. The King was forced to grant concessions, and in the autumn of 1931 he proclaimed a constitution (the 'Octroyed Constitution'), which loosened the policy of strict absolutism.[*] A Senate and National Assembly were established and political activities on a limited scale were again allowed. This brought about little change because supreme state

---

[*] The King remarked sarcastically that there should be no intermediaries between him and the people.

power was still vested in the King who had competence in legislation, administration and the judiciary; the government was responsible to him alone. Yugoslav national unitarism became the official
ideology. At elections for the National Assembly at the end of
1931 only one (pro-regime) list was put forward, headed by the
prime minister, General Petar Živković. Voting was public and
oral, and civil servants and many others were under pressure to
vote. Nevertheless, in the Primorska *banovina* there was only 34
per cent turnout and in the Sava *banovina* 54 per cent – much
lower than in other parts of the country.

The main opposition force in Croatia, the Peasant-Democratic
Coalition, was not allowed public expression till 1932. In that
year it issued the *Zagrebačke Punktacije* (Zagreb Points), strongly
condemning the King's absolutism and Serbian hegemony and
demanding the reorganisation of the state on federal lines, but
with none of the federal units predominating over others. This
was the basis for the activities of Croatian parties until the Axis
invasion in 1941. The text was published abroad and it influenced
opposition parties in other parts of Yugoslavia. Vladko Maček,
leader of the HSS and one of the main signatories of the Points,
was imprisoned again, this time for two years.

However, repression did not end with imprisonment, nor were
Communists the only victims. In 1931 Milan Šufflay, a member
of the Croatian Party of State Right, a prominent writer and
historian, and a rare student of Albanian language and culture,
was killed in the street in Zagreb. The killers were never found.
Two years later the same fate befell Josip Predavec, vice-president
of the HSS. In 1932 demonstrations broke out in various parts
of Croatia, mostly organised by HSS supporters, with the
demonstrators carrying Croatian flags and national slogans. In some
places the police intervened, and some people were killed. New
clashes with the police took place in 1935 during the election
campaign, and again the police over-reacted and altogether there
were twenty victims in various places.

In the autumn of 1932 a group of Croatian émigrés attacked
a police station in the Lika village of Brušani, and the police
made great efforts to catch the perpetrators. Most were arrested,
while some fled abroad. In addition, the harsh behaviour of the
police against the local population aroused resentment and poisoned
relations between the Croats and the police and, even more

important, Serbs and the state generally. This event is known as the Velebit uprising, and members of the Ustasha movement regarded it as the formal birth of their organisation.

This throttling of individuality and aspirations for national freedom provoked extreme nationalist reactions. In 1932 the first number of the paper *Ustaša – Vijesnik Hrvatskih Revolucionaraca* (Ustasha – Herald of Croatian Revolutionaries) was published in Italy by the Ustasha headquarters, Glavni Ustaški Stan. In this and some other documents, editorials signed by '*Poglavnik*' (the Leader) advocated the most radical methods in the struggle for an independent Croatia, not excluding terrorism. The next year saw the publication of *Principles of the Croatian Ustasha Movement*, which called for national exclusiveness (recognising the rights of no other peoples in Croatia except the Croats, and limiting decision-making on state and national affairs to 'members of the Croatian people by descent and blood'), state-right historicism (relying on Croatia's historical state right and the right to all territories that had ever belonged to it or been inhabited by Croats throughout history), and the unconditional rejection of any common state with other Yugoslav peoples. Right from the start, the Ustashas goaded people against the Serbs, and the promotion of violence was inherent in their movement. 'Dagger, revolver, machine-gun and time-bomb, these are the bells that will announce the dawn and the RESURRECTION OF THE INDEPENDENT STATE OF CROATIA,' wrote the *Ustaša-Vijesnik* in 1932. Most of the Ustashas were at that time living in – and supported by – Austria, Germany, Hungary and especially Italy, where they had training camps in which they prepared themselves to fight in their homeland. However, the degree of support for them fluctuated as relations between those states and the government in Belgrade warmed and cooled.

In 1934 the Ustashas and Macedonian nationalists assassinated King Alexander in Marseilles, also killing the French Foreign Minister Jean-Louis Barthou. This created an international scandal. Italy was forced to arrest Ustashas, who ended up in Italian prisons or being confined in camps. After that the Ustashas increasingly began political agitation in Croatia, but their success was modest. The organisation did not develop, and newspapers and pamphlets written under their influence had only a small circulation. The police harried them, but they also sometimes turned a blind eye to their activities if this would harm the popularity of the HSS.

After the death of King Alexander the state was ruled by regents acting on behalf of the Alexander's son King Peter II, aged eleven at the time of his accession. Opposition parties, though officially still banned, participated in the elections of 1935. The Peasant-Democratic Coalition appeared with middle-class parties from other parts of Yugoslavia, and Vladko Maček headed the list. Maček's list won 37.4 per cent of the vote, and the pro-regime Yugoslav National Party, led by Bogoljub Jevtić, 60.6 per cent. Because of the unequal electoral law, Maček's list obtained only sixty-seven seats, and Jevtić's 303. In Croatia about three-quarters of the votes were for Maček's list, although voting was public. The entire opposition, including Croatian parties, demanded the abolition of the constitution, voting on a new one without any party having an in-built majority, a new electoral law and new elections.

In Croatia national and social problems were intertwined. In the 1930s the HSS founded the *Gospodarska Sloga* (Agricultural Co-operative) to improve the lives of the peasantry. This systematically worked on increasing the prices of agricultural produce, introducing electricity to villages, health protection, and eradicating livestock diseases.

The Communists were also very active – in 1937 the Communist Party of Croatia and Slovenia was founded within the Communist Party of Yugoslavia (KPJ). This showed that they allowed the formulation of national policies and had a greater understanding for national problems than was sometimes claimed. At that time a Croat, Josip Broz (1892-1980), who had taken part in the October Revolution, became secretary of the KPJ. He was a capable organiser and politician, and under his leadership the party grew in strength during the immediate pre-war years. About 700 volunteers from Croatia (a total of 1,200-1,300 from Yugoslavia), most of them Communists, managed to overcome government-imposed obstacles and went to fight on the Republican side in the Spanish Civil War. More than half were killed, but those who returned had gained experience that was to prove valuable for the war of 1941-5.

In the 1930s social themes were prominent in Croatian art and literature. In 1929 left-wing painters, sculptors and architects founded Zemlja (Earth Group), through which they tried to document reality and express a critical attitude to the social order of the time. The government banned the group in 1935, but its members retained their influence. In 1936 Miroslav Krleža published *Balade Petrice Kerempuha* (Ballads of Petrica Kerempuh). Through the figure of Kerempuh, a wily and rascally peasant, Krleža spoke with bitterness but also with humour of the Croatian people's position from the time of feudalism to the present. Those were also the years of 'conflict on the literary left wing'. Krleža proclaimed the predominance of aesthetic criteria in evaluating art and denied that social (and political) views could be used as a measure of value. Party-oriented Marxist critics opposed him, but he was an excellent polemicist whom it was difficult to oppose, and the positions he adopted found their way into Party circles. Krleža's humanistic view of socialism and Communism contributed to the gradual shift of Yugoslav and Croatian Communists away from Stalinist practice even before 1948.

*The Croatian banovina of 1939: a treaty of doubtful value.* Preparing for elections in 1938, and aware that it stood no chance by itself, the Peasant-Democratic Coalition joined forces with the 'Allied Opposition' in Serbia. Thus the opposition went to the elections with a single list under the name 'National Democratic Block', headed by Vladko Maček. The opposition demanded that a government should be formed consisting of parties 'rooted in the people'. They also demanded the abolition of the constitution, a new electoral law, and elections for a constituent assembly. The results obtained in the preceding elections were more or less repeated. Pro-regime parties won the great majority of seats in the Assembly but in Croatia, despite being under pressure from the government, Maček's list won some 80 per cent of the vote. The increasing tension in Europe and difficult conditions in the country forced the government into negotiations with the opposition – primarily the HSS, which through Maček most closely reflected Croatian public opinion.

At the beginning of 1939 Dragiša Cvetković became prime minister, and talks about a solution to the Croatian question became more serious. Maček tried to persuade the Allied Opposition to join the negotiations and allow him to speak in their name, but part of that group in Serbia persisted in its belief that establishing party-political life and democratisation should take priority over the Croatian question.

After several months of negotiations, an agreement was reached in August 1939 to establish the Croatian *banovina* covering the territory of today's Croatia and some parts of Bosnia-Hercegovina with a Croatian majority. It was an attempt to solve the Croatian national question as a whole. This agreement (*sporazum*) – between the Croatian political élite and the court in Belgrade – defined the boundaries of the Croatian *banovina* only approximately. This élite agreed to form a common government with Maček as vice-president and five more places for the Peasant-Democratic Coalition. Some competences were transferred to the *banovina* authorities, and a method was worked out to resolve disputes between the *banovina* and the state. A *ban* responsible to the King and the *Sabor* headed the *banovina*; its government had eleven departments including internal affairs, education, judiciary, industry and trade, and finances. The problem of finances was the most difficult to solve. In principle the *banovina* was to take over some taxes from the state, but no final arrangement was ever reached. Maček's political goals were realised when he achieved Croatian autonomy within Yugoslavia. Even in 1941 he did not want an independent Croatia that would depend on the Axis powers.

It seems that this solution, probably realistic and beneficial, came too late because internal tension and outside pressure were too great even for the wisest political solution to prevail. In order to placate Germany, in the autumn of 1940 the Yugoslav government passed, among other measures, the first anti-Jewish laws: a *numerus clausus* at universities and a ban on Jewish involvement in the wholesaling of food. At the beginning of 1941 it introduced coupons for flour and bread.

In foreign policy Yugoslavia's situation was extremely shaky. The Balkan Agreement (Entente) which also included Greece, Romania and Turkey, which Yugoslavia's royal regime had signed to strengthen its defence, and the Little Entente (Yugoslavia, Czechoslovakia and Romania) were worthless. In the summer of 1940 Yugoslavia established diplomatic relations with the Soviet Union, but this too was more a formality than any real support. In 1934 Yugoslavia had signed a trade agreement to supply Germany with Yugoslav agricultural produce in exchange for industrial goods, and at the end of the 1930s German influence in Yugoslavia was on the increase, helped by a degree of sympathy in the top echelons of the Yugoslav government for German policy. Hungary and Italy began to challenge Yugoslavia's territorial integrity more or less openly despite the 1937 Italian-Yugoslav agreement on the honouring of frontiers and co-operation.

At the beginning of 1938, through the Austrian *Anschluss*, Germany became in effect Yugoslavia's neighbour. By the beginning of 1941 it had mastered much of Europe. Hungary, Romania and Bulgaria were forced to join the Tripartite Pact, and Italy had already occupied Albania and was campaigning in Greece. Yugoslavia was thus completely surrounded. In 1940–1 the Third Reich was at its peak, with only Britain still resisting. The Soviet Union was temporarily Germany's ally. The pressure on Yugoslavia was irresistible.

# 8

# 1941-5: THE TRAGEDY OF THE SECOND WORLD WAR

## The capitulation of Yugoslavia; establishment of the Independent State of Croatia

After several months of German pressure and obvious political *rapprochement* between the Yugoslav government and the Axis powers, the kingdom of Yugoslavia signed, in Vienna on 25 March 1941, the Protocol by which it joined the Tripartite Pact. On that day demonstrations broke out in Belgrade and the larger Serbian towns which were partly spontaneous and partly engineered by either the British and partly by the Communists (in Croatia there were almost no demonstrations, only some minor protests organised by the Communists). The marchers carried the slogans *'Bolje rat nego pakt'* (Better war than a pact) and *'Bolje grob nego rob'* (Better a grave than a slave). This was a turning point after which things changed dramatically. A group of pro-British army officers staged a coup proclaiming King Peter of age, whereupon he assumed full royal prerogatives. A broad coalition government under General Dušan Simović was formed, consisting of parties and politicians whose views varied considerably, even on basic questions. Maček and the HSS faced several options, none of them good, so the lesser evil had to be chosen. The HSS formally remained in the government and had five ministers, with Maček as deputy prime minister. However, he quickly resigned and returned to Zagreb.

Germany and its allies considered what had taken place in Yugoslavia as a direct challenge, and war became inevitable. Belgrade was bombed on 6 April, and at the same time German, Italian, Hungarian and Bulgarian land forces entered the country from all sides. The Yugoslav army had no chance of putting up a defence, and capitulated without even token resistance. The army was demoralised by the enemy's superiority and eroded from within

131

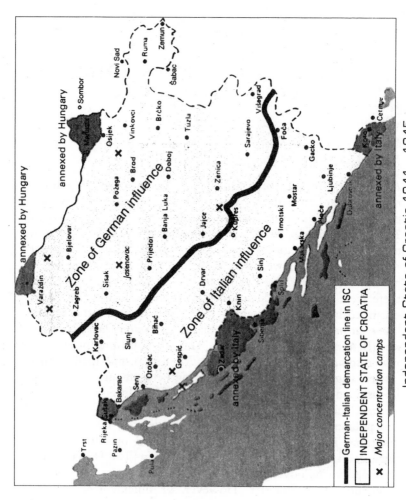

Independent State of Croatia 1941 - 1945

by national strife. The Serbs accused the other nations, especially the Croats, of treason, and it is true that the Croats did not want to fight for a country they did not consider their own. On 14 April King Peter and the members of his government fled abroad, first securing the safety of a large amount of treasure. Three days later the Yugoslav army signed an unconditional surrender.

The Germans had entered Zagreb on 10 April, and the former Austro-Hungarian Colonel Slavko Kvaternik, one of the leaders of the nationalist movement in the country, read on Croatian radio the 'Proclamation on Establishing the Independent State of Croatia': 'Croats! The providence of God, the will of our allies, the arduous and centuries-long struggle of the Croatian people and the great self-sacrifice of our leader Dr Ante Pavelić, and of the Ustasha movement in the country and abroad, have ordained that on this day, the eve of the day that celebrates the Resurrection of the Son of God, our country, the Independent State of Croatia, shall also be resurrected' (Easter that year fell on 13 April). Kvaternik assumed power and the command of the armed forces in Pavelić's name. The Germans did not succeed in persuading Vladko Maček to form a HSS government. Although he did not wish to compromise himself by collaborating with the Germans and Italians, and counted on the HSS retaining popular support during the war, he nevertheless called on 'all Croats to obey the new government' and on 'all HSS supporters in positions in the administration...to cooperate sincerely with the new national government'. At that moment the confused Maček may have thought that the Ustashas were a fortunate solution that would enable him to avoid complicated dilemmas and the burden of responsibility. However, in a week or two he probably realised that he had been too hasty, and retreated into passive resistance.

Ante Pavelić and about 300 Ustasha exiles came to Croatia from Italy via Rijeka, accompanying the Italian army; about the same number of Ustashas came from Germany and other countries. Before that, the only Ustasha operation was when they worked undercover to persuade two Yugoslav army regiments – a total of 8,000 soldiers – to rebel on 8 April and refuse to fight. On 15 April Pavelić came to Zagreb and the first government of the Independent State of Croatia (*Nezavisna Država Hrvatska* – NDH) was formed. Pavelić took the title of *poglavnik* (leader) of the state, and became prime minister and foreign minister. Judging from how they greeted the German army in Zagreb and some other towns, and from various other events in those days, most of the Croatian population were pleased at the defeat of Yugoslavia and the establishment of the NDH. Pavelić was welcomed by about 2,000 'sworn' Ustashas who had been working underground in the country: these made up the backbone of the new government. People immediately flocked to join the movement, so that by May 1941 it already had 100,000 members who had sworn the Ustasha oath. The Ustashas had most of their sympathisers among the less educated classes, and in some poor regions of the Dinaric mountains where Serbs and Croats lived mixed. Many people were also pleased that the NDH included Bosnia-Hercegovina.

However, disappointment soon set in and sympathy evaporated. The first great blow to Croatian national feelings was the Rome agreement of 18 May 1941, which ceded almost all of Dalmatia, much of the Croatian Primorje and a small part of Gorski Kotar to Italy, although the population of all those regions was about 90 per cent Croatian and just under 10 per cent were Serbs. There was a negligible number of Italians. Thus Pavelić and the NDH gave Italy almost the entire Croatian Adriatic coast, all the islands except Pag, Brač and Hvar, and all the major towns and ports (Pula, Rijeka and Zadar already belonged to Italy, which now also got Split, Šibenik and Trogir) except Dubrovnik, which remained part of the NDH but was strategically isolated in the far south. Somewhat later the NDH gave Medjimurje and Baranja to Hungary. Quite quickly, other disappointments followed. Racial and ethnic persecution of Serbs, Jews and Gypsies, and cruel terrorising of political opponents, antagonised most of the Croatian population and gave them a deep sense of insecurity. This was accompanied by grave economic troubles: the NDH had to bear the expenses of all the German occupying troops, and part of the Italians on its territory. Italy took over Croatia's maritime economy and shipbuilding, Hungary the best-developed agricultural areas, and (somewhat later) the Partisans almost all the agriculture, forestry and communications. The urban population became impoverished, and many were hungry. The sudden appearance and steady growth of political and armed resistance to the Ustasha regime and foreign occupation are clear indicators of the political disposition of the Croatian and non-Croatian population in the NDH.

## Establishment of rule and genocide

Because Pavelić and his close associates had prepared their political programme exhaustively as emigrants, and planned the most important laws and the form of administration they would introduce, the new political and state authorities were organised very quickly. They established a 'new order' which mirrored the contemporary Italian-German model and had the cult of the nation, the state and the leader at its centre. Their programme of June 1941 expressed the totalitarian idea concisely: 'In the Ustasha state, created by the *poglavnik* and his Ustashas, people must think like Ustashas, speak like Ustashas, and – most important of all – act like Ustashas. In a word, the entire life in the NDH must be Ustasha-based.' Soon the Ustasha Corps (Ustaška Vojnica), was formed, in which only members of the Ustasha movement could serve. The NDH armed forces also included, as its regular army, the re-mobilised Domobrans – the home guard created after 1868 as the nucleus of a Croatian army – who were to prove unreliable especially towards the end of the war.

The Muslims of Bosnia-Hercegovina, of whom at that time there were just over 700,000, were considered part of the corpus of the Croatian nation. A special policy of winning them over was initiated: they were called the 'flower of the Croatian nation', and Bosnia was called the 'heart of Croatia'. The Ustasha authorities were sensitive about culture and tried to win over writers, artists and other cultural figures, expecting that they would promote the national spirit in their work. They banned all political parties and all existing newspapers, turned all the printing presses into state property, and put Ustasha commissioners with almost unlimited authority in charge of all institutions. They named deputies in the Croatian *Sabor*, but it only met three times – at the start and end of 1942 – and had no power. The Ustashas laid great emphasis on the introduction of traditional symbols and old Croatian words. They demanded the 'purity of the Croatian language', which was to be cleansed of all 'Serbisms'. Archaic words and neologisms were introduced, along with the archaic orthography which was considered not to be tainted by the Serbian orthographic system.

From its foundation at the beginning of the 1930s, the Ustasha movement was radically nationalistic, and extremely intolerant of any kind of Yugoslav idea and the Serbs. It wanted an independent Croatia with a 'pure living space'. Anti-Semitic and racist program-mes were added at the end of the decade, influenced by the alliance with the Third Reich.

On the day after they had established their government (17 April 1941) the Ustashas proclaimed the *Zakonska odredba za obranu naroda i države* (Legal provision for the defence of the people and state), the basis for their system of political terror: the institution of concentration camps and the mass shooting of hostages. They introduced irregular as well as regular courts. Any threat to the survival of the NDH or the state, which even included listening to banned radio stations (e.g. the Partisan radio and the BBC), was treason and punishable by death. On 30 April racial laws were proclaimed, defining Aryan and non-Aryan origin, and these were the foundation for all later anti-Jewish measures. In a short time the NDH had adopted the Nazi legal system, and in some areas even exceeded it. Only two months after the establishment of the NDH, the Jews lost their citizenship rights; they were forbidden to sign business contracts, ordered to wear yellow armbands and compelled to undertake forced labour; and their property was requisitioned. Provisions were enacted for sending them to camps. On 14 April the synagogue in Osijek was burnt down, and during 1941 synagogues in other towns were demo-lished, some for 'reasons of town planning'. The Zagreb Jews handed 1,000 kilos of gold over to the Ustasha authorities to save themselves from persecution, but this did not help them: of almost 40,000 Jews in NDH territory before the war only about 9,000 survived, and of them only a few hundred were still in occupied territory at the end of the war, thanks to personal and family connections, corruption and intercession by the Catholic church, especially the Archbishop of Zagreb, Alojzije Stepinac. Fewer than 1,000 returned from concentration camps. At least 7,000 saved themselves by joining Tito's Partisans or fleeing to the Italian-occupied zone or to Italy itself. Although some Croats actively participated in killing Jews, there were also many who tried to save them and succeeded. At times the German army judged that, despite all their cruelty, the Ustashas were not carrying out the 'final solution' thoroughly enough; they themselves organised raids and deported the remaining Jews to their own death camps. The racial laws also applied to Gypsies, and almost all those in the NDH, some 15,000, were killed.

Special legal provisions were also passed imposing various limitations on the Serbs, but the Ustasha authorities did not have a precise or officially verified plan for dealing with the 2 million Serbs in their power. The unwritten Ustasha plan, often mentioned and implemented in practice, was to kill one-third of the Serbs, banish another third to Serbia, and force the remainder to convert to Catholicism. The more moderate Ustasha leaders were for mass deportations into Serbia and conversion. The 'hard core', headed by Pavelić and his émigré followers, advocated the 'use of all means, even the most terrible' (from a 1932 editorial by Pavelić in the paper *Ustaša*), i.e. death. Pavelić entrusted the organisation of the killing to a special secret service within the Ravnateljstvo za javni red i sigurnost, known as 'Ravsigur' (public order and security department) and the Ustaška obrana (Ustasha defence), which was the third division of the Ustaška nadzorna služba – UNS (Ustasha supervisory service). The 'Ustasha Himmler', Eugen Dido Kvaternik, headed both services. On 27-28 April the Ustashas committed their first mass crime at Gudovac near Bjelovar (80 km. east of Zagreb): in retaliation for the killing of a Croatian soldier by an unknown person, they killed 196 Serbian men from Gudovac and the surrounding area. This was followed on 9 May by the slaughter of 400 Serbian peasants from the Kordun village of Veljun and its surroundings, and on 13 May 260 Serbs at Glina in Banija were killed. Because of this Archbishop Stepinac wrote a letter to Pavelić, protesting for the first time at the Ustasha's crimes. As summer approached, in June and July, mass murders became more frequent, now also of women and children, in Serbian villages in Lika, Kordun and Banija, and in the Dalmatian interior. Especially terrible were the crimes committed by mostly Muslim Ustashas in eastern Hercegovina in 1941, but by the winter of that year the Chetniks were returning measure for measure in eastern Bosnia, in the valley of the Drina. Thus a vicious circle of revenge set in from which the Partisan movement managed largely to distance itself for some time. The violence set off a wave of refugees, and in August 1941 the German occupation authorities in Serbia registered 180,000 Serb refugees on their territory, most from the NDH.

On 29 April the first concentration and work camp in the

NDH was formed at Danica near Koprivnica, 90 km. north-east of Zagreb, and about 5,000 prisoners, including 500 Jews passed, through it. In the following months other concentration, work and death camps were formed, totalling about thirty. The largest, Jasenovac on the river Sava, which included the old Stara Gradiška prison, was set up in September 1941. During NDH rule, between 80,000 and 100,000 people – Jews, Serbs, Gypsies, Croats and others – were killed there.

Following Maček's recommendation to the people on 10 April to cooperate with the new authorities, many Croatian Peasant Party (HSS) members helped establish the Ustasha regime. However, after making this compromising proclamation, he no longer wanted to cooperate with the authorities and turned to passive resistance. Thus the Ustashas began to look on him and many HSS members as opponents. Some were interned, others were even liquidated, and Maček himself spent five months in Jasenovac concentration camp, and after that was placed under house arrest on his estate near Zagreb. By the end of 1941 the great majority of HSS members had distanced themselves from the Ustasha movement, and from 1942, but especially in 1943 and 1944, a considerable number joined the Partisans. Most of the HSS leadership advocated a waiting policy, secretly expressed sympathies for the Western Allies (Britain and the United States), and tried to establish connections with them through various channels to create a base from which their party might be able to influence the post-war arrangement of the country.

The Ustashas were especially cruel to Communists and other anti-Fascists, and towns were covered with announcements of mass executions of imprisoned hostages in retaliation for Communist actions. As the anti-Fascist struggle grew, Ustasha massacres in Croatian villages that supported the Partisans were also not unusual.

In the name of the Catholic church Archbishop Stepinac had publicly expressed his support for the establishment of the NDH on 12 April, and satisfaction with it. Already by this time some priests were active supporters of the Ustasha movement, and in 1941 they were joined by many others. However, the Catholic church opposed the enforced conversion carried out by the regime, and in 1941 made several official protests. Stepinac himself, first in talks with and letters to Ustasha officials, and later in public sermons, expressed opposition and protested against the Ustasha policy of violence and racial intolerance. Often he intervened personally, on some occasions with the help of Vatican representatives, and managed to save persecuted individuals and groups. Among others, he saved from the Holocaust many Jews in mixed marriages and fifty-five inmates of a Jewish home for old people, whom he sheltered on a church estate near Zagreb. At the same time, Stepinac remained consistent in his radical anti-Communism and his Croatian-national orientation, and although he criticised the Ustasha regime he did not distance himself from the NDH as a state. He considered the Communist-led Partisans the 'anti-Christ' and the main enemy. Most Catholic priests in the NDH went through a similar evolution. Only a minority remained closely linked to the Ustasha movement, and an even smaller number joined or cooperated with the Partisans between 1943 and 1944.

The international position of the NDH was hopeless. Created under the patronage of the Axis powers, it remained throughout its whole existence part of Hitler's war machine. It joined the Tripartite Pact on the Soviet Union, even sending two of its regiments to the Eastern Front – they fought before Stalingrad – as part of the German army. On 8 December 1941, the day after Pearl Harbor, it declared war on Britain and the United States. Right up till the very end of its existence, in most of their operations in Croatia NDH units were under the command of, and often also part of, German military units. The Germans and Italians divided NDH territory almost exactly through the middle into the northern (German) and southern (Italian) spheres of interest, in which their troops took over power on certain occasions, and where they exploited forests, ores and labour to the full. By the end of the war over 200,000 men and women from the NDH were taken to Germany as cheap labour. Only twelve countries recognised the NDH, all of them signatories of the Tripartite Pact, i.e. members of the Nazi-Fascist coalition, and only eight established diplomatic relations with it. The Vatican sent its permanent legate to Zagreb but did not recognise the NDH and retained diplomatic relations with the royal Yugoslav government in London. It thus recognised Yugoslav continuity. As the war progressed and Allied victory became certain, various small groups appeared in Croatia that wanted to overthrow the Ustasha regime but save the NDH as a state. However, in the existing situation this was doomed to failure. All the three great anti-Fascist powers and their allies recognised Yugoslavia as a state, as the forcibly dismembered victim of Nazi-Fascist aggression and as their ally, whose full state sovereignty would be regained immediately after the war. The question was only what kind of government this post-war Yugoslavia would have and what would be Croatia's position in it.

*The liberation war*

In the early summer of 1941 armed resistance broke out against the Ustasha authorities and foreign occupation. The main organisers were the Communists, but it was the Serbian population in central parts of Croatia and in other parts of the NDH who provided numbers and the main support. They took up arms to defend their very lives from Ustasha genocidal terror. Croatian democratic and anti-Fascist patriots also took part, at first mostly in Dalmatia, the Croatian Primorje and Gorski Kotar, where they rebelled against Italian rule, and later in increasing numbers in other parts of Croatia.

When Yugoslavia broke up in April 1941, the Communist Party of Yugoslavia was the only political party whose organisation covered the entire country. The Communist Party of Croatia was its most numerous and best organised part; at the time, the Yugoslav Party had 6,000-8,000 members, one-third of whom formed the Croatian Party. To them must be added about 10,000 other active sympathisers and members of the Communist Youth organisation in Croatia. Most were revolutionaries used to underground work and ready to do what their party ordered in a disciplined, almost fanatical manner. When the NDH was proclaimed, the Yugoslav Party leadership and Tito were in Zagreb. A month later they went to Belgrade, from where they continued to maintain regular courier contact, and later a scrambled radio-link, with the Croatian Party leadership in Zagreb, and with Party organisations elsewhere in Yugoslavia. Throughout the war the Croatian Party, as part of the Yugoslav Party, implemented the general directives of the Yugoslav Central Committee and Tito in a disciplined fashion, at the same time adapting with great skill to specific circumstances in Croatia.

Up till 22 June 1941, while the pact between Germany and

the Soviet Union held, the Communists refrained from open action against the German occupying forces and their allies. Nevertheless, they made preparations, secretly gathering weapons, organising military committees and extending their underground network among the increasingly dissatisfied population. The German attack on the Soviet Union and the call to Communists in occupied Europe to 'fulfill their international debt by defending the main stronghold of the world proletariat, the USSR' was the signal for the Croatian Communists to act. On the very day of the attack, 22 June, without waiting for instructions, about fifteen Croatian Communists from Sisak, about 50 km. south-east of Zagreb, moved into the nearby forest, founded the first guerrilla detachment, and on the following day carried out the first armed action by blowing up the railway line that passed close by. In succeeding days there were a series of diversions by Communist shock groups in some Croatian towns, mostly in Zagreb, Karlovac and Split. They tore down telephone lines and electric cables, attacked soldiers and mined railway lines. The most spectacular event was on a Zagreb football stadium where the Ustasha officials tried publicly to separate Zagreb secondary school pupils according to nationality. Members of the Communist Youth persuaded the youth of Zagreb, most of whom were Croats, to move on to the side of the field that the Ustashas had set aside exclusively for the Serbs and Jews. However, in the middle of July the Communist leadership sent their combatants into mountain villages and regions to start widespread resistance and a guerrilla war, and this proved much more efficient than diversions in the towns.

Fleeing from Ustasha massacres, Serbian peasants hid in the forests and were organised by the Communists who led them in attacks on minor Ustasha and police garrisons and in other guerrilla actions. During the summer the rebellion flared up in central parts of Croatia (Kordun, Banija, Lika), and even more in the neighbouring Bosnian border region and eastern Bosnia-Hercegovina, where there was a relatively large Serbian population who were in immediate danger. Military activities were commanded by experienced Communist fighters – former volunteers in the Spanish Civil War – and by a certain number of officers from the royal Yugoslav army who managed to avoid being taken prisoner in the April war.

In Italian-occupied Croatian Primorje and Dalmatia, the situation was only slightly better. The Italians gave Dalmatia special bilingual status and tried to win over the local population through special consultation bodies (*Consulta*), without much success. When the first diversions began they did not react as brutally as the Ustashas and the Germans, but even this did not win them any sympathy. The Communists' call to fight against the Italians was effective. In Split a general strike was organised in August in protest against Italian occupation, and later a ship loaded with material for the Italian army was set on fire. Communist shock groups were organised into seven Partisan detachments, which suffered considerable losses fighting a much stronger enemy. However, resistance in Dalmatia grew and was no less than in other parts of Croatia.

From the beginning the Comintern sent messages to the Yugoslav Communist Party warning them 'in the present stage to concentrate on liberation from Fascist occupation, not on a socialist revolution'. This accorded with earlier assessments by the Croatian and Yugoslav Communists that they should place themselves at the head of a pan-national resistance. At that time Croatian (and Yugoslav) Communist propaganda and proclamations made no mention of the 'class struggle', 'overthrowing the bourgeois order' or the socialist revolution in general. The calls to resistance were exclusively anti-Fascist and patriotic, against foreign occupation and the Ustasha regime. Aware of the widespread dissatisfaction that had existed in pre-war Yugoslavia, the Communists used the argument of a struggle for a better post-war order in the country: democracy and a fairer inter-ethnic balance. On 13 July 1941 the Central Committee of the Communist Party of Croatia issued a proclamation outlining the goals of the national liberation struggle as 'liberation of the country from foreign rule and domination' and the establishment 'of a new democratic Yugoslavia of free and equal peoples, with a free Croatia built on the basis of self-determination'. With these slogans anti-Fascist armed resistance gradually spread to Croatian regions – first the coastal belt in the south and in 1942 the north, including some regions around Zagreb. In the autumn of 1941 resistance fighters organised themselves into companies, battalions and detachments they called 'Partisan'. On 26 October 1941 the 'General Staff of the National Liberation Army and Partisan Units of Croatia' was founded on Petrova Gora mountain in Kordun. The commander, political commissar and operations officer – Ivo Rukavina, Marko Orešković and Franjo

Ogulinac-Seljo – were all members of the Croatian Communist Party and had been officers in the Spanish Republican Army. All subordinate units had political commissars, who without exception were Croatian Party members, as were most commanding officers. Thus the Communists retained positions of command and a decisive influence on the Partisan movement.

By the end of 1941 Partisan units in Croatia already had about 7,000 armed combatants, to whom must be added at least three times more organised helpers and the support of the population in most Serb villages and some Croat ones. The Communists also had strong underground organisations in most of the towns. The winter of 1941-2 was especially long and harsh, with great difficulties in communications and supplying the population. The Partisans also suffered severe hardships, but by this time they already controlled extensive rural and mountain areas far from the main lines of communication, and several small towns in the centre of the country along the border with Bosnia-Hercegovina.

During the whole of 1942 the national liberation struggle gradually increased in intensity in Croatia, and its influence – and the extent of the liberated areas – spread northwards. In addition to units linked to a more limited territory, the Partisans, in the summer and autumn of that year, formed their first brigades – mobile units of 800-1,000 combatants. By the end of 1942 there were eighteen brigades in Croatia: four in Lika, three each in Kordun, Banija and Dalmatia, two each in Primorje-Gorski Kotar and Slavonia, and one in Žumberak about 30 km. from Zagreb. They were relatively well armed, with weapons captured from the enemy mostly in guerrilla attacks and by overpowering small garrisons. At the end of 1942 the Partisan brigades, detachments and independent battalions in Croatia counted some 25,000 armed fighters. In neighbouring Bosnia-Hercegovina, which had its own general staff, there were many more Partisans, but the organisation was weaker. In Slovenia there were far fewer Partisans, but with far superior organisation, especially in Ljubljana. From the end of 1941 to the summer of 1944 the supreme command headed by Tito moved from one location in Bosnia-Hercegovina to another.

In liberated villages and small towns the Partisans established *Narodnooslobodilački Odbori* (people's liberation committees – *NOO*) which, as well as providing services behind the lines for the Partisan army, also became the civilian authorities. The Communists held key positions in both the army and the NOOs, but they still kept to their national liberation programme instead of a revolutionary-socialist one. However, it was clear that they intended not to let the reins of government slip from their fingers.

## Ethnic and civil war

The war that raged in Croatia from 1941 to 1945 was part of the war throughout the whole of Yugoslavia, and what happened in other regions of the country often influenced the situation in Croatia. In the late summer of 1941 fighting began in Serbia between the Chetniks under the command of Draža Mihailović and the Partisans, who had earlier fought side by side against the Germans and their collaborators. The conflict soon spread to Montenegro, eastern Hercegovina and Bosnia, and by the spring of 1942 it had reached Croatia. Everywhere it developed into a violent civil war between the former short-lived allies.

The Partisans under Communist leadership were relentless in their use of offensive tactics, regardless of their casualties and those caused in addition by enemy retaliation against the civilian population. The Chetniks, on the other hand, were opposed to offensive actions against the Germans, Italians and other superior armies. They considered that this caused too much suffering, especially after 16 September 1941 when Hitler ordered the execution of 100 civilian hostages for every German killed, and of fifty for every German wounded. They advocated a tactic of 'waiting for the propitious moment for a general uprising'. Until then they embarked on the task of defending the Serbian population from Ustasha genocide in the NDH and retaliating against Croats and Muslims. They had already given an example of this on 15 April 1941 when a Chetnik unit, retreating from Mostar before the Ustashas who were taking over the town, killed several dozen Croat civilians in the surrounding villages and set fire to a large number of houses. In 1941 there were several more individual actions of a similar nature, and at the end of 1941 and in 1942, after breaking off their alliance with the Partisans, the Chetniks began genocide on a more mass scale, especially against the Muslims in eastern Bosnia. The Partisans opposed this with their Yugoslav programme of 'equal nations' and the slogan 'brotherhood and unity', and through their ethnically mixed units, particularly in Croatia; from 1941 they also undertook some retaliatory actions of burning and killing. In Croatia Chetnik mass crimes against the Croats remained limited to the Dalmatian interior, Knin and 'a small part of Lika.

The differences in the long-term goals of the Partisans and the Chetniks were even more crucial. Draža Mihailović proclaimed that the Chetniks were the 'Yugoslav army in the homeland', and under the slogan 'For King and Country' they fought for the continuity and renewal of royal Yugoslavia. The Partisans openly opposed the King and the government-in-exile, and any renewal of the old Yugoslav order.

The Chetniks envisioned post-war Yugoslavia as a Greater Serbia that would include Bosnia-Hercegovina, Montenegro, Macedonia, Dalmatia and Croatia up to the Virovitica-Karlobag line, with a corridor through Lika and Gorski Kotar for a direct link with Slovenia. The Partisans supported a 'Yugoslavia with six equal federal republics' and a democratic system, although their Communist leadership indicated that the latter would be a Communist kind of democracy. When Tito and Mihailović met in western Serbia in the autumn of 1941 they recognised each other as the main rivals in the struggle for power after the war, and a clash between them was inevitable.

In the nineteenth century, when the Serbs were rebelling and fighting wars for liberation from the Ottoman Turks, their élite guerrilla units were called Chetniks. In royal Yugoslavia the Chetniks became an organised radical Serbian nationalist movement, and even gave their name to some élite military units in the royal Yugoslav army. They were also organised in Croatia in areas settled by Serbs. They considered themselves the nucleus of the royalist movement and of Serbian domination over Yugoslavia, including unreliable Croatia where they had to be the protectors of the threatened Serbs. In their war-time propaganda they claimed to be continuing this tradition.

With this programme the Chetniks had more supporters in Serbia and Montenegro in 1942 and 1943 than the Partisans. However, in the NDH the Partisans defended Serbian villages from Ustasha terror much more efficiently and, except in the Knin area, enjoyed much stronger support among the Serbs in Croatia than the Chetniks. When resistance began in 1941 the

Chetniks did not have special units in Croatia. Some of them joined the Partisans individually or in groups, while others laid low waiting for further developments. In August and September 1941 the Italians could clearly see that Ustasha atrocities were causing unrest and disorder in their sphere of interest, and accordingly moved their troops to cover a larger area in southern Croatia and protected some Serb regions from further Ustasha terror.

This led to the first differentiation among the resistance fighters. The Chetniks and their sympathisers considered that they should only fight against the Ustashas, while they cooperated with the Italians in protecting Serb villages. The Communist-led Partisans, on the other hand, said that they were fighting against all Fascist forces, including the Italian occupiers. In the winter and spring of 1942 these differences grew into open war between Chetniks and Partisans in Croatia, like that which had already started a month or two earlier in Serbia and Montenegro. The Chetniks in Croatia found refuge in Italian garrisons (Knin, Gračac, Plaški, Gomirje and others), where they received all their supplies, and fought the Partisans under direct Italian control. They completely stopped fighting the Ustashas – and the Germans, with whom they established direct cooperation after the Italian capitulation in 1943. They justified this as 'making use of the enemy of the moment' (the occupiers and Ustashas) to destroy the 'long-term enemy' (the Communist-led Partisans).

In 1942 it was already clear that Ustasha rule and the NDH were in crisis. The Partisans held much of the agricultural land and forests, and many mines and sawmills, and blocked road and railway traffic in most of the country. The towns were short of food and of many industrial goods. The violent methods of the Ustasha authorities alienated the population. In the spring of 1942 a group of prominent theatre artists left Zagreb to join the Partisans, and founded the 'national liberation theatre' on Partisan territory. In the autumn of 1942 Vladimir Nazor (1876-1949), the most distinguished older Croatian poet, and Ivan Goran Kovačić (1913-43), one of the most talented and best-known young poets, joined the Partisans. In 1943 Nazor became president of the ZAVNOH, the supreme body of Partisan civil government in Croatia. Kovačić wrote *Jama* (The Pit), the most moving poem about Ustasha crimes, while he was among the Partisans; he was later killed by the Chetniks. Miroslav Krleža, the greatest of all Croatian writers, spent the war in Zagreb but refused to cooperate with the Ustasha authorities in any way and did not publish a single line in their papers.

Already in their early reports German representatives in the NDH, especially the military representative General Glaise von Horstenau, warned that the 'bestial behaviour of the Ustasha authorities is causing unrest and rebellion' damaging to German interests. Instead of the NDH being a growing military and economic aid to the German war machine, as had been planned, the Germans increasingly had to struggle as the war progressed to keep Pavelić's state alive. In 1942 they put pressure on Pavelić, and to some extent he changed his policy towards the Serbs: he proclaimed them 'Croats of the Orthodox faith', promised to stop religious persecution, and founded the Croatian Orthodox Church for the NDH territory. He picked on Dido Kvaternik as the main scapegoat and dismissed him, and disbanded the notorious Ustaška Nadzorna Služba (Ustasha Supervisory Service). However, by then the Ustasha regime was so badly compromised that such measures could not succeed in giving it any credibility among the Serbs, or among an increasing number of disillusioned Croats.

## The decisive year: 1943

At the end of 1942 the Partisans held a large and compact area in central parts of the NDH: from Livno and Glamoč through Drvar and Bihać to Korenica, Slunj and Vojnić. The Ustashas and Domobrans (home guard), with the help of the Germans in the north of the country and the Italians in the south, held all the large towns with strong garrisons and some of the main communications, but Partisan-controlled territory already covered more than half of the NDH, including smaller enclaves in the north. In November 1942, in the presence of about 100 representatives of the Partisan movement from all parts of Yugoslavia, Tito founded the Anti-Fascist National Liberation Council of Yugoslavia (AVNOJ). This was to be the supreme representative body, and the nucleus of Yugoslavia's future government. Although the programme still concentrated only on anti-Fascism and the slogans were democratic, it was clear that the Communists held the

monopoly in decision-making and that they would not let power
slip out of their hands.

The mere fact that this meeting was held signalled that the
German occupation system was facing breakdown. That autumn
Hitler himself instructed his commanders to bring about the 'complete destruction of Communist resistance'. In the middle of winter,
in January 1943, the Germans launched their great Operation
Weiss to destroy the main Partisan forces in the NDH. For this
they assembled three operational divisions and one reserve division,
the Volksdeutscher SS-Division Prinz Eugen, a Croatian legionary
division and selected units of the NDH army. The Italians
cooperated with three complete divisions and parts of three others
that joined later. A total of 120,000 troops attacked the central
Partisan force of almost 40,000 directly under the supreme command and Tito. In five weeks the more numerous and better-armed
Germans captured Partisan territory and pushed the main Partisan
force several hundred kilometres south-eastwards to the valley of
the river Neretva in Hercegovina. Ivan Rukavina, general staff
commander of the Partisans for Croatia, took two Croatian divisions
and attacked the advancing enemy in the rear, using guerrilla
tactics and avoiding direct confrontations. Although he thus
managed to preserve the nucleus of the Croatian Partisans from
heavy losses, the supreme command rebuked him for this operation
and demoted him to become commander of the first Croatian
Partisan Corps.

The Germans and their allies managed to concentrate their
forces and once more encircle the main Partisan force. The decisive
battle took place in the valley of the river Sutjeska, on the border
between Bosnia and Montenegro. Showing great heroism (the
fighters from Dalmatia were especially notable) the Partisans
managed to break out of the ring, but suffered great losses: at
least 7,000 dead and as many wounded. During their campaign
to destroy the basis of the Partisan movement, the Germans and
their allies burnt down several hundred villages and committed
countless atrocities on the population. However, as soon as the
offensive passed and the three German divisions went to other
fronts, the Partisans retook their territory first in Croatia and then
in Bosnia, and the movement healed relatively quickly. In June
1943, in newly-liberated territory in Lika, they founded the
Regional Anti-Fascist National Liberation Council (ZAVNOH),

their supreme representative body of Croatia. Its decisions and declarations reconfirmed the federal organisation of the future Yugoslavia, with Croatia as a federal unit.

The capitulation of Italy on 8 September 1943 was one of the crucial events in the four years of war. The Partisans disarmed many Italian units and acquired a great amount of weapons, ammunition, food and various kinds of equipment. Besides superiority in weapons, Partisan units now also became superior in manpower. Most of Dalmatia was liberated, with Split and all the islands, most of Istria and the Croatian Primorje. The ZAVNOH proclaimed all previous treaties with Italy null and void and announced the decision to annex Istria and all the Italian-held areas to Croatia. Pavelić proclaimed similar decisions, but the NDH had never established its power in most of the formerly Italian-held areas. Because of danger that the British or Americans might disembark on the eastern Adriatic shore, the Germans were forced to relocate seven divisions from other fronts, and at the end of 1943 and beginning of 1944, helped by the NDH army, they managed to force the Partisans back from most of the former Italian territories. However, they too gradually had to retreat from those areas.

After the Italian capitulation many Croats from coastal regions joined the Partisans, and on the whole the liberation struggle in Croatia went from success to success. The number of Partisans kept growing: from 7,000 in 1941 to 25,000 in 1942, 100,000 in late 1943 and 150,000 in 1944. By the end of the war this number had grown even higher through systematic mobilisation. The process was mirrored in the manpower situation of the other side. The numbers of the regular NDH army, the Domobrans, reached their peak at the end of 1943 with 130,000, but a year later it had halved. The élite voluntary Ustasha units had most soldiers at the end of 1944: about 76,000. These included Croats and a considerable number of Muslims from Bosnia-Hercegovina, whereas the Partisan statistics mentioned above include only combatants from Croatia.

The Croatian Peasant Party meanwhile drew closer to the Partisans in its policy, and HSS individuals and groups increasingly expressed loyalty to them. In September 1943 the HSS broke off the last contacts between its prominent members and the Ustasha government over a possible coalition government, and a month later members of the HSS executive committee met on liberated territory and expressed their support for the Partisans. April 1944 saw the setting-up of the HSS executive committee for liberated areas.

In November 1943, at its second session in Jajce, central Bosnia, the AVNOJ was constituted as the supreme representative legislative and executive body of Yugoslavia. It confirmed that the Partisan movement was part of the anti-Fascist coalition and was resolved to fight against Nazism and Fascism to the end. It was decided that Yugoslavia should be reconstructed as a federal republic with six units, whose borders were also in principle delimited (these were the so-called AVNOJ borders later used as the basis for delimitation after the dissolution of Yugoslavia in 1991-2). The AVNOJ established the National Liberation Committee of Yugoslavia as its executive body with the powers of a temporary government. It divested the royal government-in-exile in London of the right to represent the country, and forbade King Peter II to return to Yugoslavia. A general election or a referendum would be held after the war to decide the fate of the monarchy. Josip Broz Tito was given wide powers: he was named supreme commander, army minister with the rank of marshal, and prime minister. Although the AVNOJ included individuals from various political parties, it was completely under the influence of Communists, who retained key positions in the government. They still supported general anti-Fascist and democratic programmes and slogans, but were leaving no doubt that they would hold on to power after the war.

The Communist leaders in the future republics, including Croatia, behaved like the leading Communists at the federal Yugoslav level. After 1942 Andrija Hebrang was secretary of the central committee of the Communist Party of Croatia, and thus the most influential person in the Croatian Partisan movement. His authority and work methods promoted a relatively independent Croatian policy. Disputes between Hebrang and other Communist leaders became more frequent in 1944 (his opponents accused him of insufficient 'Yugoslavism'), and Tito decided to post him to Belgrade – where, however, he and Tito continued to have disagreements. Vladimir Bakarić (1912-83) became the leading figure in Croatia, and so remained till his death. As Tito's close associate, he held various offices (secretary of the Croatian central committee, Croatian prime minister, and the like) and was thus the main promoter of the leader's policy in Croatia. He coldly distanced himself from all 'deviations' and in every situation took an authoritarian stance.

At its third session in May 1944, the ZAVNOH was constituted as the supreme representative legislative and executive body, and thus the highest body of state authority, in democratic Croatia. This was the first stage of creating the new federal Croatia in the 'second' or 'socialist' Yugoslavia. The session was held in Topusko, only about 60 km. south of Zagreb, and attended by Randolph Churchill, son of the British prime minister, then head of the British mission in that area. In his report to his father he wrote: 'If you want to find a peaceful place in Europe, come to Topusko.'

# 9

# 1944-8: THE SOCIALIST REVOLUTION – FROM ELEVATED IDEALS TO REVENGE AND TOTALITARIANISM

To win the war the Partisans needed further military victories and international recognition, especially from the three leading Allied powers which maintained close contact and diplomatic relations with the exiled Yugoslav government in London throughout the war. Until the spring of 1944 the Yugoslav government unreservedly backed the Chetniks and Draža Mihailović.

In the spring of 1942 the British first learned of the Chetniks' lack of fighting resolve and collaboration with the Italians, and the military superiority of the Partisans. The political sympathies of the British government were still with the Chetniks, who were anti-Communist and loyal to the monarchy, but military arguments increasingly tipped the balance towards the Partisan side. The following spring, in 1943, the British parachuted the first military intelligence mission to the Yugoslav Partisans. The agents, three Canadians of Croat origin, landed at Lika, in Croatia. Only later were Allied missions sent to Slovenia and Bosnia. After Italy's capitulation the British began to supply the Partisans liberally with weapons and other equipment from their base in the Italian Adriatic port of Bari; a Partisan base was also set up there, which organised help and coordinated the reception of wounded and refugees from the German offensive and famine in Dalmatia. El-Shatt in Egypt was selected to accommodate them, and about 28,000 went there. At the beginning of 1944 the Allies broke off all contact with Draža Mihailović's Chetniks.

The Soviets pursued an insincere policy, fearing that Tito might outgrow the role of pawn which they intended for him. The Americans were the most passive, leaving Yugoslav affairs for the British to took after. After 1943, and especially after 1944, the

Allies accepted Tito and the Partisans as the only liberation movement in Yugoslavia and Croatia.

The exile government in London had to renounce Mihailović
in order to remain in the diplomatic game, and it nominated the
Croat Ivan Šubašić, former *ban* of the Croatian *banovina*, to become
its new head. In June 1944 Šubašić met Tito, and they agreed
to cooperate in strengthening the national liberation struggle, but
not to form a joint government. In August Šubašić issued a declaration calling on people to join the struggle against the occupier
under Tito's leadership. Whether their agreement would be
honoured or not depended on the balance of forces, which was
greatly to the benefit of the Communists. Šubašić and his supporters
had no military back-up, and it was impossible for the masses to
feel loyalty towards them. Šubašić could only count on tepid
British and American diplomatic support, which was obviously
not enough. In contrast to all the other East European countries,
the Communists in Yugoslavia and in Croatia were an indigenous
force, aware that they had much of the population behind them.
They were convinced that the right was on their side, and that
their movement must win. Thus Tito could allow himself to
arrest August Košutić, vice-president of the HSS, in September
1944 after the failure of negotiations between them. Even the
appeals of Croatian politicians to Winston Churchill himself did
not help Košutić.

The Tito-Šubašić agreement was signed in November 1944
in Belgrade. It laid down the establishment of a joint government
and the convening of a Constituent Assembly, and again King
Peter was forbidden to return to Yugoslavia until the people
made their final decision known. In February-March 1945 the
government of Democratic Federal Yugoslavia was formed, and
the portfolios were distributed on a basis of realism: Tito became
prime minister and defence minister, and the Communists held
almost all the other most important portfolios. Ivan Šubašić became
foreign minister, and members of parties that 'followed the policy
of the National Liberation Movement' also entered the government.

After 1944 the Partisans, and with them the government that
was being created on the basis of their liberation war, slowly lost
their revolutionary appeal. They had fought to renew Yugoslavia
– not as a royalist state but as a federation. However, this idea
was outmanoeuvred because post-war Yugoslavia, though federal

in name, was nothing of the sort in practice. It was a centralised state, completely in the spirit dictated by the Communist Party, centrally constituted with one man at the head of a small group who decided all essential questions. At that time the Partisans also stopped adhering to their earlier democratic proclamations and promises, and were seen to be establishing a dictatorship on the Soviet Communist model.

The Yugoslav Communists were setting up their rule while the war was drawing to a close, and the regime became increasingly authoritarian and then totalitarian. From the principle of free will the Partisans turned to recruitment and mobilisation; from relying on villages that supported them and supplied them with as much food as they could spare, they now introduced forcible requisitioning and left the population without even the necessary minimum. Some Partisan commanders, including Tito himself, showed that they wanted not only to become leaders but also to live in luxury, which was at odds with the proclaimed principles of social justice and equality.

This new atmosphere began to be felt in Serbia more or less as soon as the Partisans entered Belgrade on 20 October 1944, and in Croatia especially after May 1945. They began to rule on the Stalinist Soviet model. Enemies and potential enemies were killed or persecuted without trial, and their property was confiscated. Many people were evicted from their homes. This period lasted till 1949-50, when new forms began to be sought following the break with Stalin and the Soviet Union, and changes began which at the time were called liberalisation. A modest shift took place towards the rudimentary elements of a market economy. This lasted till 1953-4, when there was another wave of autocratic constraint after the Djilas affair and reconciliation with the Soviet Union. At the end of the 1950s, tentative liberalisation set in again. These successive waves of freezing and thawing were one of the characteristics of Tito's dictatorial rule.

Some of the final operations in Yugoslavia, such as the liberation of Belgrade in October 1944; were carried out with the help of the Soviet army. The Croatian Partisans had liberated most of southern Croatia by the end of 1944, but the German army tried to keep control of the railway line from Zagreb to Belgrade and on to Greece, which they needed as a line of retreat for their army. It therefore dug in and fought a frontal war in Srijem which the Partisans readily accepted, wanting to show that they could win in that way too. The northern and western parts of Croatia were thus mostly not liberated till April and the beginning of May 1945 after heavy fighting and great Partisan losses. Zagreb was liberated last, on 8 May.

## Bleiburg and 'squaring accounts with the enemies of the people'

The NDH caved in along with its Nazi ally. After repeated Partisan calls the Domobrans flocked to join Partisan units. In the summer of 1944 two of the more moderate NDH ministers (Vokić and Lorković) conspired to remove the most compromised and radical Ustashas from power, hoping to establish contacts with the Western Allies and save the NDH from the Yugoslav Communist Partisans. With the Germans' help the Ustasha hard core headed by Pavelić put down the conspiracy, executed its leaders, and remained faithful to the Third Reich right up to their common end. When the Partisans reached the outskirts of Zagreb, the NDH leaders, Domobrans, Ustashas and many civilians, including the HSS leader Vladko Maček, did not wait for the new authorities. Fearing retaliation, they fled through Slovenia in the hope of reaching Austria and surrendering to the British, whom they expected to treat them better than the Partisans or the Soviets. They were joined by about 40,000 German soldiers, a small number of Slovenian collaborators and civilians, and Serbian Chetniks and civilians (not more than 5,000–10,000 of each). Altogether there were between 100,000 and 150,000 refugees, probably around 134,000. However, at the request of the Yugoslav army, the British army in the Austrian border region (Bleiburg and Viktring) handed back the fleeing soldiers and civilians. Some of the more important prisoners were singled out, taken to prison and legally tried, but many of the anonymous refugees were killed on the spot. The others were taken on death marches, called the 'Way of the Cross', to various parts of Yugoslavia, and the guards were ordered to kill those who could not keep up or became exhausted. Some lucky survivors walked up to 1,000 km. to the final goal. According to the most precise research published to date (Žerjavić, 1992), 45,000–55,000 former Domobrans and Ustashas were killed around Bleiburg and on the Way of the Cross, and the others were sent to prisons and prison camps. Only a small minority were immediately released.

Full of the fervour of revolution, victory and vindictiveness, the new authorities thought they had the moral right to square accounts uncompromisingly with 'bands' and 'class enemies', and this continued even after the war ended. Exactly how many people were killed like this in Croatia and other Yugoslav republics is unknown, but the estimate for all of Yugoslavia, which may be exaggerated, is 250,000. It seems that quite a large number of people were killed in all areas of Yugoslavia and in every one of its nations, and it is difficult to say that this 'revolutionary enthusiasm' was targeted exclusively or mainly against any single nation. The relations that developed with church communities were in line with this campaign. The Catholic church was treated with particular harshness in comparison with other church communities because some of its clergy cooperated – actually or allegedly – with the Ustashas in Croatia and Bosnia-Hercegovina. However, the conflict was really founded on the fact that the Catholic clergy were hostile to the ideology of the new authorities. They supported free Catholic press, schools, associations and charitable activities, personal freedom and the return of confiscated property. In 'squaring accounts with the enemies of the people' several hundred priests and monks were killed, some churches were destroyed, and monasteries, convents and seminaries were closed. Propaganda and intimidation were also used to suppress the activities of the Orthodox church. As for the Islamic community, the new authorities fought against 'ancient backwardness' and destroyed traditional manifestations of Islamic culture: the veil was banned, and dervish orders, Koranic schools and courts of Islamic law were abolished. The 1946 constitution included the usual article about honouring religious freedom in Yugoslavia and the separation between church and state, but in practice things were different. There was an unwritten rule that members of the Communist Party could not be believers; furthermore, not only could they not be married in church or have their children baptised, but they were not even allowed to enter a church for celebrations organised by their friends or relations.

Concentration camps were set up, and victims also died in prisons. Some people were simply killed in the street or in their homes, although such cases were relatively rare and happened only immediately after the Partisans and the OZNA, the notorious Communist secret service, arrived in a region. A federal decision in September 1945 curbed the lawlessness somewhat: camp and prison commandants were required to keep precise evidence of the number of prisoners, and thus made impromptu executions practically impossible. In the following years concentration camps were abolished, with the inmates being gradually released, or sentenced to long terms of imprisonment. The military court in Zagreb sentenced to death former ministers and prominent NDH officials handed over to them by the British, including Pavelić's first deputies Slavko Kvaternik and Mile Budak. Pavelić himself, his home minister Artuković, the 'Ustasha Himmler' Eugen Dido Kvaternik and a large number of former NDH ministers, Ustasha officials and senior military officers managed to escape in the post-war confusion. Using illegal channels, they managed to reach Argentina, Paraguay, Australia, the United States and Spain.

## The trial of Alojzije Stepinac

The peak of the legal 'settling accounts with the enemies of the people' happened in 1946, when members of the Quisling armies were tried at around the same time in Serbia, Slovenia and Croatia. In Belgrade the Chetnik General Draža Mihailović was among those sentenced to death. The Archbishop of Zagreb, Alojzije Stepinac, was tried in that city together with members of the Ustasha regime. He was accused of 'activities against the people and the state', i.e. aiding the Ustashas even after the war and cooperating with them during the war. Stepinac denied all the charges: he was an anti-Communist, but his fault in the complicated events of the war could only be political; he could not be criminally tried. Nevertheless, he was sentenced to sixteen years of prison and forced labour, and five years' loss of political and civil rights. Thus the Communists created a stumbling-block for relations between the church and the state that lasted a long time, and Croatia acquired a national hero and martyr.

Similar repression was undertaken against HSS members. In 1945 all their activities were completely blocked (the paper published by Radić's wife Marija was banned after its first issue), and in 1948 twelve members of the party were tried with the intention of compromising the whole party as collaborators. The first defendant, the attorney Tomo Jančiković, was sentenced to ten years in prison.

## Consequences of the war

The war on NDH territory and in Croatia had terrible consequences: since this was the site of most of the war operations, there were proportionally most victims and most destruction. Of a total of 2,100,000 Serbs approximately 330,000 were killed – 82,000 as Partisan combatants, 23,000 as Quislings and collaborators (i.e. as victims of Communist revenge at the end of the war), and 217,000 as victims of Nazi terror. Most of the victims (124,000) were killed in their own homes or in their towns and villages; a smaller number (about 93,000) were taken to prisons or concentrations camps and killed there. Of more than 3,400,000 Croats on NDH territory, about 46,000 died as Partisans, 46,000 in the places where they lived, 19,000 in prisons and camps where their bodies were thrown into mass graves, and about 70,000 as Quislings and collaborators. Throughout Yugoslavia over 80 per cent of the Jews, 7.3 per cent of the Serbs, 5 per cent of the Croats and 8.1 per cent of the Muslims (mostly as victims of Chetnik terror and as soldiers in NDH units) were killed.

Many people fled or had to leave Yugoslavia and Croatia, among them about 90,000 ethnic Germans (*Volksdeutscher*). People blamed this community as a whole for the crimes of the Nazi occupiers (many of them actually did belong to military and paramilitary formations), and the Communist authorities passed laws that bolstered this attitude. Some Germans were collectively relocated to Germany after October 1944. When the war ended, German property was confiscated and nationalised, and many of the *Volksdeutscher* – the term acquired a pejorative connotation – were interned in camps. Later population censuses showed that only a few hundred remained. Mass colonisation by people from poorer and overpopulated regions was organised in the late 1940s in places the Germans had vacated, primarily in Vojvodina and northern Croatia. Most came from the Dinaric mountain region, but also from Zagorje and elsewhere.

The fate of the Italians was similar in some ways and differed in others. After the capitulation in 1943 they began to move out of Croatian areas that had been incorporated into Italy in 1918, and when the war ended mass emigration began, especially from Rijeka and Istria. Official emigration began in 1947-8 and lasted till 1954-5. No one was forced to leave, but there was a general will not to live under Communism. Many people were deprived of their property – land, factories, shops and any apartments in excess of one to live in – and thus had no reason to stay. Emigrants, known as 'optants', were obliged to renounce their real estate and their right to return. Croats and Slovenes also emigrated in this way for political, economic and ethnic reasons. The exact number of emigrants was never established, estimates ranging from tens of thousands (which is more probable) up to 200,000. Be that as it may, some parts of Istria became deserted; Pula's population fell from 45,000 to barely 20,000, and the pre-war population level was not reached again till the 1960s.

## Republican boundaries

The boundaries of the newly-established republic of Croatia were finally fixed in 1945 (in 1991 they suddenly became a subject of contention again), although on the whole they had been formed much earlier. For example, most of the border with Slovenia dates from the Middle Ages, as does that in the south between Dubrovnik and the areas that are today parts of Montenegro and Bosnia-Hercegovina. The border between Croatia and Bosnia-Hercegovina is the result of delimitation with the Ottoman empire, and mostly dates from the end of the seventeenth century. Only that with Serbia (i.e. with the former Autonomous Province of Vojvodina) had to be settled on the basis of the report of a federal commission that used an ethnic criterion. Most of eastern Srijem was under Croatian sovereignty in the Middle Ages and again after 1699, but it became part of Vojvodina because since the end of the nineteenth century Serbs had been the majority population there – in some places merely relative to other groups and in others absolutely since they formed over half of the population. The border regions that became part of Croatia (site of the fiercest fighting in 1991) – notably Vukovar and its surroundings – had a large percentage of Serbs, but Serbs were never the majority population in the region as a whole.

*Revolution and violence*

The violent methods used by the Communists at the end of the
Second World War and immediately afterwards did not end even
after they had consolidated their power. In 1945-6, a year of
famine, livestock and wheat were massively 'requisitioned' from
peasants, who did not have enough even to feed themselves.
Property was nationalised consistently and on a wide scale and
the process was more or less completed within only a year or
two after the new authorities had taken over. Opposition activities
and any kind of criticism were systematically blocked, and propaganda drives and 'spontaneous' demonstrations were often organised
against them. Merely owning material possessions of any kind,
which meant that one belonged to the 'bourgeoisie', was regarded
with suspicion and could be dangerous, regardless of the political
affiliation of the 'bourgeois' in question.

Elections for the Constituent Assembly were held at the end
of 1945. All the seats went to candidates of the National Front,
a branch of the Communist Party. At the federal level and in
Croatia, the Communists and their sympathisers won over 90 per
cent of the vote, and the turnout topped 80 per cent. The electoral
law made the Communist victory easier and there can be no
doubt that in the absence of a neutral electoral commission the
votes were manipulated. Most political parties that did not belong
to the National Front abstained, and the existence of a 'box without
a list' only formally enabled a choice to be made between different
political programmes. Before the elections Ivan Šubašić and all
the other middle-class politicians left the government on the
grounds that the Tito–Šubašić agreement was not being honoured.

The economy had been devastated by the war and any kind
of improvement, however small, made life easier. Rijeka's port
had been destroyed and mined and remained out of use till the
beginning of 1946. In that year, too, the Zagreb-Belgrade railway
line was re-opened to traffic. In 1947 the Federal Assembly adopted
the first five-year development plan on the Soviet model, which
encouraged the growth of heavy industry. The International Zagreb
Fair was also opened, thus renewing the city's tradition as a centre
of trade fairs. Some West European countries took part. In principle
the Yugoslav government agreed to negotiations on the Marshall

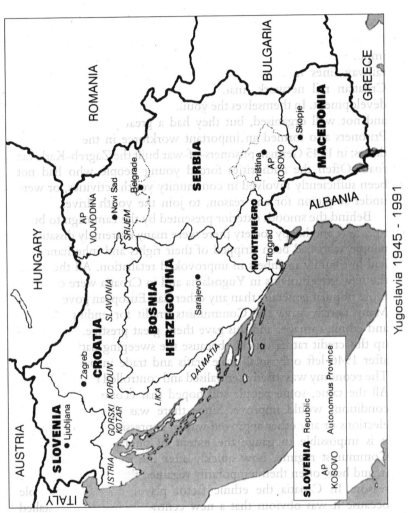

Yugoslavia 1945 - 1991

Plan, but later rejected it under Soviet pressure on the grounds that the aid provided was hedged about with political conditions.

'Youth work drives' (*radne akcije*) began to be organised after 1946; these consisted of work on the building or rebuilding of the infrastructure, especially roads and railways. The three most important, a modern road from Slovenia to Macedonia and two railway lines in Bosnia-Hercegovina that linked up with the Croatian rail network, made a great contribution to Croatian development. In themselves the youth drives were rather expensive and not well organised, but they had a great propaganda effect. Prisoners also formed an important workforce in the 'voluntary' drives; in 1945 German prisoners-of-war built the Zagreb-Karlovac road. Often the authorities forced young people who had not been sufficiently involved in community youth activities, or were under suspicion for any reason, to join the youth drives.

Behind the smooth exterior presented by the campaign to build up a new and happy society there were many extremely dissatisfied people who had been stripped of their rights and inheritance, or had lost family members in unprovoked retaliation. All the same, the new governments in Yugoslavia and in Croatia were certainly more popular generally than any other East European government. Many people gave the Communists credit for ending the war and ethnic carnage, and this gave them great prestige. They used up this credit rather quickly because the sweeping nationalisation after 1946 left only small-scale crafts and trade in private hands. The economy was strictly centralised and controlled from Belgrade. All the same, some people still hoped that economic and social conditions would improve. Since there was no system of free elections or any other approved way of expressing public opinion, it is impossible to gauge the extent of public support for the Communist regime, how quickly after the war the regime lost it, and how often then temporarily regained that support for some reason. In Croatia the ethnic factor played an important role because it was obvious that a new centralism had been installed in spite of political slogans proclaiming the contrary – namely, equality between the republics. Some measures were indeed received enthusiastically. One was the introduction of compulsory seven-year schooling in Croatia in 1946 (previously no more than four years had been compulsory). In 1951 this was extended by a further year. At the beginning of 1949 a broad effort was launched to eradicate illiteracy, which brought almost 70,000 people (nearly 2% of the population) into literacy courses.

At the end of 1945 the Constituent Assembly began to function. It proclaimed the Federal People's Republic of Yugoslavia (FNRJ) to be a 'federal people's state of the republican form, a community of equal peoples who had freely expressed their wish to remain united in Yugoslavia'. King Peter II and the Karadjordjević dynasty were divested of all their rights. The new constitution promulgated in January 1946 – a faithful copy of the Soviet constitution passed about ten years earlier – was designed to give an organised autocratic system constitutionality and legality. On the one hand, the text was swollen with bombastic declarations and hollow phrases about civil, national and confessional freedom, and on the other it defined the position of the National Front as the broadest political organisation, although it was in fact no more than a mask for the Communist Party. Only education and culture, health, social welfare and municipal affairs remained republican competences; this was insufficient for them to express any kind of republican or national individuality. Elections for the Constituent *Sabor* of the People's Republic of Croatia were held at the end of 1946 (several candidates stood in almost all the constituencies, but all were National Front members), and at the beginning of 1947 it promulgated the Croatian constitution as confirmation of the existence of Croatian statehood, i.e. sovereignty within Yugoslavia. However, this was no more than a show of democracy, strictly on the Soviet model, and for about the next twenty years Croatian history was closely tied to what happened at the Yugoslav level.

In 1947 a treaty with Italy was signed at the Paris Peace Conference, which confirmed that all the territories on the eastern Addiatic coast which before the war had been under Italian occupation – Rijeka, the Kvarner islands and most of Istria – had formally become part of Croatia and Yugoslavia. Trieste and its environs were still disputed, as were the Slovenian coast (Koper and other towns) and north-western parts of Croatian Istria (Buje and its surroundings), which were claimed by both Yugoslavia and Italy. No definite solution could be reached at that time, and therefore the Free Territory of Trieste was formed, with a division into Zone A and Zone B. After much contention, which even threatened to escalate into armed conflict, it was agreed in 1954 that most of Zone A (Trieste and its surroundings) would be awarded to Italy and Zone B to Yugoslavia. This finally defined the Yugoslav-Italian border, and the future border between Croatia and Slovenia in Istria.

## *1948: resolution of the Informbureau*

The Yugoslav Communist movement enjoyed greater independence than others in Eastern Europe because it had largely fought its way to power. Tito had come to Yugoslavia in 1938 as a Soviet Communist agent, but his war victories helped him to transcend that early role and he became an extremely self-confident leader who would not allow the Soviet Union and Stalin to dictate to him. His ambitions also grew. He tried to achieve domination over Albania, and planned to make himself head of a Balkan federation that would include Bulgaria. He also complained to the Soviet authorities when they imposed on Yugoslavia unequal economic relations bordering on exploitation. All this made Stalin and the other Soviet leaders regard him with suspicion, and they began to exert pressure on the Yugoslav leadership in various ways.

In March 1948 the Soviet government recalled its military and civilian advisers from Yugoslavia, with the excuse that they were being subjected to hostile treatment. Further escalation came quickly. A week later the Central Committee of the Soviet Communist Party wrote to its Yugoslav counterpart criticising the Yugoslav leadership. The Soviets made the remarkable claim that there 'was not enough democracy' and that 'capitalist forces were growing stronger'. The correspondence lasted till June, with Soviet criticism becoming ever sharper and more far-reaching. The Yugoslav leadership rejected the accusations while endeavouring to remain part of the international Communist community. Only Party committees and military commands knew what was going on – the general public had no inkling whatever, which made the shock that came at the end of June all the greater. When the Information Bureau of Communist Parties (Informbureau) sent Yugoslavia a resolution summarising all the earlier accusations and criticism concerning conditions in the Communist Party of Yugoslavia, Tito and the Party leadership had the courage to publish it in newspapers and broadcast it on the radio. The resolution called on 'healthy forces' in the Communist Party to force the leadership to admit to their mistakes and rectify them. Two days after the resolution, the Yugoslav Central Committee rejected the charges as unfounded and slanderous, and in July organised the Fifth Party Congress in a tense and uncertain atmosphere. The great majority of delegates backed the Yugoslav leadership headed by Tito, after which the Soviet Union and other Communist states immediately severed all economic, cultural, scientific, sport and other connections with Yugoslavia. A propaganda war began and there were frequent incidents on the borders with Hungary, Romania and Bulgaria in which people were killed or wounded. The Yugoslav leadership withstood this pressure, but within the country they began at the same time to persecute all declared resolution supporters and others they considered suspect, even those who could not have anything to do with those events. This was another difficult period for Yugoslavia and Croatia. Many so-called 'Informbureauists' from all over Yugoslavia were sent to the prison on Goli Otok near the island of Rab in the Croatian Primorje, which became a symbol of Communist repression. It was a place from which many of its inmates never returned, and where those who survived suffered terribly, just as people were suffering under Stalin – against whose measures the Yugoslav Communists were fighting.

In May, at the height of the Soviet-Yugoslav altercation, Andrija Hebrang was arrested in Belgrade. Hebrang's position in the Party and state hierarchy had steadily declined since 1944 and his arrest was not unexpected. However, the basic reason for his removal at that moment was fear that the Soviets might try to use him as a rival to Tito. He was detained and accused both of being an Ustasha spy and of siding with the Soviet Party, and was killed in prison without ever being tried, probably in 1949; the official version was that he had committed suicide. This was the cruellest liquidation of a Croatian official in the Communist period, and in later decades Hebrang became a kind of symbol for Croatia's difficult position within Yugoslavia.

There were proportionately fewer 'Informbureauists' in Croatia than in other republics. The best-known case connected to these events, other than that of Hebrang, was in 1950 when the Central Committee of the Communist Party of Croatia expelled from the Party three well-known Serbian Partisans, former ministers in the Croatian government, because they were alleged to support Serbian nationalism and the Informbureau resolution.

Some of the Ustashas who had managed to escape abroad in 1945 found refuge in Italy and Austria, from where they tried to organise diversions in Croatia. The first groups who hoped to lead a revolt entered the country in July 1948 – perhaps in co-operation with the Soviets – just when the crisis of the Yugoslav Communist leadership was approaching a climax. About fifty Ustashas, mostly former officers, entered Yugoslavia at that time planning to lead the uprising. However, all fell into police traps and were arrested, tried by court-martial and sentenced to death.

At that time Croatian post-war exiles, scattered through many European and more distant countries, started the first cultural activities abroad and began to write books. The common denominator of all these efforts was the desire to do away with the Communist system and a more or less acknowledged hope that they would be able to return to their homeland.

# 10

## 1948-66: THE BEGINNINGS OF DEMOCRATISATION AND YUGOSLAVIA'S SEARCH FOR ITS OWN COURSE

Yugoslavia was the first Communist state openly and successfully to oppose the Soviet Union, and this ultimately led to the development of a freer and richer society in Communist Yugoslavia, independent of the Soviet model. However, Yugoslavia did not immediately find a new way, and after the break with the Eastern countries there was at first no alternative social model to follow. Furthermore, in 1949 the Yugoslav leaders tried to prove their ideological purity by establishing peasant co-operatives (*seljačke zadruge*) on the Soviet model and forcing peasants to join them. The resulting dissatisfaction was immense and at times erupted into open rebellion; the largest incident was in western Bosnia on the border with Croatia, when eighteen death sentences and about 100 prison sentences were pronounced. After a time the leadership, and especially Tito, realised that this policy was creating unnecessary resistance and great damage without a counterweight in greater productivity. The mistake was never publicly acknowledged, of course, but after 1951 the co-operatives began to be abandoned and the peasants were again allowed to work their land individually. The co-operatives were transformed into voluntary communities, but in practice they were abolished.

By that time, at the beginning of the 1950s, Yugoslavia was already searching for ways to overcome the Soviet concept of social development. The first move came in 1950, largely on the initiative of the Slovene Boris Kidrič (1912-53), who directed the Yugoslav economy after 1946, and the Montenegrin Milovan Djilas (1911-95), then the Party's leading ideologue. A law was passed subjecting businesses to 'social ownership' and handing them over to workers to manage. Although businesses still depended greatly on centralised planning, this gave birth to the idea of

167

Administrative Division 1955-1962

self-management. A self-managing society began to develop and became the dominant social model in the next four decades. Although in time it became bureaucratised and inefficient, and 'social ownership' was shown to be 'no one's ownership', a recipe for neglect, this system nevertheless resulted in the creation of independent economic entities: they were forced to fend for themselves and be responsible for their activities.

The dominant atmosphere was now one of gradual political liberalisation and positive economic expectations, but the standard of living was still low and the country faced great difficulties. The economic blockade imposed from the East forced the Yugoslav government to seek and receive financial and other aid from the

United States and Western Europe. In 1950 a great drought took place, and a large amount of food was imported to prevent hunger. A national loan was initiated, and the realisation of the first five-year plan was delayed.

A fresh approach to art developed. In 1950 the younger generation of artists in Zagreb (earlier than elsewhere in Yugoslavia) began to resist the concept of Socialist Realism and created the first works embodying free artistic expression. They were influenced by Constructivism and the Bauhaus, and promoted Expressionism and abstraction. Krleža was the central figure at the Congress of Yugoslav Writers in 1952 in Ljubljana, and the speech he delivered there marked the final decline of Socialist Realism. But even then not everything ran smoothly because in that year a very entertaining Croatian film comedy, *Ciguli-Miguli* by Branko Marijanović, was banned from public display for allegedly 'affirming a petit bourgeois attitude'.

In 1951 the first signs appeared that the rigid Communist attitude to the church was thawing. Stepinac was released from Lepoglava prison and interned in his native village of Krašić in Žumberak, where he died in 1960. On the other hand, whenever relations with Italy deteriorated due to the Free Territory of Trieste, invective against the Vatican became part of the propaganda campaign. In 1952, when the Vatican began procedures to make Stepinac a cardinal, Yugoslavia broke off diplomatic relations and expelled the Catholic theological faculty from Zagreb University. In 1954 a new law was passed that once again guaranteed all religious communities freedom of confession, and in the 1960s this made possible the reactivation of the Catholic church.

Yugoslavia's world isolation lasted for several years after 1948. In 1951 it signed an agreement on military aid from the United States, and at the same time established diplomatic relations with the Federal Republic of Germany. In 1953 Tito went to Britain on his first official visit to a Western country and his first trip abroad since 1948. The West openly expressed its interest in Yugoslavia remaining outside the direct reach of the East.

The next step forward came from the East. In 1955 and 1956 Tito and Khrushchev met in Belgrade and in Moscow, and two declarations were signed to normalise relations between Yugoslavia and the Soviet Union and other East European countries. The Soviets recognised that there could be different paths in the development of socialism, and that co-operation between Communist parties should be based on free will and equality. But even after this opening it was clear that Yugoslavia would remain somewhere in between; the fear of Soviet domination was too great for the self-assured Tito to allow a new rapprochement with the East, yet the ideological component was too great for warmer relations to be established with the West. This logically resulted in growing links with developing countries (at first Egypt and India), which developed into the policy of Non-Alignment (with the Eastern and Western power blocs) which achieved great international prominence in the 1960s and '70s.

Tito behaved in a way typical of capable dictators, alternating periods of relative liberalisation with ones of restriction. This helped him to keep the different ideological currents in the leadership in check and prevent potential inter-republic confrontation, and at the same time strengthened his own position. One of the greatest upsurges of liberalisation, immediately followed by a clampdown, happened in the autumn of 1953 when Milovan Djilas, one of Tito's closest associates, began publishing a series of articles in the Belgrade paper *Borba* (The struggle) on the need for radical democratisation. Djilas maintained that the Communist Party should renounce its political monopoly and initiate, with certain limitations, a gradual transition to a multi-party system. His ideas aroused a wave of enthusiasm and hope among the educated population, especially in Croatia, and the weekly *Naprijed* (Forward), the official organ of the Communist Party there, began to promote them openly and resolutely. *Vjesnik u srijedu* (Wednesday Herald – circulation 300,000 copies) of Zagreb, the top-selling Yugoslav weekly, did the same several times. Three months later Tito and the Politbureau stopped Djilas's campaign and at a spectacular session of the Central Committee that was broadcast live, relieved him of all functions. However, he continued his dissident activities, publishing books and giving interviews abroad, and this earned him a total of nine years in prison. At that time he was one of the best-known heretics of any Communist country. Those of his more prominent supporters in Croatia who would not publicly repent were thrown out of office and expelled from the Party, and some were arrested. The editorial board of the *Naprijed* was dissolved and the paper ceased publication.

Tito's personality cult was a creation of the 1950s, and in some aspects it intensified as the years passed. His birthday (25 May) became a state holiday called Youth Day, for which a Youth Relay Race (*Štafeta mladosti*) was organised. A baton carried through all Yugoslavia with the good wishes of the Yugoslav youth and pioneers (children) and handed over to the President at a magnificent rally in Belgrade. He had many residences in various parts of Yugoslavia, most of them in Croatia (a summer residence on the Brijuni islands near Pula, the Zagorje villa in Zagreb, the Dalmatia villa in Split etc.). In every town the main street or square was named after him, and each of the Yugoslav republics had a town to whose name Tito's was added (in Croatia this was Titova Korenica).

Tito's birthplace, the small Zagorje village of Kumrovec about 40 km. from Zagreb on the border of Croatia and Slovenia, developed into a kind of pilgrimage centre visited by tourists and school excursions from all parts of Yugoslavia and even from abroad. The house where he was born became a museum, and in the 1970s a Political School was opened in an impressive building nearby, giving six-month courses in Marxism and socio-political education for young Communist cadres. The Feelings in Croatia about the Tito cult in Yugoslavia and abroad ranged from pride to contempt.

In 1958 another step was taken towards liberalisation when the Programme of the League of Communists of Yugoslavia was adopted at the Party Congress. In it the Party was defined as the initiator of further social democratisation in all areas of life: economic, social and cultural. In the Soviet Union and other Eastern countries the Programme was called revisionist. The liberalisation in the 1950s opened up possibilities, albeit still on a limited scale, for some independent and individual stands to be expressed in Croatia. Student demonstrations in Zagreb in 1958 were triggered by bad food in the student restaurant, but their deeper reasons lay in social and national dissatisfaction.

From 1952 to 1963 Većeslav Veco Holjevac (1917-70) was mayor of Zagreb. Unlike most Communist officials, he opposed excessive institutional centralisation in Belgrade as the capital and was not satisfied merely to be a channel for transmitting the will of higher authorities. Acting independently and resolutely, he implemented bold town-planning projects in Zagreb: the city spread to the south bank of the river Sava, the Zagreb Fair acquired large new grounds, and so on. At that time economic, scholarly and cultural factors started to shape Zagreb into a large city (television, the rapid growth of the university, large industries etc.). Holjevac was too different from the ruling Communist establishment, too much of a free-thinker, for Yugoslav political leaders to accept. For the Croatian Communist leadership, headed by Bakarić, he was a dangerous rival because of the great popularity he earned with his policies. In the 1960s his career took a downward turn, and in 1967 he was removed from his last position of influence.

In 1963-4 professors at the Zagreb faculty of philosophy opened a summer school on the island of Korčula and started publishing the journal *Praxis*. Their thinking never went beyond the bounds of Marxism and socialism, but their reformist ideas and vehement theoretical criticism of existing conditions set a precedent in socialist countries. The school became known by the name of its journal and greatly contributed to democratisation in general. Orthodox Communists in Croatia and Yugoslavia and in all European Communist parties looked on *Praxis* thought as heretical, criticising it openly, and Bakarić and Tito attacked its proponents. However, reformist Marxist philosophers, sociologists and political scientists throughout the world (Bloch, Fromm, Habermas, Marcuse, Goldman and others) strongly supported and co-operated with the *Praxis* group. Thanks to this international reputation and support, *Praxis* and the summer school in Korčula managed to survive for ten years.

The new Croatian constitution enacted in April 1963 (the Yugoslav constitution came into force two days earlier) defined social management (self-management – *samoupravljanje*) as the basic management system. In the long run this weakened the conservative current headed by the second man of contemporary Yugoslavia, Aleksandar Ranković, who endorsed centralism in state affairs, a controlled economy and the leading social role of the League of Communists.

In 1965 an economic reform was initiated in Yugoslavia which brought in new changes. Its purpose was to increase the market orientation of enterprises and so make their involvement in the international economic system easier and less painful for them. Although these goals were only achieved in part, the changes that took place in the following years were important.

# 11

## 1966–80: DECENTRALISATION
## AND REPRESSION

Ranković's influence in Yugoslavia was so great that everyone spoke of him as Tito's certain successor. The security service, under his permanent patronage, was already secretly taking certain practical steps to ensure his succession, and even bugged the leader's residence. Tito's patience snapped. Conflict due so different views of how the country should be run grew into personal conflict among state and Party leaders that could no longer be kept secret. In July 1966 a session of the Central Committee was called at which Ranković and his sympathisers were forced to resign, allowing the movement for further democratisation, which Tito then supported, to prevail.

However, this democratisation had limits, as the authorities quickly demonstrated. In Zadar a group of young intellectuals, mostly teachers in the Zadar Faculty of Philosophy, tried to establish an opposition party and launch an independent paper, but nearly all were arrested. However, only Mihajlo Mihajlov, the best known among them, was given a prison sentence.

With the favourable effect of the economic reform and the fall of Ranković, the 1960s brought the greatest economic growth in post-war Croatia and Yugoslavia. Liberalisation was best seen in the almost complete freedom of travel to and from the country, and a relaxation of border control. The economic reform brought much unemployment, and a large number of Croats from Croatia and Bosnia-Hercegovina (in higher percentages than from any other Yugoslav nation) went for 'temporary work' abroad, mostly to West Germany and Austria, France, Belgium, the Netherlands and Scandinavia. These 'guest workers' (*Gastarbeiter*) often turned their temporary stay into a permanent one, but they maintained links with the homeland and repatriated substantial amounts of money. Regulations were passed enabling them to send their earnings to Yugoslav banks. They built houses and bought a variety of goods such as cars and household appliances, and between the mid-1960s and about the mid-1980s many undeveloped areas were transformed due to their inhabitants having gone to work abroad. By the end of the 1960s saving in foreign-currency bank accounts was also legalised for all citizens, without any need to show the origin of the deposits. The foreign currency reserves thus created were one of the motors of development, and a new class of managers developed in Croatia. Growing relations with the West and open borders brought in Western influences ranging from newspapers to rock music.

In the mid-1960s the Adriatic coast road, Jadranska Magistrala, from the Italian border to Dubrovnik was finished and airports were opened in Dubrovnik and Split. In the 1960s tourism developed faster in Croatia than elsewhere. From 2,800,000 'tourist nights' in 1938 the figure had risen twenty years later to 8,100,000 and by 1969 to over 28,000,000. The increase of foreign tourists was especially important. In 1958 foreigners accounted for hardly 1.8 million tourist nights in Croatia, which was under a quarter of those spent by domestic tourists. By 1969 over 60 per cent of the tourists were foreigners. At the end of the 1950s and in the following decades about one-third of foreign tourists came from Germany, with Austria providing the next highest percentage. In the 1960s many Czechoslovaks came, but after the 1968 Soviet intervention few of them could do so any longer. Italians were also traditionally good guests, always accounting for almost 10 per cent of foreign tourists.

In the 1960s relations between the Vatican and Yugoslavia improved, influenced partly by liberalisation in Yugoslavia and partly by the Second Vatican Council (1962-5), which also enhanced the position of the Catholic church in Croatia. The church had always published a newspaper, and in 1962 *Glas Koncila* (Voice of the Council) began to come out, at first fortnightly and then weekly, becoming the most important church paper. Many religious periodicals were then founded or renewed. In 1966 Yugoslavia signed a protocol with the Holy See agreeing to safeguard the position of religious communities in conformity with the constitution, while the Holy See would ensure that the Catholic clergy confined themselves to religious matters and that the church condemned every act of violence. However, diplomatic relations were still not established at that time. In 1968 the first complete translation of the Bible into Croatian was published in Zagreb, resulting from the combined work of many language and literary experts, theologians and biblical scholars. A meeting between President Tito and Pope Paul VI in 1971 also had a positive effect.

## Between extensive urban development and rural ruin

The boom in the 1960s had side-effects which would have dramatic repercussions in Croatia in later decades. Much of the rapid industrialisation was not based on market principles; instead, priority was given to the extensive employment of people who had moved into the towns from the countryside, and whose productivity was often very low. This had the worst possible results, as the villages lost their economically and demographically most productive people without providing a foundation for healthy long-term economic and social development in towns. This led not merely to the marginalisation of agriculture, but to its collapse. In the 1950s co-operatives were not structured for market competition, and the peasants were too poor and weak for it without help from the state and banks. The top limit of 10 hectares of land for a family farm had been designed to prevent farmers from getting rich, but it actually led to catastrophe. The government treated this difficult situation lightly and gave their backing exclusively to agriculture on large factory farms (*poljoprivredni kombinati*), mainly for cereal production. In maritime Croatia the situation was even worse than in the continental region. Agricultural production dwindled, and terraced fields and dry-stone walls that had been maintained for centuries quickly deteriorated. Ancient cultures like the vine were now mostly grown for home use or as an additional occupation for employees. Olive production, the mainstay of agriculture in the Adriatic parts of Croatia for two millennia, practically died out. In the 1980s some islands where tourism was strongly developed produced only 5-10 per cent of their needs in fruit and vegetables although they had fed themselves for centuries.

The living standard increased greatly but the money that people earned could not be invested because of the strict limits on private initiative. They did not even buy apartments because of a ramified system in which enterprises and institutions assigned free tenancy rights in apartments which they owned to their employees. In this, party membership was important but not decisive; about 10 per cent of the adult population were members of the League of Communists of Croatia, but tenancy rights were assigned on a much broader basis.

The consumer mentality that washed over Croatia at that time led to highly irrational spending on shopping expeditions to neighbouring countries, primarily Italy (Trieste) and Austria (Graz). People also built holiday houses (*vikendice*). Banks did not work on market principles, approving loans to enterprises at the request of politicians even though the enterprises were not profitable. Some people obtained very cheap (almost free) loans to build holiday houses and for other needs.

The irrationality of this development can be seen from the fact that in the 1970s there were twice as many cars in Croatia as telephones, because the purchase of cars reflected the level of people's personal standards, while the development of the telephone network reflected social standards.

Self-management as a system was only slightly more efficient than the Soviet model. It was bureaucratised and cumbersome and could not compete with Western economies. People could obtain so much free or for less than the market price (e.g. apartments) that they began to believe, as in other socialist countries, that things could be obtained without work. All this made the settling of accounts in the 1980s and in the post-socialist age more difficult.

## The issue of language

In the mid-1960s political and economic changes in Yugoslavia created a new atmosphere in which people began to raise matters that had previously been taboo. One of them was the question of inter-ethnic relations, which could be discussed most freely in the context of the language problem. There is no doubt that the Croatian and Serbian standard languages are very similar, but differences do exist. After 1918 the Yugoslav administration and close cultural contacts decreased the differences naturally and through indirect compulsion, and these tendencies continued in the 1950s. The Croats wanted to call their language Croatian and leave the Serbs free to call theirs whatever they wished, but the official name of the language was Croato-Serbian or Serbo-

Croatian. In the 1950s it was agreed that the language of the Serbs and the Croats was the same, with two pronunciations (*Ijekavski* in Croatia, *Ekavski* in Serbia) and two alphabets (Latin and Cyrillic) that were equal in status.

After the fall of Ranković the need was felt for decentralisation and federalisation, and accordingly public discussion began concerning constitutional amendments. In this context, a Zagreb literary weekly published at the beginning of 1967 a document called the 'Declaration concerning the Name and Position of Croatian Standard Language', signed by 180 scholars and cultural institutions in Croatia, who wanted to establish the equality in status and use of Slovenian, Croatian, Serbian and Macedonian in federal institutions and the consistent use of the Croatian standard language in Croatia. The publication of this text had broader implications since it indicated national inequality, especially suppression of the Croats and the Croatian language. The government branded the 'Declaration' as tendentious and politically damaging, and some of the most important national institutions were accused of spreading such ideas. The signatories were subjected to political pressure and removed from public life. Although events connected to the 'Declaration' had an unsuccessful outcome for Croatian interests, they heralded what was to take place throughout Croatia soon afterwards.

## Towards an outcome in 1971

At the end of the 1960s social life centred around the wish for more democracy and decentralisation, and there were demands in the League of Communists for the discussion of issues concerning self-management, banks and inter-republic relations.

The student movement that arose in Yugoslavia in 1968 reflected similar developments in Europe (mainly France and Germany) and the United States (demonstrations against the Vietnam war). It reached its height in Belgrade, but also came to Zagreb where a partial strike took place, and lectures and events were organised in the Zagreb student centre. A growing section of the student body became politically aware, which worried the political leadership in Croatia. The students' political stands varied, with emphasis on the social aspect ('down with the red bourgeoisie').

In 1968 the Soviet Union and its allies intervened in Czechoslovakia

and thus greatly influenced events in Croatia and the whole of
Yugoslavia. The highest Yugoslav state and Party bodies condemned
the intervention, and spontaneous demonstrations broke out in
some towns in support of the peoples of Czechoslovakia. Czechoslovak tourists who happened to be in Yugoslavia at this time
(most were in Croatia) found themselves very warmly received.
Some returned home, others went to the West, and yet others
remained in Croatia and other Yugoslav republics. In Croatia the
Czechoslovak example, the 'Prague Spring', was seen as a possible
model for democratisation. Yugoslav–Soviet relations deteriorated
sharply and there were even threats of Soviet intervention to
remove the last 'bastion of revisionism'. This made Yugoslavs
even more suspicious of the Soviet model.

It was concerning the priority of road-building that in 1969
differences of interest between the republics and federal bodies
emerged clearly for the first time. The federal government supported
construction being spread equally in all parts of Yugoslavia. The
most developed republic, Slovenia in the north-west, considered
that priority should be given to construction there because that
was where there was most traffic on the roads, which had to be
linked up to Austrian and Italian motorways. This was a clear
indication that the wave of democratisation would make preservation of the sacrosanct 'brotherhood and unity' (*bratstvo i jedinstvo*)
dogma, on which Yugoslav society had functioned for over two
decades, extremely difficult. Even if federal officials had been
consummately just and impartial in relation to all the republics,
in practice this desire for unification and 'not rocking the boat'
favoured the largest nation – the Serbs. In Slovenia and Croatia
as the richest republics, and especially among the Croats who
were the second largest nation, this was bound to cause an adverse
reaction.

In 1969 the Ninth Congress of the League of Communists of
Yugoslavia was for the first time organised after the congresses
of republican Leagues of Communists had taken place (previously
it had been the opposite way round). For the first time also there
was republican parity in the central bodies of the League of Communists. Some months later a National Defence Act was passed,
continuing the decentralisation of defence that had begun on a
small scale in the 1950s. For the first time republican defence
acts were enacted: these introduced units of territorial defence in

each republic in addition to the regular Yugoslav People's Army (JNA). The territorial units were under the command of republican headquarters, and became the embryo of the national armies of Slovenia, Macedonia and partly of Croatia.

In those years government in Croatia was gradually being dominated by a democratic and nationally-oriented leadership headed by Savka Dabčević-Kučar, who became Central Committee president in the republican League of Communists. This circle of people – among its outstanding figures were Mika Tripalo (Yugoslav Presidency member for Croatia), Ivan Šibl and Pero Pirker – worked to achieve a radical transformation of the economic system and a move to political democratisation. By the end of 1971, when the movement called the 'Croatian Spring' was forcibly suppressed, it had been spontaneously joined by a large part of the Croatian nation and enjoyed great popular support. Various ideological, national and social aspirations came to expression in that relatively short but eventful period, but two basic ideas dominated: the national and the liberal-democratic. With different people and on different occasions one or the other would be expressed more strongly, but usually they surfaced together, with the national idea uppermost. Even these two basic ideas were never clearly defined and analysed, and many people were afraid to say all that was in their minds. In public the wish for further democratisation was presented exclusively as reform within the socialist system, but some people obviously believed that this should lead to the development of a pluralistic liberal democracy. And although the publicly avowed goal was a more independent Croatia within Yugoslavia, between the lines of some writing and in some incidents the wish for complete Croatian independence could be discerned. Later events – mainly after 1990, when people were freer to speak and act as they wished – suggest that two visions of the Croatian state were present at that time. One was democratic, with an anti-Fascist and democratic identity, while the other was based on Croatian exclusionism and in some ways continued the traditions of the NDH.

Most Serbs were wary and took no active part in the movement. In some villages they even took the precaution of acquiring arms, remembering the tragic events of some thirty years earlier. Regardless of whether they were manipulated by outside forces or acted on their own initiative, there was hardly any justification for this.

True, there were some inappropriate anti-Serbian acts, but anti-Serbian feelings were of little significance in the 'Croatian Spring'.

This Croatian-Serbian problem in Yugoslavia and especially in Croatia, was rooted in the nineteenth century. It escalated in the time of the Yugoslav kingdom and had tragic consequences in the wars of 1941-5 and 1991-2. In the 1981 census Serbs accounted for 11.6 per cent of the population in Croatia, and in the 1991 census they had increased to 12.2 per cent. To this number must be added some people who for various reasons declared themselves to be 'Yugoslavs', so the Serbs probably made up 14-15 per cent of the population. They had an absolute majority in eleven of Croatia's 114 municipalities, but were disproportionately represented throughout the post-war period in the Croatian police force (estimated at 76 per cent), in state bodies (about 24 per cent in the republican administration), in the ruling League of Communists, and even in controlling positions in the economy; the inclination of Serbs to enter government service has a long history. They had above-average representation in the Croatian Partisan movement in the Second World War. However, in this period some new reasons must be added to the historical ones. Serbs always felt threatened as a minority – which, however, does not mean that there was any real threat. They felt safer if they acquired positions in the administration which, in a one-party dictatorship, was necessarily repressive. Because of this, they appeared to those of other nationalities, especially the Croats, as being pro-regime and with a partiality for privileges and undemocratic government. This created new mistrust and further deepened existing antagonisms.

At the end of 1969 Vladimir Bakarić, ever cautious, denied charges that nationalism had taken over in the Croatian League of Communists. Not much later, in January 1970, the Croatian Central Committee rejected claims made by Miloš Žanko, a Croat and deputy speaker of the Federal Assembly, that Croatian nationalism was on the increase and that the new Communist leadership had given nationalists free rein and were not merely tolerating but actually supporting them. The most important conclusion of that session (the tenth) was that 'unitarism' as an ideology, and 'bureaucratic centralism' as a practice, represented the greatest danger to the development of self-management and stability in Yugoslavia. They demanded a share in discussing the way the state's financial resources (tax revenues etc.) were redistributed, and the foreign currency system – the two central problems. Translated from dry bureaucratic language, this meant that the Croatian Communists had made public their independent vision of Croatia's development in Yugoslavia. The leaders of the other republics and the federation received this with misgivings. Tito was then almost eighty, but all major decisions were still his. For a time he wavered and showed a somewhat conciliatory attitude towards the Croats. At a meeting with Zagreb Communists in September 1970 he announced the reorganisation of the state, primarily by allowing the republics to become responsible for their own development and for the development of the whole of Yugoslavia. Intensive preparations began for comprehensive amendments to the Yugoslav constitution, and these were enacted in June 1971. They introduced, in addition to the President of Yugoslavia Josip Broz Tito, an eight-member Presidency, one member from each of the six republics, and one from each of the two Serbian autonomous provinces (Kosovo and Vojvodina); for some issues consensus between the republics and provinces would be necessary. In general, the competences of the republics were increased, and this was considered a particular success for the Croatian leadership.

The Croatian national movement gained momentum. In the spring of 1971 a new nationally-inclined student leadership was elected at Zagreb University. The Matica Hrvatska[1] began to publish the *Hrvatski Tjednik* (Croatian Weekly), which became the public platform for the non-Communist intellectuals of the 'Croatian Spring'. The paper addressed various aspects of democratic development and Croatian national issues, and specially emphasised the indivisible sovereignty of the Croatian nation in Croatia. At the same time, it wrote, minorities (in the first place Serbs) would be guaranteed free and equal expression concerning all aspects of ethnic individuality. On the wave of the new freedom there were incidents in Zagreb and in other Croatian towns which the Croatian communist authorities could no long control. Some articles in *Hrvatski Tjednik* (e.g. one demanding that Croatia, like Ukraine and Belarussia, should be a member of the UN and another explaining the bad performance of certain enterprises by their

[1] Literally, the 'Croatian Bee'. This society, founded in 1842, existed to promote culture and education, and in some cases, such as this, to raise political questions.

relatively high percentage of Serbian executives) and certain high-spirited excesses (singing songs like 'Croatia gave birth to two bandits – Ante Pavelić and Marshal Tito') provoked a reaction both in Croatia and in other republics. There was mounting pressure on Tito to do something.

In July Tito again met the Croatian Communist leaders, who by then were clearly divided, some of them openly speaking against 'nationalism and separatism in public life'. It was decided that two economists, who were the most outspoken concerning Croatia's unequal position in Yugoslavia, should be expelled from the League of Communists and from public life. All the same, during the summer things grew more strained, attitudes to current economic and social problems increasingly diverged, and emotions built up on both sides.

It seems that the big manoeuvres of the Yugoslav army called 'Freedom 71', held in October 1971 in central Croatia, were apparently a rehearsal for some form of armed intervention. They were intended to be a final warning. Bakarić believed that he was losing control, and persuaded Tito to act. In November Tito decided to break the Croatian movement, and the events of the next few days increased his determination.

At the end of November the Zagreb students decided to go on strike. Their demands were a synthesis of the immediate and strategic goals of the 'Croatian Spring'. They called for Croatia to become the sovereign state of the Croatian nation (they supported the Croatian leaders and President Tito!), demanded that opponents of reform be ousted from office, and denied charges that they represented 'nationalist-chauvinist and separatist forces'. They demanded a complete change in the political and economic system, a re-orientation of foreign policy, and a change in the foreign currency system so that those who earned it could dispose of it themselves. They claimed that the foreign currency earned by Croatian tourism and the advanced Croatian economy ended up in the federal coffers, from which it was then shared out unfairly. They also demanded reforms in the army, which they considered predominantly 'Serbian' – for example, they demanded the use of the Croatian language in the army and that Croatian citizens should do their army service in their own republic. The strike included most Zagreb students and some from other universities.

The student strike exacerbated the already tense situation in

Croatia and the whole of Yugoslavia. Even some of the student leaders cautioned against taking to the streets. On the one hand the students were allies of the Croatian Party leadership, but on the other the leadership were alarmed at student radicalism, and feared that the strike was playing into the hands of opponents of the 'Croatian Spring'. The students wanted to establish contact with other parts of Yugoslavia but, apart from muted echoes in Ljubljana, no one else took action. The student leaders then decided to end the strike 'to avoid excesses and express confidence in the leaderships of the Leagues of Communists of Croatia and of Yugoslavia headed by Savka Dapčević-Kučar and Tito', but it was too late by that time. On 1 December 1971 President Tito convened the Presidency of the Communist Party of Yugoslavia (CPY) in Karadjordjevo (near Novi Sad), and the leaders of the Croatian Communists were sharply reprimanded for not resisting the 'growth of nationalism, chauvinism and the class enemy'. Tito assessed the student strike as a long and carefully prepared counter-revolutionary activity initiated from abroad. Party meetings were organised throughout Croatia, at which over 400 people were forced to resign or were expelled. Spontaneous demonstrations broke out, first among Zagreb students. Police repression throughout Croatia increased an several thousand people were detained, harassed in various ways or forced into the sidelines of public life. The leaders of the 'Croatian Spring' – Tripalo, Dapčević-Kučar, Pirker, Haramija and their closest associates – were removed from all offices, pensioned and banned from every kind of public activity. Trials of prominent cultural figures in the Matica Hrvatska, editors of the *Hrvatski Tjednik* and student leaders were rigged and most were sentenced to between two and four years in prison. A large number of people fled the country. Croatia descended into political apathy from which it did not emerge for almost two decades.

## The 1970s: apathy between intellectual repression and relative economic progress

In the summer of 1972, nineteen well-armed members of a Croatian right-wing organisation entered Yugoslavia illegally from Austria. All were originally from Bosnia-Hercegovina, and they intended to raise a rebellion when they reached central Bosnia, wrongly assuming that the Croats (and Muslims) there were so dissatisfied that they would join them. They did not manage to get anyone on to their side, and the JNA organised a manhunt in the mountains of Bosnia-Hercegovina in which 18,000 people took part. All the members of the group were either killed or, if caught alive, sentenced to death and shot, except for one who was sentenced to twenty years in prison because of his youth.

At the height of the 'Croatian Spring' in 1971, two Croatian exiles assassinated the Yugoslav ambassador in Sweden. In 1976 a group of Croatian exiles hijacked a TWA plane and demanded that leading US newspapers publish data which they would supply about Yugoslav repression of their people. A bomb was set off at the same time at Kennedy airport in New York which killed a policeman. These terrorist activities made the presenting of reasonable and logical Croatian demands for liberalisation and economic reform much more difficult and created the impression in Western countries that extremism dominated the Croatian move-ment to the exclusion of other options. The West's strong support for Tito's policy and Yugoslav integrity was partly the result of this extremism. It was obvious, in addition, that Moscow supported some Croatian right-wing organisations in the 1970s.

The terrorists were usually members of émigré organisation that supported the unconditional creation of an independent Croatia either as an immediate objective or as a long-term one. The main difference between these groups was in the extent to which they approved of the use of force to achieve that goal. Croatian right-wing organisation certainly created the most mayhem, but there were others too. In 1960 Jakša Kušan started in London the moderate, democratic, non-party monthly *Nova Hrvatska* (New Croatia), which for about thirty years remained the most widely-read paper in the Croatian diaspora. It expressed the standpoint of middle-class Croatian emigrants whose primary goal was democratic and economic reform in Croatia. They considered an independent Croatia unrealisable, and in practice did not even think on those lines. In 1963 a group of Yugoslav exiles (Serbs, Croats and Slovenes) founded the Democratic Alternative in Britain, upholding a democratic Yugoslavia that would be a pluralist and polycentric community.

Despite the fundamental ideological differences between these initiatives, the Communist authorities anathematised all of them without exception. The Croatian public usually learned of their existence only from ideologically-charged commentary in the media.

## The new constitution: towards the confederate idea

The educational reform of the 1970s caused great dissatisfaction in Croatia. It was planned on the Yugoslav level, but was drawn up (after 1972) and rigidly implemented (after 1974) only in Croatia. The basic idea was to equalise the level of education offered by the allegedly élite grammar schools, and by other secondary schools that trained pupils for workers' occupations. Public anger was directed particularly at Stipe Šuvar (born 1936), the young and ambitious minister of education and culture.

Although the Yugoslav leadership had crushed the Croatian movement, of which one goal had been decentralisation, they could not turn a blind eye to the fact that the centralised federal state and economy were functioning badly and that changes leading to decentralisation were necessary. These changes were implemented in the constitutional amendments of 1971, and especially in the new constitution adopted in 1974. The latter confirmed the statehood of the republics and provinces and introduced a new mixture of federal and confederal elements. As well as the Yugoslav Presidency, the federal government was also constituted on the principles of equal republican representation. Finally, a system of self-management was designed, which in some cases brought decentralisation to an absurd level – the latter became even clearer in 1976, when the Associated Labour Act was passed. The constitutions of all the republics, including that of Croatia, affirmed the idea of statehood, and indeed in many aspects the republics had become states.

Political apathy may partly have been the result of economic progress in the 1970s, which was to a large extent due to taking excessive foreign loans and allowing a quantity of imports that could not be covered by exports. All the same, for Yugoslavia and Croatia the 1970s, right up till 1978-9, was the period when the standard of living was at its highest. It seems that the aged Tito, who resisted any restrictive economic measures, contributed to this policy that was suicidal in both the short and the long term.

In 1972 the first freeway was opened in Croatia, between

Zagreb and Karlovac. It was 38 km. long and part of the Zagreb-
Rijeka and Zagreb-Split roads. However, roads through central
Croatia leading towards the sea (especially in the direction of
Split), which were planned by the 'Spring' leadership, were labelled
'nationalistic' and their construction was stopped. During the boom
years of the 1970s construction was only allowed to continue on
the Ljubljana-Zagreb-Belgrade freeway, and by the end of the
1980s over 200 km. had been completed. This road was ideologi-
cally more 'correct' because it was considered to support Yugoslav
territorial unity. The 1970s saw the construction of relatively
good roads from Zagreb and Karlovac to Rijeka and Split, and
of tunnels and bridges on the coast. A road network in Bosnia-
Hercegovina was also built. All this ended the isolation of the
southernmost parts of the Croatian coast, and accelerated their
tourist development. An important section of the Croatian ethnic
corpus in central Bosnia and western Hercegovina now had better
traffic connections with Croatia.

At the end of the 1960s and in the '70s tourism prospered.
Through that decade the number of 'tourist nights' almost doubled:
from 28.5 million a year in 1970 to 42.5 million in 1975 and
49.5 million in 1978. With minor variations, the total tourist
traffic increased each year by almost 10 per cent. In 1970 large
luxurious hotels began to be built, and these, together with the
roads leading to the sea, were decisive in the rapid growth of
tourism.

At the beginning of the 1970s three new universities were
founded – in Rijeka, Split and Osijek. Although some faculties
had been opened in those three towns in the 1950s and others
did not become operative till the '80s, the new universities contributed significantly to more balanced regional development in
Croatia and to decentralisation.

At that time some sections of the Croatian economy came to
have an international profile. These were mainly construction
firms that did work in Arab and East European countries, and
on a smaller scale in Western Europe. Important results were also
achieved in shipbuilding and the oil, pharmaceutical, chemical
and metal industries. The oil pipeline through Croatia was completed; running inland from Rijeka, it supplied much of Yugoslavia
and some central European countries.

## Tito's death and its consequences

Tito became gravely ill in the autumn of 1979 and in the following months his condition gradually worsened. The whole country followed his treatment with acute attention, realising that a new age, an 'age without Tito', was relentlessly approaching. He died on 4 May 1980, a few days short of his eighty-eighth birthday. The train carrying his body began its journey in Ljubljana. In Zagreb there was a great ceremony when it came though, and as it travelled on through Croatia to Belgrade, where he was to be buried, many people from nearly towns and villages spontaneously stood along the railway line to pay their respects.

Many people claimed that it was largely due to Tito that the ethnic bloodshed in the Second World War had become a thing of the past, and that after the war something approaching trust had come to exist among the formerly warring peoples. This would have meant that Tito found a solution to the fundamental problem of Yugoslavia. However, it seems in retrospect that his solution actually helped to sow the seeds of the conflict that erupted in the 1990s. A multi-ethnic community can only function in a healthy way with genuinely democratic institutions, which Tito's Yugoslavia did not have. It is true that much was done with the best intentions and with a feeling that it was 'fair', but often arbitration 'from above', however benevolent, is a poor alternative to open discussion and freely co-ordinated opinions on the most difficult problems. In Tito's system no interests or ideas could be expressed in a truly democratic way. This did most harm where feelings of ethnic identity were concerned because their suppression led to the growth of extreme nationalism. Furthermore, the economic failure of Tito's system, most clearly expressed in the protracted crisis of the 1980s, left people who, even if they were not poor, were disillusioned and open to manipulation by demagogues. Finally, Tito's practical solutions ensured that he would retain unlimited power during his lifetime, but foreshadowed the problems that would come after his death. During the war he chose associates who were usually about twenty years younger than himself, so that none of them could rival him in the coming power-struggle. Whenever it seemed that someone – like Hebrang, Djilas and Ranković – might even think of challenging his authority, a way was found to eliminate him. Tito's death was a turning-point and showed that a system depending on one man could not work. Although Tito involved himself in internal affairs very little after the 1970s (to the extent that his mental and physical capacity allowed, he was still engaged in the Non-Aligned movement), he remained a unifying factor, and all the power in Yugoslavia was concentrated around him. He had no real heir because after his death supreme power passed to a collective Presidency consisting of eight very mediocre politicians with great ambitions but mostly also without any serious potential.

The entire political and economic organisation made decision-making in the guise of self-management extremely bureaucratic. Necessary changes in the system could not be introduced because they required a complicated procedure and republican consensus, which the ruling bureaucracy was neither able nor willing to achieve. Tito left a system in a state of paralysis, unable to cure itself. Croatia was in an especially difficult position because Krleža died in 1981 and Bakarić was ill for a long time, finally dying in 1983. Thus figures who had dominated Croatian cultural and political life for decades were gone. The collective leadership system included obligatory rotation, and the presidents of the collective bodies rotated every year or two, which lessened the possibility that a strong figure would emerge, even if one had existed. Furthermore, the period of office under the system of rotation was too short for any important initiative or long-term plan to be implemented.

Meanwhile, the economic and political crisis deepened, apathy increased, the socialist ideology decayed, the League of Communists lost respect and, slowly but surely, the entire state and social structure were eroded. In these circumstances conflicting interests among the republics burgeoned and became increasingly bitter. The federal constitution demanded that all important decisions at the federal level had to be reached through a consensus of republican delegations who, as the 1980s progressed were able to agree on an ever smaller number of issues although they all belonged to a single party. It usually happened that Slovenia was in the minority (7:1); alternatively, it would be Slovenia and Croatia (6:2).

# 12

## 1980-9: OVERALL CRISIS GROWS

After Tito's death the Yugoslav economy faced catastrophe. Immediately following that event, the federal government realised that it could not repay almost US$20 billion of external debt. Difficult negotiations with international banking institutions continued for years. They were prolonged for political reasons: the West wanted Yugoslavia to remain as it was, more democratic than the other countries of the East, and different from them. They therefore granted partial moratoriums. Nevertheless, in Yugoslavia as in other East European and developing countries, debt pressed heavily on the economy during the 1980s. Thereafter the fact that most of the loans had been obtained by the federal government, and it was very difficult to establish in which republic the money had been spent, additionally aggravated relations among the republics and the different ethnicities.

The lack of foreign currency made it impossible to import sufficient quantities of oil, and already in 1980 there was a shortage of petrol and other oil derivatives. Economising in their use, which could not be a lasting solution, caused great damage. Goods that were partly or completely imported, such as coffee, chocolate and washing powder, disappeared from the shops. These shortages encouraged shopping trips abroad and caused a further foreign currency outflow.

Because of its specific nature, the Croatian economy faced additional difficulties. Construction, one of its main branches, was the first to be hit by the slump and money shortage. Major new contracts that had been planned failed to materialise and firms set aside ever less money – e.g. for building apartments. The metal and machine construction industries lost their previously assured markets in the Soviet Union and other East European countries because of the crises there. The Croatian shipbuilding industry, at one time third in volume in the world, began to decline. It cannot be said that nothing was done, but everything that was done was wrong or came too late. Initiatives by experts and independent intellectuals outside the ruling Party circle were usually greeted with suspicion, if not hostility. In 1984 the society of Spanish Volunteer veterans sent a letter to the Presidency of the Central Committee of the Yugoslav League of Communists from its convention in Sarajevo, in which they wrote in unusually strong terms about the social, economic and moral crisis, and demanded an extraordinary congress of the Yugoslav Communists. The regime-controlled press raised a hue and cry against the signatories without ever publishing the letter itself. The Central Committee set up a kind of commission that expressed itself unfavourably and inappropriately about the initiative. If the aged 'Spaniards', an unquestioned moral force and authority in Yugoslavia at that time, could be treated in this way, it was obvious that other groups or individuals would have fared no better. All this increased social apathy and inertia.

One of the principal moves for improving the economy initiated by central state and Party institutions took place at the end of 1981 when the government set up the Kraigher Commission for economic stabilisation, headed by the Slovene communist Sergej Kraigher. In June 1983 the Federal Executive Council and other federal institutions accepted part of the Kraigher Commission's report (which became known as 'the Document'). It was called the 'Long-Term Programme for Economic Stabilisation', and affirmed a market-based economy. However, the programme was internally inconsistent: it called for continued League of Communists tutelage over all aspects of social life. Its full implementation would have meant deep and painful cuts in the economy, and was therefore strongly resisted, mostly in Party committees, and produced no practical results. In the 1980s administrative measures were introduced to decrease inflation, increase exports and halt the fall in living standards (price freezes and the like). Although politicians still talked of economic laws and criteria, in practice they were given ever less attention.

The question of economic relations among the republics was especially sensitive. Public polemics concerning the need to help undeveloped republics (Macedonia, Bosnia-Hercegovina, Montenegro) and autonomous provinces (Kosovo) became increasingly frequent and heated. Croatia and Slovenia attributed about 60 per cent of the funds for this purpose, but problems were not being solved, and indeed the gap between the developed the undeveloped regions was increasing. In 1982 the social product per person was 7.4 times higher in Slovenia than in Kosovo, and the Croatian social product, especially in the most developed parts (in and around Zagreb and in the coastal regions), was only slightly below that of Slovenia. With such differences in the rate of economic development and in social interests, with ethnic conflict already in the wind, the crisis of the Yugoslav community was quickly approaching.

There is no doubt that most of Croatia's relative prosperity and wealth was due to tourism. In the 1980s Croatian tourism peaked, but it was now growing more slowly than in earlier decades. From 53.5 million tourist nights in 1980, the record figure of 67,665,000 was reached in 1985. But by 1990, because of the overall crisis in the country, unsatisfactory tour offers and other factors, the number had fallen back to 52,500,000. Croatia's participation in the world tourist traffic decreased from 1.9 per cent in 1975 to 1.2 in 1988, and in the same period its share of the total income from tourism fell from 1.4 to 0.7 per cent. At the end of the 1970s hardly any more large hotels were being built, but private initiatives took over. Family homes were enlarged to be let to tourists, apartments were built, and new cafés and restaurants opened, giving much greater variety to overall tourist purchases. A ray of light in the economic gloom of the 1980s was the income of these people, mostly operating outside state control. This uncontrolled private activity was probably the most important factor in the economic development of the entire Croatian coast. Data on the total income from tourism depend on methods of calculation, but it seems that in the mid-1980s Yugoslavia's total annual income from tourism was about $3 billion, and Croatia earned 80 per cent of this. Foreign tourists, especially those from Western Europe, brought more money than domestic ones, and 84 per cent of the Germans and as many as 91 per cent of the Austrians and Italians who came to Yugoslavia spent their holidays in Croatia.

In the 1980s Croatia made good use of its position on international traffic routes, in relation both to neighbouring Central European countries and to other parts of Yugoslavia. In the mid-'80s, 42 per cent of scheduled passenger air traffic, 74 per cent of charter and cargo, and 76 per cent of transit air traffic in

Yugoslavia went through Croatia, and about 70 per cent of the Yugoslav maritime and river traffic went through Croatian ports. In 1984, 13 million tons of cargo passed through the port of Rijeka, and when the nearby oil pipeline terminal at Omišalj was added, it became almost 19 million tons.

Rural–urban migration was greatest right after the Second World War, but it was also high in the 1950s and '60s when rapid industrialisation and economic development were in progress; only in the 1970s did it begin to ebb. The population that depended wholly on agriculture decreased from 62.4 per cent in 1948 to only 15.2 in 1981. On average, the four largest Croatian towns (Zagreb, Split, Rijeka, Osijek) doubled their populations during that period; Osijek grew by 78 per cent (from 89,191 to 158,790 inhabitants) and Split by 143 per cent (from 97,146 to 235,922, together with the suburbs of Kaštela and Solin). Urban growth, although slowing down, continued till 1991. The broader Zagreb area also went through a considerable population growth, from 448,444 in 1948 to 855,568 in 1981 and 933,914 in 1991.

Smaller Croatian towns grew in size and number of inhabitants, and developed economically. This usually happened when a large industry, or more than one, opened in a town or its immediate neighbourhood. Since many of these plants could not compete on the world market (although mostly built to export) wages were low and household incomes could not satisfy the increasing needs of the consumer society. This resulted in a relatively numerous suburban population whose primary employment was in industry, but who also engaged in agriculture or some other side activity. While this increased their standard of living, it was harmful in the long run because such workers did not give their best efforts to their factory jobs.

Between 1955 and 1984 employment increased by 150 per cent, but unemployment increased almost sixfold (it had barely existed in 1955). The clearest indicator that the country was sliding towards economic disaster in the 1980s and '90s was unemployment, which doubled again between 1984 and 1992. However illiteracy decreased in Croatia from 16.3 per cent in 1953 to 5.6 per cent in 1981 – when the rate in Kosovo was 17.6 per cent and in Slovenia 0.8 per cent. Infant mortality decreased from 91.8 per 1,000 in 1954 to 15.8 in 1984. Life expectancy increased over the 1953-81 period from fifty-nine to sixty-seven for men, and from sixty-three to seventy-five for women.

The drastic fall in the birth-rate began to threaten population renewal because the natural birth-rate fell from 12.1 per 1,000 in 1954 to 2.3 in 1984, with an indication of further decline to come. Severe depopulation, called the 'white death', swept some Croatian regions, especially the mountains (Like and partly the Dalmatian interior) and islands. On some of the islands the demographic situation was catastrophic: in the 1980s the average age of their population was sixty, and they had dwindled to no more than 10% of their numbers in earlier times. Industrial and tourist development and other economies helped stop the population decreasing on some islands after the 1970s, and selectively it even began to grow again, but the highest numbers reached at the end of the nineteenth century and in the first half of the twentieth have not yet been equalled except in Rab, where the population has constantly increased since modern population censuses were introduced in 1857.

The falling-off of the natural population increase in the 1980s would not have been so dangerous had people not continued to emigrate at the same time. In the 1960s it was mostly manual workers and craftsmen who went abroad, but in the '80s it was professionals and academics in search of a higher living standard and better chances of promotion. These were mostly young people with or without children, which additionally worsened the demographic scene. The population decrease and the brain drain remained a painful Croatian reality in the 1990s.

The demographic aspect of relations between Croats and Serbs is a subject in itself. Various interpretations, often inexpert and occasionally ill-intentioned, have fanned misunderstandings. In the nineteenth century Serbs accounted for 26 per cent of the population in Civil Croatia and 20 per cent in Dalmatia. Post-war censuses showed that the number of Serbs in Croatia increased from 543,000 in 1948 to 627,000 in 1971, but their percentage gradually decreased because of the faster increase of the population in general. From 15 per cent in 1953 and 1961 it fell to 14.2 in 1971 and 11.6 in 1981 but by 1991 it had risen again to 12.2 per cent. The decrease in the number of Serbs in 1981 is explained by the fact that many declared themselves to be Yugoslavs (as many as 8.2 per cent of those living in Croatia did so – many of them were children of mixed marriages), while the increase in 1991 is the result of the decrease of Yugoslavs (now they make up barely 2.2 per cent). Some identified declared themselves as Yugoslavs due to political persuasion or to further their careers: Yugoslavs were considered to advance more quickly in government service, especially in the JNA and the police.

Rapid urbanisation brought equally rapid changes in population distribution. Analysis of migration processes must cover the whole territory of Yugoslavia, or at least that predominantly inhabited by Serbs and Croats (the republics of Serbia, Bosnia-Hercegovina and Croatia). Generally, Serbs moved in the direction of Serbia and Croats in the direction of Croatia. There were also some specific features at the republican and regional levels: in Croatia, Croats moved into large towns, and Serbs, as well as doing the same, also moved from villages into small towns where the Serbian population was already in a majority or becoming so. Thus Knin,* Obrovac, Petrinja and Benkovac changed from being small towns with a majority or at least a significant percentage of Croats into larger towns with a Serbian majority. The 'each to his own' tendency is seen even in the growth of these towns.

The number of Croats in other Yugoslav republics also clearly shows this principle. Although the Bosnia-Hercegovina Croats had a high birth-rate (between 1948 and 1981 their number grew from 614,000 to 758,000), as a percentage of the total population they decreased between 1948 and 1991 from 23.9 to 17.3 per cent. In the Serbian autonomous province of Vojvodina there were 145,000 Croats (7.8 per cent of the population), in 1971, and only 110,000 (5.4 per cent) in 1981. This decline was caused partly by there being fewer births than deaths, but most of all by migration into Croatia.

The evils of Stalinist totalitarianism were mitigated in Yugoslavia and in Croatia by occasional and piecemeal moves in the direction of greater liberalisation. People lived at a much higher economic and cultural level than in countries under Soviet control, especially in the 1970s and '80s. At that time autonomy increased in many fields—notably health, science and university curricula—where criteria of professionalism had largely replaced the principle of

---

* In 1880 its population was 58:42 in favour of the Croats; in 1953, it was 57:37 in favour of the Serbs; in 1981, 89:11 in favour of the Serbs.

'moral and political correctness'. At the beginning of the 1970s medical science came closer to world standards: the first kidney transplant took place, and in the 1980s the first 'test-tube' baby was born and the first heart was transplanted. Health care was free, and health insurance was paid through the taxation system so that it covered the entire population (although farmers benefited from these rights less than other groups).

In the 1980s the Croatian civil society acquired new qualities. The first alternative radio stations appeared, and newspapers not under direct Party control – in particular the Zagreb weeklies *Danas* (Today) and *Start* and Split's *Nedjeljna Dalmacija* (Sunday Dalmatia) –attained a high professional standard.

The Catholic church remained the only guardian of the Croatian spirit in the national apathy that spread during the 1970s. As Communist morale and the revolutionary system in general decayed, Christian ethics were reborn, and many home and foreign circumstances left the regime unable to limit church activities from the 1980s onwards. In 1976 the Croatian bishops published the pastoral letter 'Thirteen Centuries of Christianity among the Croats', and in that year too they prepared a great celebration of the 900th anniversary of King Zvonimir's coronation at Solin near Split. Three years later in 1979, at Nin near Zadar, the 1100th anniversary of the founding of the Nin bishopric was marked in an event called Branimir's Year. Unlike celebrations organised by the authorities which passed virtually unnoticed, these church events attracted vast crowds, thus indicating a renaissance of the church in Croatia. The peak came in 1984 when the national eucharistic congress of the Croatian church was organised in Zagreb and in the nearby pilgrimage shrine of Marija Bistrica, where the final jubilee for 'Thirteen Centuries of Christianity' among the Croats was attended by 400,000 people, 1,100 priests, thirty-five archbishops and bishops, and five cardinals.

The authorities stuck to their dogmatic attitude towards the church, although it was weakening. It was still very difficult to obtain a permit to erect a church building. The return of the church to towns (its influence had always been strong in the villages) was reflected in the increasing percentage of folk or church names being given to children, and the increase in infant baptisms and church weddings.

A highly important occurrence in this process was the apparition

in 1981 of the Virgin Mary in the village of Medjugorje, a part
of Bosnia-Hercegovina inhabited exclusively by Croats. The village soon became a place of mass pilgrimage, although political
and internal church disputes continued over whether the Virgin
had really revealed herself or not. The village became the most
profitable tourist destination in Bosnia-Hercegovina (at the end
of the '80s its income was estimated at about $80 million a year,
all without any major investment beyond hotel building).

Despite all these relative benefits, Communist Yugoslavia was
still a totalitarian state. The Communist monopoly continued in
the '80s, but now was increasingly limited to the police, the
army, the legal system and the state budget. Ideological constraint
gradually loosened because the state and Party structures were no
longer sufficiently strong or respected to impose themselves. All
that they could still manage was partial control over the media.
The regime's impotence was most clearly seen in its attempts to
cover up the real problems, to keep the many unsolved issues
hidden from the public eye. Up till 1987-8 attempts were made
to hide ethnic problems, and their suppression then was one of
the crucial reasons why they erupted with such violence in 1990-1,
leading to the dissolution of Yugoslavia and war.

In the 1980s Croatia was ruled by people who considered the
'struggle against nationalism' their principal goal. They were more
rigid than the Communists who ruled Serbia till 1987 and more
so, especially, than those in Slovenia. Political trials were rare,
but two prominent men who had been imprisoned for their activities in 1971, Vlado Gotovac and Franjo Tudjman, were jailed
again (for two years) because of an interview the former gave to
Swedish television. In the opinion of the court, they spoke in
an improper manner about conditions in Croatia.

In March 1984 the Information and Propaganda Centre of the
Central Committee of the League of Communists of Croatia
issued a paper or 'White Book' entitled 'Concerning some Ideological and Political Tendencies in Art, Literature, Theatre and Film
Criticism, and the Public Declarations by a Number of Cultural
Figures that Contain Politically Unacceptable Messages'. It contained political criticism of about 200 cultural figures all over
Yugoslavia, and included quotations, interviews and aphorisms
they had published. By issuing this index of politically unsuitable
people the Croatian Communists took over the banner of ideological

dogmatism in Yugoslavia. Reactions to this move were largely negative because it was already felt by this time that such a policy had no future. The general scorn felt for Communists spread, and, however much noise they made, the writers of the 'White Book' did not have the power to call to account or pass sentence on a single person listed in it. One of the last moves by the 'dogmatic' forces occurred in 1987-8 when *Život sa stricem* (Life with Uncle), a film script by Ivan Aralica, was attacked as anti-Communist because it analysed repression in the first years of Communism. In 1988 the director Krsto Papić made the film anyway and it was distributed to cinemas and shown in the normal way. In the same year the director Branko Schmidt filmed the play *Sokol ga nije volio* (The falcon did not love him) which had already played in theatres. It was the first Croatian film about the fate of Croatian Domobrans and Ustashas on the death marches (the 'Way of the Cross') in 1945. The making of these films showed that the influence of the 'dogmatists' was rapidly weakening.

The system of socialist values did not include the right to strike. For a long time, right up till the 1980s, strikes were considered counter-revolutionary and their organisers and the strikers themselves always risked various kinds of harassment. The few strikes that did break out were not mentioned in the media. Party committees usually appeased the demands of strikers for a better life by securing urgent bank loans whose repayment they could not guarantee. In 1987, in one of the first major and long-lasting strikes in Croatia, some 1,000 coal miners ceased work in the Istrian town of Labin. The media could not, and some would not, hide what was happening. The strikers first demanded an increase in wages and a decrease in administrative personnel. The official trade union was not on their side, but the basic demands were satisfied. The authorities were afraid of a broader social revolt erupting, and even ethnic strife because most of the miners were Bosnian Muslims.

# 13

## YUGOSLAVIA AND CROATIA
## ON COURSE TO WAR

In many public speeches throughout his rule, Josip Broz Tito showed that he was completely aware of the serious nature of Yugoslavia's ethnic problems. Not knowing how to solve them democratically, he tried in the typical Communist manner to stifle them and in so doing managed to achieve a relatively successful balance. Indeed it was his shrewdness and extraordinary feeling for the balance of power that shored up Communist Yugoslavia. In Zagreb the statue of *ban* Jelačić was removed, and throughout Croatia streets and squares named after him were given new names. The names of Ante Starčević and Stjepan Radić and their ideologies of, respectively, state rights and general human rights were allowed or at least tolerated, but they were served to the public in strictly measured quantities. At the same time, amnesia concerning almost all its imperial glory was imposed on Serbia. To curb the Greater Serbian spirit, legendary military commanders were slowly relegated to the background, and in return the Serbian *nomenklatura* were bribed by the excessive development and glitter of the capital, and by ambassadorships, military careers and senior positions in the civil service.

From the moment the 1974 constitution in Serbia was passed, there was latent dissatisfaction with it especially because of the excessive competences given to the autonomous provinces, which thus became practically detached from the republic of Serbia's jurisdiction. The Serbs complained that Kosovo and Vojvodina had been given all the attributes of states. After Tito's death, the apparent peace and internal balance of power were upset in the spring of 1981 in Kosovo: the Albanian majority demonstrated, demanding greater autonomy within the republic of Serbia, and even calling for their own independent republic. This was the beginning of a long period of rebellion and resistance against the

Serbian authorities, taking various forms. After the Kosovo demonstrations, views on Serbia's unsatisfactory position in Yugoslavia came into the open, being first aired at a session of the Central Committee of the League of Communists of Serbia at the end of 1981, and thereafter repeated ever more often and quite openly. In November 1984 the Serbian Central Committee again demanded tighter internal integration of the republic and a better position in the federation. They sensed that strong processes of disintegration were at work in Yugoslavia, and for the first time submitted a 'platform for reintegration'. Although no one yet publicly challenged the essence of the 1974 constitution, it was obvious that Serbian nationally-coloured demands were increasing.

Evaluation of the disorders in Kosovo was contradictory. For the Serbs it was 'genocide against the Serbs', for the Slovenes 'natural emigration of Serbs' and for the Albanians 'terror and suppressions against the Albanians'. Controversy among proponents of the conflicting views increased tension within Yugoslavia, and the Serbs in their propaganda began to exert direct pressure on other Yugoslav nations and republics to speak out against the Albanians.

## The myth of a genocidal nature

One of the main supporting arguments behind the contention that the Socialist Republic of Serbia, and the Serbs, were at a disadvantage in Yugoslavia was a reinterpretation of history at variance with the ruling dogma. The new approach was a form of mystification that accentuated the cult of self-sacrifice and was obsessed with the past. It was based on a concept that the writer Dobrica Ćosić (President of Yugoslavia in the 1990s) had already formulated in the late 1960s and continued to develop: 'In today's world the Serbian nation is probably best known for its great sacrifice and suffering for freedom, which is the ideological substance of Serbian collective spirituality and ethics.'[1]

Interest in other previously forbidden subjects also awoke in Serbia and among the Serbs. One of them was the Chetnik movement, whose negative image based on Communist historiography

---

[1] D. Ćosić, *Stvarno i mogue* (Ljubljana–Zagreb, 1988), p. 188.

they wanted to reinterpret. In September 1986 a Belgrade daily published the unfinished text of a 'Memorandum' written in the Serbian Academy of Sciences and Arts. The Serbian authorities mostly reacted unfavourably to this text, but the authority of its authors and its nationalistic inspiration overpowered the tepid official criticism. The document first analysed the Yugoslav crisis in detail and then outlined what was in fact the Greater Serbian national programme. It openly accused Tito of wilfully weakening Serbia, and spoke of nationalism 'from above', alleging that other Yugoslav nations were developing their ethnic identities with the blessing of 'higher circles' but that this was forbidden to the Serbian nation. It called all the others 'anti-Serbs' because they supported or tolerated Albanian protests in Kosovo. It also claimed that a disgraceful programme of assimilation was being implemented in Croatia with the ultimate object of Croatising the Serbs. The basic idea underlying the 'Memorandum' was that the Serbian nation was a kind of primary entity in Yugoslavia with special rights transcending all usual political and geographical divisions: 'The integrity of the Serbian nation and its culture in all of Yugoslavia is an essential issue for the survival of that nation.' It recommended strengthening the Yugoslav federation, but in the perspective of the 1990s 'integrity' may be interpreted differently, as the creation of a Serbian state in areas inhabited by the Serbs.

At the same time, by no means inadvertently, another Belgrade paper published an article by the historian Vasilije Krestić, an academician and university professor in Belgrade, entitled 'Concerning the Genesis of Genocide over the Serbs in the NDH'. He was the first to give a rounded formulation of what is called the genocidal nature of the Croats: 'It is quite certain that the origin of genocidal acts against the Serbs in Croatia should be sought ... in the sixteenth and seventeenth centuries, when the Serbs began to settle Croatian lands.' He then cited many instances of Croatian-Serbian disputes in Croatia in the second half of the nineteenth century and the early twentieth, always blaming the Croats and imputing to them a wish to destroy the Serbs. Serbian authors belonging to this movement considered that the great number of Serbs killed by the Ustashas in 1941-5 made the Croats collectively guilty, and that their nation was genocidal in character. The effort to prove the latter contention focused on the camp at Jasenovac. In 1946 it was claimed that 46,000 people had been killed there, but in following decades estimates of the number of victims grew till 600,000 or 700,000 were claimed, even in official publications. An exhaustive investigation in the 1960s into the killings at Jasenovac and Stara Gradiška could not bring to light more than 59,000 names. If victims whose names could not be found are added to these, we come closer to establishing the real number of victims. However, the results of the investigation were not made available to the public because they differed from the generally-accepted opinion. Scrupulous demographic and historical analysis shows that about 83,000 people were killed in Jasenovac (Žerjavić). In the 1980s some historians and quasi-historians addressed the Serbian death-toll in the Second World War, especially in the Jasenovac camp, and enlarged the already inflated claim that 700,000 Serbs had been killed to one million, then to more than 1.1 million. Finally it was said that 'it will never be possible to discover' the exact number of victims.

At the end of the 1980s, more incendiary articles appeared in the Serbian press. Various publicists used the 'Memorandum' as a starting-point for trying to prove, on the basis of data taken out of context, exaggerated, distorted and even fabricated, that the Serbs had been 'cheated', 'short-changed', 'killed', 'destroyed even after the genocide' and, finally, that they were eternal winners in war and losers in peace. All this led to theories of a worldwide anti-Serb conspiracy.

This 'newly written history' might have remained no more than a specific cultural phenomenon had the passage of time not disclosed the politically volatile nature of these 'scholarly' evaluations, especially after Slobodan Milošević came to power in 1987. A year or two later they began to be used to justify the wars of conquest started by Serbia, Montenegro, the JNA and some of the Serbs in Croatia and Bosnia-Hercegovina in 1991-5. The repetition of these views had menacing undertones with the allegation that the Serbs deserved the greatest credit for the existence Yugoslavia, and that Yugoslavia had treated them unjustly. The Serbs had liberated all the other Yugoslav peoples, and in return had been subjected to exploitation, genocide and the break-up of their national territory. Their conviction that whatever they did to balance the account would be justified grew more intense.

Vindictive rage over 1941, the year 'that had never been repaid', was awakening.

## 1987: the crisis intensifies. Slobodan Milošević comes to power

In 1987 Slobodan Milošević (born in 1941) began to emerge in Serbian political life. He was an exceedingly ambitious and rather capable bank manager, and a career Communist. He was relatively young, and he immediately won people over because he told them what they wanted to hear. In the spring of 1987 he was elected President of the Central Committee of the League of Communists of Serbia, and in the autumn of that year he staged a typical party putsch to 'cleanse' the Central Committee and the Belgrade Municipal Committee of more liberal non-sympathisers. He then began to rule with a 'firm hand'. Using the slogan 'No one is allowed to beat the people', which later became a popular saying, he supported the Kosovo Serbs against the Albanians, and skillfully combined Communist and authoritarian methods with nationalistic slogans and demagogy. Most Serbs soon accepted him as the man who was protecting their interests not only in Serbia but throughout Yugoslavia. This included the Serbs in Croatia.

In the summer of 1988, helped by groups of militant Kosovo Serbs, Milošević began to organise mass meetings in all the major Serbian towns, at which his supporters threw yogurt at local leaders who supported autonomy and opposed his centralism (the so-called 'yogurt revolution'). In the following months these methods brought about the resignation of the local leaderships in the autonomous provinces of Vojvodina and Kosovo, and in the republic of Montenegro, thus annulling the autonomy of the provinces. According to official statistics, almost 100 Albanians were killed in the disturbances in Kosovo in 1989. It was obvious that Milošević would not stop at this. His demagogic utterances could be interpreted in various ways, but since he often mentioned Yugoslavia as the stage on which his activities were being played out, it was obvious that the leaderships of the other republics could soon expect the beginning of Serbian pressure on federal bodies.

Milošević's statement of 1988 was a true announcement of what was to come: 'The problem of Yugoslavia will be solved by the policy for which most people in this country have opted, inside and outside institutions, statutorily and unstatutorily, in the streets and indoors, as a popular movement or confined to the élite, with or without arguments, but always by making it clear that it is a policy for a Yugoslavia in which people will live richer and more cultural lives in unity and equality.' A year later, at the celebration on 28 June 1989 of the 600th anniversary of the Battle of Kosovo in Gazimestan, he spoke of the lessons of this battle for the 'modern battles Serbs are waging', and called on their courage, resolution and self-sacrifice. He emphasised that 'even armed battles are not out of the question'. In a later stage of the war in Croatia and Bosnia-Hercegovina (and in Kosovo after 1998), this statement was interpreted as a declaration of war.

In the 1990 election campaign many political parties publicly proposed a confederate Yugoslavia; so too did the newly elected governments in Slovenia and Croatia. Milošević said that in that case he would challenge the boundaries between the republics. Supporting the allegedly just demands of the Serb minority, he and his supporters left no doubt that if Yugoslavia were not organised according to their demands, they would create a Greater Serbia that would include large parts of Croatia, even those in which the Serbs were a minority. They did not rule out the use of force. Milošević's policy was of a kind that allowed no compromise.

When, at the end of the 1980s Communism collapsed throughout Europe, the Serbian Communists became transformed into nationalists who even adopted some elements of Fascist and Nazi policy: hatred for others, fuelled by a clear *Blut und Boden* ideology ('Serbia reaches to wherever there are Serbian graves'), police repression and a militaristic policy of expansion. At meetings in 1989 the crowds chanted 'We want arms!'

Both as a kingdom and as a socialist state, Yugoslavia was a fragile entity; it was only built to withstand a bare minimum of nationalism, if any at all. The Communist leaders in each of its constituent nations seem to have felt this, and in their rigid way knew what degree of national aspiration could be accommodated and how much should be said about ethnic relations. Milošević's violent movement was designed to destroy Yugoslavia or to transform it according to the Milošević measure.

In the mid-1980s any will that remained to preserve Yugoslav unity had already largely disappeared. In 1985 the last congress of the Yugoslav Association of Writers was held, at which republican delegations expressed irreconcilably different attitudes to literature and politics. At that time other professional associations went through a similar process. Professional journals on a federal level ceased publication. The Yugoslav Film Festival in Pula and the Eurovision Song Contest had become forums where republics could vote each other down.

When Milošević moved to transform Yugoslavia in the late '80s, the erosion of the remaining Yugoslav institutions – the League of Communists and the Yugoslav People's Army – was part of a strategy designed to preclude a compromise being reached in those organisations. At the same time the Serbian leaders and the JNA generals were eager to preserve a socialist state. One of the propaganda means used to achieve this was to present all other options, such as Albanian resistance and the Slovenian reform policy, as ultra-nationalistic.

## Towards a multi-party system

This was the atmosphere in which the first steps to found opposition societies and parties began in Slovenia and Croatia at the end of 1988 and beginning of 1989. The first meetings were held under the threat of police obstruction, but the relative speed of demo-cratisation and change was such that it could not be stopped. In Croatia all initiative was centred in Zagreb.

The newly-formed opposition had the twin goals of establishing a multi-party liberal democracy and solving the Croatian national question, and from the beginning opposition associations and parties expressed these priorities. The Association for Yugoslav Democratic Initiative (UJDI), as its name suggests, demanded a democratic transformation throughout the whole of Yugoslavia – which in itself would solve the national question. It was founded in February 1989 in Zagreb – branches appeared in other republics – but its leaders would not transform it into a political party. Later most of its members joined left-wing civil parties.

The Croatian Social Liberal Party (HSLS) was founded in May 1989. It supported the development of a liberal democratic society in Croatia and all of Yugoslavia in the belief that this was the best way to express the true interests of Croatian citizens and Croats in general, and would be the basis for a solution to the

Croatian national question. Their 'programmatic declaration' said that 'the HSLS starts from the principle that only a community in which every individual is free and socially secure can be free' and that 'the national question in Yugoslavia can be solved only by federalism based on consensus with the right of nations to self-determination and secession.' As soon as they were founded, the Liberals were joined by many figures in public and cultural life. In 1989 they showed themselves to be moderate and won respect. They failed to win the 1990 elections, and during the next five or six years were always the second strongest party.

Finally, the Croatian Democratic Union (HDZ) placed its main emphasis on finding a solution to the national question, although its programme did not omit to mention democracy. The 'draft of the basic programme', published in February 1989, made the general statement that 'a way out of the chasm of overall crisis...can only be found by honouring all the civilisational and democratic achievements of human society', and then went into detail about the Croatian diaspora and Croatia's economic difficulties in Yugoslavia, with a strong accent on the national aspect: 'Croatian national consciousness developed around, and should continued to be based on, the positive, revivalist and freethinking traditions of Croatian historical state right as formulated by Starčević; universal, humanistic, democratic republicanism as formulated by Radić; and the vision and experience of the Croatian left, the Marxists and Communists.' On the future of the Yugoslav community it said: 'The Socialist Federal Republic of Yugoslavia, established as a self-managed and federal state, can survive only if it assures the freedom and sovereign rights of every individual nation.'

The HDZ, like the Liberals, was afraid that its founding assembly might be banned, but it was finally constituted in Zagreb in June 1989, and Franjo Tudjman (born 1922) was elected president. He had fought in the National Liberation Struggle during the Second World War and until the late 1950s had lived in Belgrade, where he had an outstandingly successful military career, becoming a general aged thirty-eight. When he came to Zagreb he became director of the newly-founded Institute for the History of the Workers' Movement. He was ambitious and hard-working, and his historical texts were primarily those of a politician who wanted to adapt the interpretation of history to suit his political goals.

After the 'Declaration' was published in 1967 he was removed from his position as director of the Institute but continued to study history, elaborating a kind of Croatian national programme. Even in the 1960s the idea of the Croatian *banovina* of .1939 fascinated him, and he considered it an acceptable model for a future solution of the Yugoslav question. Even then, some of his statements showed that he was convinced Bosnia-Hercegovina could not survive as a single entity. He did not think Yugoslavia could do so either.

The difference between the HSLS and the HDZ in their approaches to specific issues was most clearly expressed in October 1989, when the HSLS took the initiative for the return of *ban* Josip Jelačić's statue to Zagreb's main square from which the Communist authorities had removed it in 1947 because they considered Jelačić 'politically unsuitable'. The Liberals' petition read: 'We, the undersigned citizens, consider that the statue of Josip Jelačić should be returned to Republic Square, and placed where it used to stand.' In the immediate vicinity HDZ members were handing out a proclamation that contained the following: 'The fate of the unhappy *ban's* statue has become the symbol of how Croatian national feelings were trampled on in socialist Croatia, a symbol of a policy of heartless hatred for one's own nation, its history, culture, heritage.' On a rainy morning about 70,000 citizens signed the Liberals' petitions – the clearest indication up to that time of what people were thinking before the 1990 elections. It also seems to have been the key moment in conquering the fears of people in Zagreb and other towns about joining opposition parties. After October 1989 HDZ branches and members multiplied incomparably faster than those of the HSLS. Most Croatian political exiles, especially those with Ustasha leanings, supported the HDZ. The financial and other aid that this party received from the Croatian diaspora helped its growth, especially later during the election campaign.

The chances of official recognition of the political parties were at first slim; then a compromise formula was reached whereby the parties would act within the Socialist Alliance. However, conditions in Croatia and Yugoslavia were changing rapidly. The 'silent opposition' of Communists from the inside and the pressure of Milošević's policy from the outside led to the announcement of free elections in Croatia and Slovenia at the end of 1989. At the beginning of 1990 the authorities legalised all political parties without exception.

## Towards the dissolution of Yugoslavia

In October 1988 the anti-Milošević block in the League of Communists of Yugoslavia arranged for a vote of confidence on the top-level leadership. Only Dušan Čkrebić, a proponent of the Serbian policy, failed this test, but in the event Milošević managed to outmanoeuvre the decision and Čkrebić returned to office. This was the clearest indiction of how parts of Yugoslavia outside Serbia regarded Milošević's policy.

In the autumn of 1989 after a campaign through Serbia and Montenegro, Serbian propaganda was stepped up against the other Yugoslav republics, especially Slovenia, which had the most liberal political and economic policy in the 1970s and '80s. In the '80s especially, the institutions of a civil society, such as freedom of the press and public opinion, developed there, resulting in extreme sensitivity to the populist harangue coming from Serbia. Resistance to Milošević was unanimous. In reply Serbia applied pressure in a variety of forms: a boycott of Slovenian products, and accusations of 'separatism' and 'breaking up Yugoslavia'. The Belgrade media wrote of the Serb-Slovene friendship dating from the Second World War, which the Slovenes were now betraying.

In the following months pressure on Croatia also grew. The Serbian media called the introduction of a multi-party system and the growth of opposition parties the 'awakening of retrograde ideas', which was especially dangerous in Croatia in view of the terrible memories of the Second World War. They claimed: 'The Ustasha spirit is stirring.' At that time the ruling Communists in Croatia enjoyed no popular support or respect, and had neither the strength nor the ability to oppose Milošević's policy. They therefore stated that they had adopted a tactic of 'Croatian silence', which in fact meant that they did not intend to offer any opposition at all, or that they would only react half-heartedly and too late. For example Stipe Šuvar, the Croatian member of the Yugoslav Presidency, announced that he would 'call a spade a spade', obviously alluding to Milošević's policy being unacceptable, but this open settling of accounts never happened.

Serbian pressure culminated at the end of November 1989

when Kosovo militants, in collusion with the Serbian authorities, announced that they would organise a 'rally of truth' in Ljubljana on 1 December, and on their way there would stop in Zagreb, where they also wanted to stir up disorder. The Slovenian authorities forbade them entry, but right up till the last moment the demonstrators kept saying that they would go all the same. They finally gave up because for the first time the Croatian authorities mustered their courage and announced that they would use police against the demonstrators. This situation and other events convinced the Croatian Communist leaders that they would not be able to endure the pressure both of Milošević and of the growing non-Communist opposition. Rather unexpectedly and quite quickly, at its Eleventh Congress in Zagreb (11-13 December 1989), the League of Communists of Croatia 'gave its support to democratic political relations, including citizens' freedom of political association in a multi-party system'. The leading Communists expressed their readiness to take part in multi-party elections and adhere to democratic principles of political competition. The way for political parties in Croatia was now open.

## *Ante Marković: swimming against the tide*

At the end of 1989, with increasing threats looming, the Federal prime minister Ante Marković (a Croat from Bosnia who had lived in Croatia for some forty years) presented in the Yugoslav parliament a programme of economic reform designed to combat hyper-inflation. It seemed that he might be the saviour who would succeed in dragging the country back from the brink of a nationalistic Balkan chasm to become a developed economy of the West European type. The exchange rate of the dinar and the German mark was frozen, and convertibility for the dinar, stabilisation of the state budget and spending, and a restrictive monetary policy were announced. Western banks promised financial support for Marković's programme. However, in the end his concept was shown to be unrealistic. He wanted to win the confidence of all or at least most citizens of Yugoslavia with the promise of economic revival, but the time had passed when they still believed in any kind of Yugoslavia. In addition, he underestimated the irrational elements that were influencing people after 1987-9, and believed that he could win voters by offering them a rational economic programme. Marković's programme collapsed in 1990 when his sympathisers (mainly ex-Communists who loudly declared their support for him) and coalition partners lost at elections in Croatia and Bosnia-Hercegovina. Another factor that made his programme unrealistic was that he had no real control over some economic institutions: at the beginning of 1991, thanks to Milošević's manipulation, Serbia removed about US$2 billion from the primary issue of the National Bank of Yugoslavia, and the property of most Croatian and Slovenian firms in Serbia was requisitioned at the same time.

The final break-up of the Yugoslav federation took place at the beginning of 1990 at the Fourteenth Congress of the League of Communists of Yugoslavia. It was convened 'to find solutions to the profound and general social crisis', i.e. to overcome the increasingly irreconcilable differences among the republics. Since no decision could be reached without the consensus of republican delegations, it was clear that Milošević's concept of a centralised Yugoslavia under Serbian domination could not be imposed. The Slovenian and Croatian Communists had already prepared for elections, accepting the concept of republican sovereignty and the market economy. After four days of fruitless argument the Slovenian delegation walked out. The Serbian and Montenegrin delegations demanded that the Congress continue working without the Slovenes, but the others did not agree. That is how the League of Communists of Yugoslavia fell apart. The only powerful organisation that still functioned in the whole of Yugoslavia was the Yugoslav National Army, the JNA.

It seems that in these months the leading proponents of Milošević's policy began increasingly to consider the alternative plan they were holding in reserve. Since by now it was obvious that they could not seize power in Yugoslavia by taking control over legal structures (the Yugoslav Presidency had no authority because republican policy was created in the republics), they began to lay the foundations for creating a Greater Serbia. Realising that all kinds of pressure would have to be used in pursuit of this goal, including force of arms, the Serbian leaders did all they could to win over the top ranks of the JNA.

*Towards the first free elections*

Milošević's pressure on Croatia and the other republics, and the complete absence of any adequate Croatian response, left Croatian voters with a growing feeling of impotence and anger. When the first free elections were announced at the beginning of 1990, it became likely that whoever managed to offer voters the most forceful defence of Croatia's endangered sovereignty and settle accounts with the hated Communists would win.

A sure favourite in this competition for the 'greatest Croat' (the exact term used in Croatian) was Franjo Tudjman. He and his Croatian Democratic Union (HDZ) were helped by the unsuccessful alleged assassination attempt on him by a Serb during an HDZ election rally in Benkovac in northern Dalmatia. Some of Tudjman's statements certainly did not show him to be a democrat ('All people are equal in Croatia, but it must be clear who is the host and who the guest' and 'Some say that my wife is Serbian or Jewish – I am happy to say that she is neither Serbian nor Jewish'). In an electoral body with no developed democratic traditions only a small number of people criticised Tudjman; most considered that his radical nationalism was the appropriate answer to the challenge from the other side.

With the majority electoral system there were two rounds, in April and the beginning of May 1990. The HDZ won 42 per cent of the vote but got 205 seats in the *Sabor*, which was 57.6 per cent of the total of 356. In the main *Sabor* chamber, the Chamber of Representatives, the HDZ even had a clear two-thirds majority.

The Coalition of National Agreement, in which the HSLS was the strongest element, represented the political centre. From 1971 it had distinguished leaders, Savka Dapčević-Kučar and Mika Tripalo, and at the beginning of the election campaign appeared to have good chances of success. However, it was seriously defeated because, despite winning 20 per cent of the vote, it only obtained a negligible number of parliamentary seats. In the Manichean scenario of many voters faced with the political programmes of various parties, the HDZ was considered to represent 'the good' and to have the potential to defeat Milošević's Serbian threat and the 'evil' of Communism. There was no room for a third party, because the Coalition did not define its option for an independent and sovereign Croatia as clearly as the HDZ had done.

The League of Communists under the leadership of Ivica Račan presented a completely new programme: resistance to Milošević's policy, support for a multi-party system, and parliamentary democracy. This was the reason for its change of name to League of Communists-Party of Democratic Change (SK-SDP); they finally dropped 'SK', remaining only 'SDP' with the new meaning of Social Democratic Party. They mostly won the votes of people who were afraid of change – Serbs and civil servants. These made a total of 30 per cent, with a good number of seats.

The Croatian Communists recognised the electoral results and surprisingly the change of government passed off without disturbances. The new *Sabor* and the new government, the first to be elected freely in Croatia for half a century, were constituted on 30 May 1990. With an absolute majority in the *Sabor* the HDZ established what was *de facto* one-party rule: all the members of the newly-formed government belonged to the HDZ or were non-party HDZ sympathisers, as too were all the top *Sabor* officials. Franjo Tudjman was elected President of the Presidency of the Republic of Croatia, the country's leader.

Most of the leading HDZ members who now took over responsible state offices were former Communists who had left the Party during the 'Croatian Spring' or later because of their nationalistic views. Under Communism these people could not have learned how to run a state on democratic lines, or obtained any practice in it. They ruled in the way that their former Party had taught them: as a one-party system. The principle of separation of powers into legislature, executure and judiciary was completely neglected. HDZ members or their close associates were soon placed in all the leading positions, and thus the institutional independence necessary for the functioning of democracy could not be established. Franjo Tudjman's authoritarian behaviour and style of governing contributed greatly to the general climate. He had absolute support and authority within his party, and transferred this style to his new state functions.

The great majority of Croats greeted joyfully the fall of Communism and the establishment of a new government with a national remit. Mass meetings and various celebrations were organised in Zagreb and throughout Croatia. A large number of Partisan war memorials placed by the Communist authorities were demolished, and there was a new emphasis on Croatian national symbols. Streets named after notable Serbs or Serbian towns were quickly given new names with a Croatian symbolism. The Square of Fascist Victims in Zagreb became the Square of Great Croats (*Trg Hrvatskih Velikana*). A number of political exiles immediately returned to Croatia from the diaspora, including some who were pro-Ustasha, bringing back with them their old extremist ideas which they were not afraid to express in public. Tudjman proclaimed a policy of 'reconciliation of all the Croats', which meant tolerance for extreme nationalism. Many members of the new government were drunk with success and behaved as if they had forgotten, or perhaps only underestimated, the fact that Croatia was still in Yugoslavia with over half a million Serbian citizens who relied on Yugoslavia and were being increasingly manipulated from Serbia.

## The Serbs in Croatia

The reactions of Serbs to the first appearance of opposition parties in 1989 varied. Those living in the large towns, especially intellectuals, had a much surer sense of the feelings of the Croatian majority than inhabitants of villages and smaller towns with a Serb majority. Some of the 'urban' Serbs joined opposition parties and regarded the Croatian majority sympathetically; nevertheless, most of them followed the new developments with apprehension and many reservations. According to the 1991 census, the percentage of Serbs in Split was 4.5, in Zagreb 6.3, in Rijeka 11.2 and in Osijek 15.3. At that time 140,000 Serbs, i.e. almost a quarter of the 581,000 in Croatia, lived in the four largest towns. Among the smaller towns Vukovar had 45,000 inhabitants and almost 15,000 Serbs (32.5 per cent), Sisak had nearly 11,000 (23.6), Karlovac 14,500 (24.2), Šibenik 4,000 (9.5), and the relatively small Petrinja 8,500 (45.1). Modern migrations, mainly due to the need to find a job, had done their work. Almost every municipality, even ones that used to be all but 100 per cent Croat, now had some Serbs.

In the parts of Croatia where they were the majority, the Serbs mostly looked on the development of political parties with misgivings and suspicion. Some began to fear a repetition of 1941 and began to 'self-organise', strongly supported by Belgrade. In

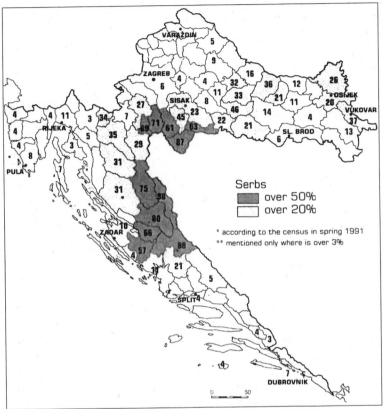

Percentage of Serbs in communities 1991

1989 and 1990 arms were distributed among them, and firms and political bodies planned how they would continue working if there were to be a state of emergency.

The Serbs in Croatia looked on socialist Yugoslavia as the guarantor of their personal and national security, and in some cases also of their economic prosperity. When they saw Yugoslavia gradually disappearing at the end of the 1980s, they lost this feeling of security and feared that they might suffer discrimination. However, Milošević's rise at the same time brought them a new sense of national identity, as and they began increasingly to look for protection to his Serbia and to the only Yugoslav institution that still existed: the JNA.

The Serbs, traditionally used to taking up arms and always strongly supported by the JNA, were unprepared for democratic dialogue and reacted instinctively. Their belief in the Communists and Yugoslavia made them put off for a long time forming a Serb party, but the Serbian Democratic Party (SDS) was finally established in Knin in February 1990. Its programme stated that the 'regional division in Croatia is outdated' and that 'it does not correspond with the historical interests of the Serb people'. They demanded a new administrative division, which foreshadowed later demands for complete autonomy or even secession. Because of the short time at its disposal, the SDS managed to nominate election candidates only in Knin and its immediate surroundings, where it won convincingly. In other parts of Croatia it organised gatherings during the election campaign that challenged the democratic changes as such, both in Croatia and in Yugoslavia. In February attempts were made to organise a 'truth rally' in four Serb villages near Vukovar, similar to ones organised in other parts of Yugoslavia, but this was prevented by the local Party organisation on the grounds that 'one-nation gatherings would only cause the relatively stable situation to deteriorate'. In March a mass meeting was held beside the well-known Partisan war memorial on Petrova Gora mountain in Kordun, about 70 km. south of Zagreb. Tens of thousands of Serbs from the surrounding areas and from Bosnia–Hercegovina and Serbia attended. Speakers expressed disagreement with the programmes of almost all the parties on the Croatian political scene. They expressed Greater Serbian aspirations (some groups shouted 'This is Serbia!', and speakers spoke in that vein), but it seems that a large map of Yugoslavia with the international frontiers outlined but the inside left blank – i.e. a unitary Yugoslavia without republics on republican borders – came closest to the 'general will'. Such a map was displayed on a poster at the meeting. Every mention of Yugoslavia, the JNA and Serbia was greeted with cheers. Tito was not mentioned once, nor was any picture of him displayed; it seems that they had already come to terms with life without him, although the break must have been painful. A message was read to the Yugoslav public: 'We reject some people's dreams about confederation and this is the last warning to those who want to break up Yugoslavia....' A noisy minority whistled down the proposal of a former Partisan general that the problems in Croatia should be settled by agreement.

After the election victory of the HDZ and the establishment of the new government, the attitudes of Serbs in places where they formed the majority or a high percentage of the population became even more radical. The nationalistic SDS quickly spread its influence at the expense of the Communists, who were now called Social Democrats and who within only a few months completely lost their earlier support in predominantly Serb communities. In this tense situation the new Croatian authorities did nothing to damp down Croatian national euphoria; they even seemed to support or incite it. Among the Serbs in Croatia suspicions grew; the introduction of the traditional Croatian flag and coat-of-arms, without Communist symbols, reminded them of the Second World War and seemed like a return to the Ustasha flag and coat-of-arms. Many government employees, especially police who were mainly Serbs and Communists, resigned under various kinds of pressure and were pensioned or found different jobs. Many were discharged. This was based on a decision that the civil service should employ numbers of an ethnic group corresponding to their percentage in the population. Croats applied first to fill the places, and this could have been interpreted as creating 'ethnically pure' units. The free press began to address previously taboo subjects, and there were attempts to rehabilitate the NDH, or at least improve its historic image. Among the Serbs this generated even greater apprehension and animosity. Some kept themselves informed through the Belgrade media, which lied about what was going on in Croatia by continually claiming that the new government was purely Ustasha and preparing genocide against them.

The Croatian authorities ignored the mindset of the Serbs, especially of those around Knin who for generations had been brought up on the myth of Serb heroism and were traditionally belligerent. Besides, the Croats considered that even if a conflict were to break out, it could never be of major proportions or last long. They naively believed that in such a conflict European democratic countries would immediately take the side of 'Croatian democracy' against 'Serbian Communism and imperialism'. Tudjman considered it was his historic mission to create an independent Croatian state and he found compromise of any kind on this issue extremely difficult. When they heard of the increasing difficulties and distress in Serb-majority regions, the highest-ranking Croatian officials, instead of going there to calm things down, appeared unconcerned or even, purposely or not, poured fuel on the flames. The right wing in the new Croatian government, some just returned from abroad, actually welcomed the incendiary Serbian policy because if conflict broke out there would be a chance for Croatia to leave Yugoslavia. By the spring of 1990 two radical policies, Croatian and Serbian, were in open confrontation, and neither could back down without losing the very reason for their existence. When the Croatian authorities began late in 1990 and at the beginning of 1991 inviting local Serbs to cooperate and assist in the quiet resolution of disputes, it was too late and in fact had no result.

The peacemakers did not stand a chance. In May 1990, at a football match in Zagreb between the local Dinamo team and Belgrade's Crvena Zvezda (Red star), a large group of supporters of the latter arrived from Belgrade. For no apparent reason, they began breaking up the seats and tried to lay their hands on the few local fans in their part of the stands. The police, who still included a considerable number of Communists, looked on. However, when the Zagreb fans started off across the football field to square accounts, there was a serious clash with the police. The match was stopped, and conditions again worsened.

One must ask whether the Croatian authorities could have prevented the Serb insurrection and the war if they had followed a more considered policy: probably they could not have done so. Documents published later and some memoirs, notably those of Milošević's closest associate Borisav Jović and the Yugoslav army minister General Kadijević, show beyond doubt that it was Milošević's policy to subjugate Croatia militarily with the help of the JNA, or at least to conquer vital Croatian territories. An important part of this policy consisted of manipulating and stoking up the rebellion of the Serbs in Croatia. Compromise with the Croatian authorities was out of the question; it had to be nothing less than total subjection to a centralised Yugoslavia under Milošević's (i.e. Greater Serbian) domination. It was impossible to expect this kind of capitulation from Croatia in view of the mood of the great majority of Croats and what they had voted for at elections. Even if a more moderate party than the HDZ had come to power, e.g. one that would have supported greater Croatian independence within a confederate Yugoslavia, the Serbs in Croatia would still have rebelled. However, fewer of them would have joined the other side if Croatian policy had been more intelligent, and the overall damage would have been less. The example of the Serbs in Gorski Kotar suggests that this was the case; Croatian representatives approached them with reasonable proposals, and there was no rebellion there. Also, the great majority of prominent Serb intellectuals in the towns did not join the rebellion but remained passive – hence a better-thought-out policy might have persuaded them to exert a calming influence on their co-nationals in rural areas.

SDS representatives kept saying that they demanded 'autonomy' for the Serb people, but their true objectives remained unclear. They never presented any detailed document outlining their wishes to the Croatian public, nor did the Serbs in Croatia resort to any of the kind of parliamentary or extraparliamentary measures that are usual in developed states. The speeches of Serb deputies in the *Sabor* were ill-prepared, with no considered strategy. At mass protests and demonstrations that took place on territory under Croatian control from the summer of 1990 till just before the war in the autumn of 1991, the main aim of the organisers and speakers was to whip up popular emotion and not to explain to the Croatian or the international public what it was that they really wanted. Everything was reduced to crude propaganda promoting a unitary Yugoslav or Greater Serbian ideology. The only thing that might be called a programme was a statement by Jovan Rašković (1928-93), the first president of the SDS: 'For every step that Tudjman's government takes to separate itself from Yugoslavia, we will take a step to separate ourselves from Croatia.' It seems that the SDS leadership were consciously making relations as bad as they could possibly be. In May 1990 it was claimed by the Serbs that unknown perpetrators had severely wounded the SDS president in Benkovac. There were no objective witnesses and it could possibly have been set up by the Serbs themselves, but whatever the truth of the matter, it gave Rašković a pretext to state that he was breaking off all relations with the *Sabor* because his life was 'under threat'. This was followed by inflammatory statements based on half-truths and outright lies that brought the Serbs to the mass psychosis of imminent war and rebellion.

*On the path to war*

On 25 May 1990 the Croatian *Sabor* promulgated amendments to the republic's constitution: it erased the word 'socialist' from the name of the state, confirmed the new coat-of-arms and flag, introduced the office of President of Croatia (instead of President of the Presidency) and ministers (instead of republican secretaries). On the same day the Serb National Council was founded in the village of Srb on the border of Bosnia-Hercegovina (scene of one of the first Partisan operations in 1941). The Council did not recognise the changes in Croatia and passed the 'Declaration on the Sovereignty and Autonomy of Serbs in Croatia', calling for a referendum on Serb autonomy in Croatia. At a rally of thousands of people (some say 100,000), Jovan Rašković proclaimed: 'The Serb nation has risen!' During August 1990 weapons were stolen from police stations according to a well-laid plan. The next days passed in negotiations between the Croatian authorities and the representatives of local Serbs in attempts to persuade them to return the weapons and defuse the situation. These were unsuccessful. The Serbian leaders called their referendum on 'Serb autonomy' for Sunday, 17 August. Several dozen Croatian policemen set off to Knin by helicopter to prevent it, but the JNA forced them back to Zagreb, threatening to blow them out of the sky, on the grounds that it was 'technically impossible' to approve the flight. The situation was exacerbated by the Serbian leaders continually alarming their people with the 'coming of the Ustashas'. Following their natural instincts, people fled to inaccessible places and the mayor of Knin, Milan Babić, proclaimed a state of war, although he had not the authority or any justification for doing so. A People's Defence Council was founded in Knin, and finally roads and railway lines of vital importance for Croatia in northern Dalmatia and the Knin, Obrovac and Benkovac areas were barricaded by logs and other obstacles. Although the Croatian media and politicians tried to present these happenings as the work of a small rebel group of drunken extremists who did not know what they were doing, it was undoubtedly a well-planned provocation organised from Belgrade. The '*balvan* [log] revolution', which began on 17 August 1990, was the beginning of the aggression against Croatia. In the mean time the JNA distributed weapons more or less openly among the local Serb population; nothing could have shown more clearly on which side they would be in the coming clash. This had many direct consequences: rail traffic via Knin ceased, the ports of Zadar, Šibenik and Split were blocked and traffic through them fell almost to zero. Many tourists hurried to leave the Croatian summer resorts. In the first week the direct and indirect damage was assessed at over $200 million.

There were no electoral registers at the referendum on the autonomy of Serb municipalities, and about 48,000 people voted in Belgrade. Almost all voted 'yes', and relations grew even worse. At the end of September the Serb National Council proclaimed the autonomy of municipalities in Croatia with a Serb population. The following months passed in a succession of road and rail blockades being built and then dismantled, and in November two people were wounded in one such incident. On 22 December 1990 the new constitution of the republic of Croatia was promulgated, which gave constitutionality and legality to the liberal and democratic reforms. The Serbs in Knin responded by proclaiming the Statute of the Serb Autonomous District of Krajina (*SAO Krajina*), and were immediately joined by representatives of five of the eleven Croatian municipalities with a Serb majority. They stopped paying taxes to the republican authorities, and the municipal police stations removed themselves from the republican system.

At that time the Serbian media worked furiously to create a psychosis of belief that Croatia was preparing for war ('the organisation of terrorist activities') and importing weapons in great quantities. This was only partly true, because at that time Croatia did not yet have an army; all it did was greatly enlarge its police force, which it armed with imported weapons. JNA units were raised to combat level. At the end of January 1991, in the presence of the Croatian delegation headed by Tudjman, the Yugoslav Presidency agreed on how temporarily to decrease tension, which each side interpreted in its own way. The Croatian authorities considered that the rebel Serbs should be disarmed, while the JNA and the Serbs considered that the newly-formed units of the Croatian police should be disarmed because they were a 'party army composed of HDZ members'. Next day *The Truth about HDZ Arming in Croatia*, a tendentiously edited film made by the Yugoslav secret service, was shown on television. It was to serve as a basis for introducing a state of emergency and arresting certain figures, first of all the Croatian minister of defence Martin Špegelj for arming the police. However, the eight-member Yugoslav Presidency, which had not yet lost all its influence, rejected the proposal of the JNA general staff and the Serbian leadership to declare a state of emergency. The Slovenian, Croatian, Macedonian and Bosnia-Hercegovinian members also voted against it, thus for the moment forestalling open conflict.

A short time later, in February, the Slovenian Assembly took momentous steps towards formal and legal separation from the Yugoslav legal system, and Croatia was placed in a situation where it had to do the same. The *Sabor* voted that no federal law or regulation that would diminish Croatian sovereignty was valid in Croatia. A few days later the Serbs in Krajina and western and eastern Slavonia took a corresponding decision and proclaimed that only Krajina and Yugoslav laws were valid on their territory. Jovan Rašković called the borders between the republics 'Titoist' borders and not state ones. The Croatian and Slovenian leaderships then proposed a Yugoslav confederation, i.e. the survival of Yugoslavia with greater independence for the republics. The Serbian leaders rejected this out of hand.

Incidents now followed one after another, each more serious than the last. At the beginning of March local Serbs disarmed Croatian police in the western Slavonian town of Pakrac, at which Croatian special police units intervened. For the first time JNA units were placed between the opposing sides, and in doing so they were in fact protecting the Serbs who were weaker. This became the model for JNA interventions in the following months, until it openly attacked Croatia in the late summer of 1991.

At the end of March 1991 rebel Serb units occupied the area of the famous Plitvice Lakes national park, and in the fighting that ensued between the Serbs and the Croatian police one of the latter and a Serb fighter were killed, the first war victims in Croatia. Soon JNA units took over the Plitvice area, allegedly to create a 'buffer zone', but in fact to ensure a more enduring occupation of Croatian territory by the Krajina Serbs. Then the Serbs began to fight in earnest to secure the territory they coveted, Krajina. They attacked Croatian enclaves within its borders, evicted the Croats who lived there, and systematically attacked and killed Croatian police in this area. After the Serbs blocked a Croatian village near Knin, demonstrations erupted in Split in which a JNA soldier was killed; this was used by Serbian propaganda for a vitriolic campaign that sounded like a real call to war. Some circles in Croatia also fanned the conflict because they wanted their nation to leave Yugoslavia at any cost. Exiles returned to Croatia with this intention in mind, and when they joined the HDZ, the JNA became additionally convinced that there could be no agreement with the Croats and that Croatian proposals for confederation were no more than a ploy. This was not the reason for the conflict, but it was a factor that added fuel to the flames.

The situation in eastern Slavonia was similar to that in the surroundings of Knin, with the difference that barricades were raised, as they had been around Knin, but were then removed. The police chief of Osijek, Josip Reichl-Kir, played an important role as an intermediary and tried to defuse the situation, but he was murdered by Croatian extremists to remove the last obstacle to outright conflict. The killer was found guilty and condemned, but never imprisoned. At the end of April 1991, after Serb militants had several times caused tension on the approaches to Borovo Selo near Vukovar, several highly-placed Croats went to the same area and fired three mortar shells at the village around midnight. There were no victims and the damage was insignificant, but this gave the Serb extremists the excuse they needed to mount a counter-attack. Members of special forces arrived from Serbia, and two Croatian policemen were seized. The Croatian police force intervened ineptly and fell into a trap, with the result that twelve police were killed and more than twenty wounded. Croatia mourned its dead, fearing that there was worse to come. In the mean time the JNA came to Borovo Selo, created a 'buffer zone' and removed the area from Croatian control.

On 15 May 1991 the scheduled rotation was due to take place at the head of the Yugoslav Presidency. According to the constitution the Croatian representative Stipe Mesić was to replace the representative of Serbia, Borisav Jović, but the exchange did not take place: it was prevented by the Serbian-Montenegrin block in the Presidency and there was a 4:4 hung vote (the representatives of Slovenia, Bosnia-Hercegovina, Croatia and Macedonia voted for the legal change). The Yugoslav Presidency and Marković's government were the only bodies in Yugoslavia that still had a common Yugoslav representation, although with decreasing authority and unity. Mesić later told how the top JNA officers kept the Serbian and Montenegrin representatives in the

Presidency informed of their plans and consulted no one else. Be that as it may, this *putsch*-like refusal to allow the legal rotation paralysed the Presidency, leaving the state without its highest authority. The *finis Iugoslaviae* was approaching.

Four days later, on Sunday 19 May 1991, a referendum was held in Croatia, in which the voters were asked whether they supported an independent Croatia or not. There was an 83.6 per cent turnout, and of those 93.2 per cent – 2,845,521 people – voted 'yes'. Thus the citizens of Croatia rejected the option of their republic remaining part of federal Yugoslavia, but left a compromise possibility for it to form an alliance of sovereign states with other republics, i.e. a kind of loose confederation. As usual, the Krajina Serbs had an answer: in the same period they organised a referendum asking 'Do you want Krajina to be united with Serbia and for them both to remain within Yugoslavia?' Allegedly, 99 per cent voters answered 'yes'.

The crisis became internationalised and was joined by a third element – the European Community – and later by the United Nations. Part of the blame for the tragic developments that followed attaches to them because they believed for a long time that a rational European approach based on economic interest and diplomacy would be acceptable to all. They only realised too late that there was nothing rational about this war. What they did was not enough and came too late. Besides, for too long they treated victim and aggressor even-handedly, and supported the existence of a fictional Yugoslavia.

## *The role of the JNA: from a liberating to a criminal army*

In the impending catastrophe what disappointed many people most was the role played by the JNA. It evolved from an organisation that supported ideological Communist purity and was considered by a good number of Croats in 1945 to be a 'liberating' army, into a criminal pro-Chetnik organisation responsible for destroying towns in Bosnia-Hercegovina and Croatia and aiding the Chetnik death squads.

After 1945 the JNA consistently implemented Tito's Yugoslav Communist policy. For a time meticulous care was taken to ensure equal ethnic representation, and many Croats served in the supreme command and in other leading positions. After the war a proportionately greater number of Serbs and Montenegrins remained in active service. This 'Serbianisation' was stopped in 1948 when several thousand mostly Serbian and Montenegrin officers were thrown out of the army because they sympathised with Stalin. There was a similar development, though on a lesser scale, at the end of the 1950s and again in 1965, which coincided with the fall of Aleksandar Ranković. The defence minister Ivan Gošnjak, a Croat and Tito's trusted ally, was in charge of obtaining a national and ideological balance among service personnel. While Gošnjak was in power, the future President Tudjman, then a colonel and later a general, held a high position in the personnel administration. In 1967 Gošnjak was replaced by the Serb Nikola Ljubičić, who favoured his own men and began to change the ethnic structure in the senior ranks of the army. Laws guaranteeing equal ethnic representation among professional JNA personnel were ignored, and numbers were never made public. It is estimated that in the spring of 1991 the JNA had 70,000 professionals, of whom 50,000 or about 70 per cent were Serbs or Montenegrins; in the highest positions this percentage was even higher. After 1980, as before, the idea was for moderate Serbs (especially those from Croatia) and Montenegrins to uphold the 'Yugoslav' line and allegedly balance Greater Serbian striving for unitarism and the Croatian and Slovenian wish for greater independence. But the two most important Croatian Serbs in the JNA in the 1980s, Branko Mamula, the Yugoslav defence minister till 1988, and his successor Veljko Kadijević (the son of a mixed marriage, but one who considered himself first Yugoslav and then Serb), failed to maintain equidistance and instead practically pushed Yugoslavia into the war.

Up till Tito's death, the JNA was never an independent political factor. The most influential military figures faithfully followed his policy, at least in public. However, in secret the army top brass were becoming increasingly dissatisfied with military decentralisation, and after Tito's death the JNA began pursuing an independent policy. Over many decisions they no longer had to check with the Presidency. During the Iraq-Iran war they sold weapons to both sides, and the JNA's exports amounted to $3 billion a year. Iraq obtained a supply of weapons from the JNA just before the attack on Kuwait in 1991.

The generals considered Slovenia and Croatia their most dangerous potential adversaries, being convinced that complete democratisation, a multi-party system and greater consideration for ethnic and republican individuality would put Yugoslavia in mortal danger. In principle they supported the 'equality of peoples and minorities' and at first viewed Milošević's populist policy with suspicion. However, Milošević's demagogy and some other circumstances gradually turned the JNA into his ally. On the first signs in 1989 that non-Communist parties were being formed, the JNA confiscated from the Croatian Territorial Defence all its weapons – enough for about 200,000 soldiers – without any protest from the Croatian authorities. However, the Slovenian authorities managed to prevent the JNA, partly at least, from seizing the weapons of their Territorial Defence, so that their territorial soldiers were well armed in the war and did not need to buy weapons abroad.

At the end of 1990, after the Fourteenth Congress and the breakup of the League of Communists of Yugoslavia, the generals founded the League of Communists Movement for Yugoslavia, which never had more than a few members outside the JNA. When elections took place in Serbia in December that year, the generals supported Milošević's Socialist Party of Serbia.

At the end of 1990 Admiral Branko Mamula, a former defence minister still influential in the army, said: 'If we have to resort to measures of repression, including the exercise of military strength, we are convinced that Yugoslavia will be capable of controlling the situation within its borders.' He also said that the 'proposal of Slovenia and Croatia for confederation is not acceptable because it is impossible to create national states of Serbs or Croats without bloodshed. It is not even possible with bloodshed.' There were no nationalists of the classic type among the army's most senior officers; they displayed no obsession with myths or romantic euphoria, but plenty of prejudice and hatred for Croatian 'nationalism' and Muslim 'fundamentalism'. Their attitude to ethnic identity was utilitarian – true, most of them were Serbs, but they preferred to call themselves Yugoslavs. Many JNA officers brought the primitivism and propensity for violence that they began to show from their home regions – most were from the Dinaric mountains. This mentality has no room for honouring individual civil rights or for respecting the traditions of urban life – hence the mindless destruction of towns.

It seems that right up till the summer of 1991 the JNA leaders did not believe that fighting on any great scale could take place. They prepared plans for crushing 'anti-Communist and anti-Yugoslav' developments in the state, and were sure they could restore order quickly and efficiently without much bloodshed, but they overestimated their strength. Also, they believed that each of the Yugoslav nations had a 'healthy core' that would realise in time all the mistakes made by their leaderships and return to the rigid JNA concept of the structure of Yugoslavia. However, the strong demonstration in Zagreb that greeted the trial in a military court of six Croats accused of smuggling weapons showed that Croatia was not afraid and that repression only stoked its defiance. By then the JNA, meting out death and devastation, had become Milošević's murderous weapon, and never stopped talking about Yugoslavia, even while striking fatal blows at it.

The political and military circles that initiated, organised and started the war in Croatia and Bosnia-Hercegovina went through a change concerning what should be its final goal. At first the 'Yugoslav' concept dominated in public discourse, although ideas of a new delimitation and granting independence to other republics were discussed in secret. As time passed, especially after the war began and it became clear that Croatia could not be completely broken, the idea emerged that the creation of a Greater Serbia incorporating the occupied areas would be much more realistic. It seems that the 'Yugoslav' option prevailed in JNA operations till October 1991, but when the planned offensives failed at that time it was rejected and the Greater Serbian variant was adopted. From that moment the JNA rapidly became a Serbian army.

Croatia began its preparation for war practically from the summer of 1990. In the following spring volunteer units were organised, mostly composed of HDZ members. Several thousand members of the right-wing Party of State Right fought in the war in special autonomously-organised units called *Hrvatske obrambene snage* (Croat Defence Forces – HOS), most of which were integrated into regular units of the Croatian army by October 1991. Their courage is undeniable, but they advocated extremism and often carried Ustasha symbols and pictures of Pavelić. In the spring of 1991 the first brigades called *Zbor Narodne Garde* (Croatian National Guard – ZNG) began to be formed. This, the nucleus of the future Croatian army, coordinated its activities with special police units. In May a parade was organised in Zagreb to show the traumatised public that a Croatian army was being created. This certainly raised their self-confidence. It became clear that two armies that both claimed certain territory could not be kept apart, and that war was inevitable.

## On the path to independence

In the spring of 1991, after the Serbian leadership resolutely rejected the Croatian and Slovenian proposal of a confederation or alliance of sovereign states, the Croatian leadership headed by Tudjman began to seek a way to 'extricate Croatia' from the Yugoslav community. There is no doubt that the idea of complete Croatian independence had smouldered among the leaders of the HDZ even before the 1990 elections. However, right up till the spring of 1991 Tudjman was also ready to accept a compromise solution that would involve greater Croatian autonomy within Yugoslavia. But, as pressure on Croatia increased and armed provocations became more frequent, it was decided to proclaim independence. On 25 June 1991 the *Sabor* enacted the Constitutional Decision on the Sovereignty and Independence of the Republic of Croatia, and proclaimed that only laws passed by the *Sabor* were valid in Croatia, and that federal regulations which it had not passed were null and void. The Slovenian Assembly took the same action on the same day. Next day the Federal Executive Council invalidated the Slovenian and Croatian decisions and ordered the JNA and the federal police to take control of border crossings in Slovenia, which the Slovenian police had taken over.

This was a key moment for the understanding of future events. The Yugoslav and Serbian side and the JNA accused Croatia and Slovenia of 'secession', thus justifying all the forcible methods they applied in the following months as attempts to preserve the 'integrity and territorial sovereignty of the Socialist Federal Republic of Yugoslavia'. At that moment they were indirectly aided by actions of the US Secretary of State James Baker, who had visited Belgrade several days earlier and unambiguously told the Serbian-Yugoslav side that they must respect the constitution and laws, above all in connection with the election of the President of the Presidency. However, he warned the representatives of Croatia and Slovenia even more clearly that the United States would not support their aspiration for independence, but those two republics made it just as clear that it was no longer possible for them to remain in Yugoslavia. The Croatian and Slovenian representatives said it was the Milošević policy and JNA violence which had driven them out of Yugoslavia and that the state had self-evidently fallen apart. Several months later the international community confirmed the Croatian-Slovenian stand, but by then there had been tens of thousands of deaths.

The JNA campaign in Slovenia ended in a rout: the Slovenian territorials were easily able to resist the small and unmotivated JNA land forces, which mostly consisted of non-Serbs and surrendered in large numbers. After five days a ceasefire was called. It seems that the JNA leaders were in a quandary and the army was not fully engaged in the Slovenian war episode. Several weeks later the Slovenian authorities and the JNA agreed that the latter should withdraw from Slovenia within three months. This was the end of Yugoslavia as it had existed for forty-six years. The JNA's shameful defeat also marked the beginning of the end for the Yugoslav option among leading military personnel. They began to adapt to the goals of Greater Serbia as outlined in the 'Memorandum' (see pages 199-202, above), which many of their subordinates had already accepted.

It is not clear to what extent Ante Marković, prime minister of the still existing Yugoslav government, was informed of the details of the planned use of force. In any case, his authority was quickly fading on all sides. He finally withdrew at the end of 1991, when the JNA had already committed many crimes in Croatia. The official explanation given for his resignation was cynical indeed – that his proposals for the 1992 budget had not been accepted.

The attack on Slovenia faced the Croatian leadership with a problem. Some military leaders, headed by Martin Špegelj, defence minister and a former JNA general, suggested that Croatia should support the defence of Slovenia by attacking JNA bases on its own territory. The political leadership, headed by President Tudjman, rejected the proposals, releasing that it would gravely impair Croatia's international position. There were also doubts and fears over whether the Croatian army was ready for such action at the very moment of its birth. Nevertheless, everyone interpreted the attack on Slovenia as a clear sign that a similar attack might soon follow on Croatia, and during the summer of

1991 hasty preparations were made throughout the country. Territorial military units and reserve mobile brigades were formed, at first consisting exclusively of volunteers who signed up in great numbers. Most of the units were ill-equipped, with only hunting weapons and small arms, but morale was high. Many Croat former JNA officers and also some Bosniaks (Bosnian Muslims), Albanians, Slovenes and even Serbs joined the Croatian army and formed the nucleus of its command structure. In September 1991 its general staff and a whole network of territorially distributed local commands were brought into being. In those summer months all of Croatia was unanimous in the resolve to defend itself, as never before or after. The usual disputes between political parties completely ceased, as did the publication of various kinds of scandals in the newspapers. Unity on the political stage was most clearly expressed at the beginning of August when the Government of Democratic Unity was formed under Prime Minister Franjo Greguric, the only government in the period of HDZ rule to which the opposition also belonged.

In July and the first half of August 1991 incidents became more frequent and more violent and grew into local armed clashes. The focal points were around Knin, in Banija around Glina and Kostajnica, in eastern Slavonia around Osijek and Vukovar, and in western Slavonia around Pakrac and Okučani. Local Serb police and paramilitary units took over police stations and evicted the Croatian policemen. The first mass crime against civilians happened on 6 July 1991 when armed Serb units burnt down the undefended village of Ćelije (between Osijek and Vinkovci) and drove out the Croatian population. Local Croatian units attacked the Serb village of Palača but JNA tanks soon arrived in the Serbs' defence. Expulsions and mass crimes against Croats followed in Dalj, Erdut, Aljmaš and other eastern Slavonian villages. Local Croatian authorities in Osijek harassed Serb citizens, who left the town in increasing numbers and went to surrounding Serb villages. In eastern Slavonia a real local war broke out in which the JNA openly supported the Serbs. Milošević and the Serbian government and parliament claimed that Serbia was not at war, but well-armed volunteer and mercenary paramilitary units commanded by the extremist politician Vojislav Šešelj and the international criminal Željko Ražnjatović Arkan came to eastern Slavonia under the patronage of the police force of the Republic of Serbia. There they committed crimes and atrocities against the Croatian population. Similarly, armed groups commanded by 'Captain Dragan' came to Banija and the Knin area from Serbia. On 26 July 1991 local Serb units in Kozibrod, a village on the river Una, murdered ten Croatian police and then seventeen civilians in the nearby villages of Struga and Kuljani. This was the first mass killing of Croatian civilians and captured soldiers, and after it similar crimes took place in Slavonian, Banijan and Dalmatian villages (Kusonje, Dalj, Tovarnik, Kraljevčani, Skela, Voćin, Škabrnja and many others), culminating on 19 November 1991 in Vukovar, where several hundred civilians and soldiers were killed after the town was taken. The greatest mass crime happened on the first night, when 260 Croatian wounded and captured soldiers were taken from the town hospital and shot.

On the Croatian side the first group killing was committed on 13 September 1991 on the bridge across the Korana in Karlovac, where thirteen Serb prisoners were killed. In late autumn a Croatian paramilitary unit surrounded Gospić and killed almost 100 Serb citizens. In the village of Pakračka Poljana in western Slavonia, in the late autumn, a special Croatian military unit killed at least twenty-two prisoners and civilians. There were also individual killings of Serb citizens in Sisak, Vukovar, Osijek, Karlovac and other places, and even in Zagreb, where an entire Serb family was murdered. On the Croatian side the perpetrators were usually suspended from the army, an investigation was started against them, but no one was sentenced and after a time they were released from detention and transferred to other duties. On the Serb side none of the criminals was accused or suspended although the crimes were much more numerous.

By the second half of August and in September 1991 a real war was raging in Croatia. Ever more openly and more often, the JNA became the main attacker: on 17 August its units took over Okučani in western Slavonia and began to attack nearby Pakrac and Nova Gradiška, on 21 August they occupied all of Baranja, and on 24 August they surrounded Vukovar. At the same time local Serb units, backed up by the JNA, took over the Croatian enclaves of Kijevo and Vrlika near Knin in Dalmatia and drove out the Croats, then moved towards the coast, threatened Zadar and blockaded Šibenik.

Intense diplomatic activity went on parallel with war operations.

*Croatia: A History*

War in Eastern Slavonia and Dubrovnik region

At that time it was the European Community that was trying to solve the Yugoslav problem, but it was later joined by the UN; the United States mostly left matters in the EC's hands. Although all sides in the conflict considered the opinion of the international community very important, they knew that in the end conditions on the ground would crucially affect any diplomatic solution. In the first stage of the fighting in Croatia the international public and diplomacy were rather confused by contradictory reports, and partly also by the claims of Serbian propaganda that what was happening was a repeat of 1941. Thus international diplomacy did not react in the optimum way for a long time. Prominent EC and US representatives came to Belgrade and Zagreb in the spring and summer of 1991, organised meetings between members of the Serbian and Croatian leadership, appealed to reason and tried to calm things down. However, they lacked a common stand and could not claim any results right up till the end of 1991. In July an EC monitoring mission came to Croatia, and although it too did not manage to reduce tension on the front lines, it obtained a better insight into the situation and sent back quite objective and informative reports. On 17 July 1991 Tudjman met General Kadijević, the Yugoslav defence minister, and on 7 September a peace conference on Yugoslavia began in The Hague chaired by Lord Carrington. Ten days later, again with Lord Carrington in the chair, Tudjman, Kadijević and Milošević met at Igalo, a Montenegrin summer resort. On 15 October Tudjman and Milošević met under the patronage of Mikhail Gorbachev – but the war in Croatia raged on uninterrupted and grew in intensity. Up till the end of 1991 a total of sixteen ceasefires were signed, none of which lasted longer than twenty-four hours. They were violated by both sides, and it is impossible to say by which side more: the Serbs and the JNA because they wanted to conquer more territory, the Croats because they wanted to retake what they had lost.

In the short term some of the events on the international diplomatic scene might have been in the interests of either side, but in the long term everything was leading to recognition of the independence of Croatia and Slovenia, and later also of Bosnia-Hercegovina. In June 1991 EC representatives requested that Slovenia and Croatia suspend their decisions on independence for three months; this meant that they were buying time and that

War in Western Slavonia, Central Croatia and Dalmatia

Slovenian and Croatian independence would sooner or later be internationally recognised. All the same, both the Croatian and the Slovenian governments knew that they would have to defend themselves militarily before this goal could be achieved.

On 14 September 1991 the Croatian leadership decided after all to blockade the JNA army bases in towns they controlled, and to call on the soldiers in them to surrender. The JNA used this as an excuse to escalate from local actions to a general offensive against Croatia. The plans had already been prepared, taking advantage of Croatia's vulnerable horseshoe shape: the country was to be severed at its narrowest points, broken up into several small enclaves and then subdued. It was anticipated that Croatian resistance could not last more than ten or at most twenty days, which NATO analyses confirmed. The offensive started in western Slavonia and in central Croatia, in the direction of Virovitica and Karlovac, with the goal of reaching the Hungarian and Slovenian borders. The coast towns of Zadar and Šibenik were attacked at the same time with the aid of the Yugoslav navy, which blockaded all Croatian ports while the air force and artillery pounded the towns. On 18 September 1991 the JNA took Petrinja, broke out on to the left bank of the Kupa, reached Karlovac, and at the beginning of October crossed the Kupa and came to a point only 30 km. from Zagreb. Artillery duels across the Kupa could be heard in the capital, which lived through total nightly black-outs and almost daily air-raid alerts. Zagreb itself was mostly not attacked, and the planes that flew over it were mostly intended only to frighten and demoralise the inhabitants. Occasionally they bombed transmitters, transformer stations and other strategic installations in the surroundings, but the only real bombing in the centre was on Tudjman's residence in the old town.

The JNA and the local Serbs expelled all non-Serbs from the territories they conquered, and by the end of the year the number of displaced persons and refugees in Croatia was almost 500,000. At the same time Serb citizens were discriminated against in various ways – fired from their jobs, bombs placed under cars and in houses – in Croatian towns, especially those near the front lines like Sisak, Karlovac, Zadar, Gospić, Osijek, Vinkovci and even Zagreb. Many of them fled to the other side, and the number of refugees there also grew to tens of thousands.

While the JNA and units of local Serbs were advancing on

the external front-lines in September and October much more slowly than planned, the siege of the JNA army bases in Croatian towns proved successful. After several days the bases in Gospić and Perušić in Lika surrendered, as did those in Sesvete near Zagreb, in Ploče port, in the area around Šibenik, and others. Somewhat later the large garrison at the corps headquarters in Varaždin agreed to surrender all its weapons and leave the town and Croatia. In all these actions the Croatian army acquired a large amount of equipment – about 200 tanks, 150 armoured personnel carriers, more than 400 guns of above 100 mm. calibre and countless light weapons, all with ammunition. This played a decisive role in the further course of the war. The advance of the JNA and Serb units was stopped on the river Kupa just outside Sisak and Karlovac, around Gospić, on the bridge leading to Šibenik, and just outside Zadar. It became obvious that JNA morale was low: many soldiers deserted, and mobilisation in Serbia was largely a failure (in Belgrade the turnout was less than 15 per cent). Disorganisation was complete and prevented the JNA's technical superiority from showing itself. While JNA manpower remained the same or decreased, the Croatian armed forces, with their newly-acquired weapons and following successful mobilisation, became numerically superior by the autumn. At the end of the year they had 200,000 men under arms and about 35,000 armed police. At that time, probably already in the second half of October, the JNA commanders fell back on a reserve variant of their plan: if they could not subdue the whole of Croatia, but would try, at the best, to secure a new border on the Virovitica-Karlovac-Gospić-Karlobag line, or, at the worst, to occupy part of eastern Slavonia with Baranja, part of western Slavonia, part of Dalmatia, and areas in central Croatia where Serbs were the majority population. In practice this was the Memorandum concept of Greater Serbia, and by accepting it the JNA turned from an army that aspired to represent the whole of Yugoslavia into an instrument of Milošević's Greater Serbia policy. It became, *de facto*, a Serbian army.

Working now to fulfill this new concept, the JNA – still much the stronger in heavy weapons, warships and planes – concentrated on rounding off the requests it had already made by cleansing unconquered 'pockets' and striving for a good outlet to the sea for the future Greater Serbia. This meant that the main force was concentrated on the north-east and south-east ends of Croatia – Vukovar and Dubrovnik.

The war in Croatia reached its peak, in both actual and symbolic terms, with the battle of Vukovar. After August 1991 the 1,500 lightly-armed Croatian soldiers in the town found themselves under fire from a vastly stronger enemy. For three months, élite JNA units pounded this town of 45,000 inhabitants with artillery and tanks, but the resistance offered by its defenders exceeded all expectations. Vukovar was completely flattened, but the attackers lost between 5,000 and 8,000 killed and about 600 tanks and other armoured vehicles. Croatia lost an estimated 2,500 soldiers (including those who tried to break through the siege from the outside and help the town), and about the same number of civilians died or disappeared. When the town surrendered, the defenders were killed or taken to Serbian camps, and the surviving civilians were maltreated, robbed and driven out of the town. Although by taking Vukovar the Serbs rounded off their conquest in eastern Slavonia, their army was now much weaker. It did not possess the morale or strength to go on to attack Vinkovci, Osijek and Djakovo.

Besides the strategic need to provide the large interior of the future Greater Serbia with a suitable port, the attack on Dubrovnik was also motivated by the long-standing urge of the Hercegovinian and Montenegrin mountain dwellers to make this beautiful city Serbian. At that time the old propaganda that 'the citizens of Dubrovnik were never Croats, but Serbs who had converted to Roman Catholicism' was vehemently repeated in Serbia and Montenegro and among the Serbs in Bosnia-Hercegovina. The plan was to cut Dubrovnik off from Croatia and force it to join Yugoslavia. The defenders of the city environs, few in number and poorly armed, were beaten within several days and the town was completely surrounded on the sea and the land sides. Most of the invaders were Montenegrin, and almost the whole neighbourhood immediate surrounding Dubrovnik was plundered and set on fire. Even the state approved this criminal behaviour – in the first days of the aggression Montenegrin television included in its news an appeal by Montenegrin school hostels to be sent several hundred pairs of trainers from the Dubrovnik area. In the fiercest and final attack on 6 December, twenty-two people were killed. Several hundred shells fell on the old city, and luxury hotels in the vicinity were completely destroyed. However, the defenders managed to hold on to the city, and the international public finally took Croatia's side more resolutely, understanding clearly who was the attacker and who was under attack. The American Sixth Fleet approached threateningly close to the front lines.

The Croats had by now built up their military strength and in December they carried out their first major counter-offensive in western Slavonia. They drove the local Serb units from the entire area of Psunj and Papuk almost to the Drava river basin and right down to the Sava. The populations of Serb villages in the region fled across the Sava into Bosnia before the advancing Croatian army that torched their houses – just as the Serbs had driven away Croatian peasants and torched Croatian villages two or three months earlier. Now, at last and for the first time, the Serbs and the JNA were ready for a ceasefire and, under pressure from the international community, Croatia also agreed. The ceasefire was signed in Sarajevo on 3 January 1992 and maintained, with greater or lesser infringements, for the next three and a half years. It was to run exactly along the line separating the warring parties. Municipalities with a majority Serb population and part of the occupied areas were to be placed under UN protection and demilitarised. Nothing was said about their future, and in the following months and years Croatian diplomacy managed, despite considerable difficulties, to achieve recognition of those areas as integral parts of Croatia.

Besides thousands of casualties, the war in Croatia also caused great destruction. Indirect damage (in tourism, transit traffic, investment etc.) is practically incalculable, and it will cost about $20 billion merely to rebuild what was destroyed (the Croatian gross national product fell from $16 billion before the war to about $8 billion in 1992, which is considered the first post-war year). About 500 cultural monuments were destroyed or badly damaged, the most frequent targets being Catholic churches. Hospitals, schools and nursery schools were also precisely targeted.

## International recognition

Among the first principles to be established at the peace conference on Yugoslavia which began in Geneva in September was that republican borders could not be changed by force and that the rights of all nations and national minorities should be protected. Several days later the UN Security Council accepted the first Resolution (no. 713) on conditions in the territory of the Socialist Federative Republic of Yugoslavia (SFRJ), which demanded an end to hostilities and the continuation of talks under EC auspices. A general and complete embargo on importing arms and military equipment, introduced at the same time, remained in force for several years. The arms embargo favoured the Serbian-Yugoslav side because the JNA could fight a war for months without becoming dependent on imports; the sides for which these were wars of self-defence – Croatia and in later years Bosnia-Hercegovina – were poor in weapons and had to smuggle them in, paying higher prices.

At the beginning of October, when Croatia was being most fiercely attacked by the JNA, Stjepan Mesić left Belgrade and his office of President of the Yugoslav Presidency. The *Sabor* was convened in an underground hall, safe from air attack, and on 8 October established that the three-month moratorium on the Constitutional Decision of 25 June, proclaiming the independence of the country, had expired. Thus they broke off all state and legal links with the SFRJ and challenged the legitimacy and legality of the constituent bodies of the former common state. At the same time they recognised the independence and sovereignty of all the other former Yugoslav republics. This was the final break with Yugoslavia, after which Croatia could only have returned to the former common state through total defeat in war. Attention now turned to the hope that the international community would sooner or later recognise the new state.

Already at the beginning of November, at the international conference in Geneva, the EC presented the fourth version of the convention proposing that the crisis in Yugoslavia should be solved by accepting republican borders as the international borders of new states, and that minority rights should be honoured. Since Serbia and (later) Montenegro rejected this proposal, a commission of arbitration was set up under the French lawyer Badinter. At the beginning of December the Badinter Commission established that Yugoslavia had dissolved (not, as the Serbian-Yugoslav side claimed, that some republics had seceded), and the EC Council of Ministers announced international recognition a month later

subject to certain conditions. For Croatia this meant that it had
to protect the rights of its Serbian minority. The *Sabor* enacted
the Constitutional Law on Human Rights and Freedoms and the
Rights of National and Ethnic Communities or Minorities in the
Republic of Croatia, of which the Badinter Commission made
a favourable assessment.

In the background to the EC's recognition of Croatia and
Slovenia were a variety of interests and much diplomatic haggling.
German intercession for the recognition of Slovenia and Croatia
was consistently and shrewdly promoted by the foreign minister
Hans–Dietrich Genscher and prevailed, although some countries
thought differently. Croatia was finally recognised by the EC
countries on 15 January 1992 (a day after the Vatican and Iceland
had done so) and in the following days by almost all the rest of
Europe. The United States, Russia and China followed in April,
by which time Croatia had already been accepted as a member
by the UN and by some other international institutions.

Croatia's entry into the international community had been made
comparatively easy, but in the following years its grave mistakes
in foreign and home policy made matters much more difficult
and slowed down the process. One of the main problems was
its inappropriate engagement in Bosnia-Hercegovina.

# 14

## THE WAR IN BOSNIA-HERCEGOVINA: THE ROLE OF THE CROATS AND CROATIA

Geopolitically Croatia lies right up against Bosnia and cannot be uninterested or indifferent to what happens there. In Greater Serbian strategy the Bosnian war was a continuation of the war in Croatia, and the Croats in Bosnia-Hercegovina were also its victims.

The first free elections in Bosnia-Hercegovina in November and December 1990 were won by 'national' parties – the predominantly Muslim Democratic Action Party (SDA) led by Alija Izetbegović, the Serbian Democratic Party (SDS) led by Radovan Karadžić, and the Croatian Democratic Union (HDZ) which had several changes of leadership until Mate Boban became president at the end of 1992. Izetbegović was elected President of the Presidency and the three parties formed a coalition, but this never took off. There were great differences in conception, first of all between the Bosniaks, who supported an integral Bosnia-Hercegovina, and the Serbs, who openly wanted to divide it and annex their part to Serbia.

At the beginning HDZ policy was inconsistent and reflected the political division among the Croats in Bosnia-Hercegovina. The majority of those in western Hercegovina and in some parts of central Bosnia close to the Croatian border following tradition, wanted to secede from Bosnia-Hercegovina and become part of Croatia. After 1990 they relied on the support of Tudjman and some of his closest associates in the new political leadership, who also supported the enlargement of Croatia and the division of Bosnia-Hercegovina, although for tactical reasons they never said so openly. On the other hand, Croats in Sarajevo, Tuzla, Banja Luka and most other towns, and in central and northern Bosnia, who for generations had been used to life in multi-ethnic communities, opposed division and supported an integral and sovereign

Bosnia-Hercegovina. The first three presidents of the HDZ of Bosnia-Hercegovina, who held office one after the other in the first two years, supported cooperation with the Muslims and the integrity of Bosnia-Hercegovina. However, at the end of 1992 Mate Boban became leader of the Bosnia-Hercegovina HDZ; he supported division and worked steadily to achieve this, at first secretly but later openly and publicly.

Because in the 1990s neither the Muslims nor the Serbs were in the majority in Bosnia-Hercegovina, it was the Croats who could tip the scales and give a majority to either side. According to the 1991 census the percentages were Muslims 39.5, Serbs 32, Croats 18.4 and Yugoslavs 7.9.

The war in Croatia had a deep impact in Bosnia-Hercegovina. In May 1991, when the JNA tried to send tanks from the latter to intervene in Croatia, several thousand Croats stopped them near Mostar because they did not believe the official explanation that they were on their way to routine exercises on the nearby artillery range. The first incident in which Croats were killed occurred in October 1991, when JNA units attacked Dubrovnik. At that time the JNA also entered the Hercegovinian border village of Ravno, inhabited by Croats, and levelled it to the ground. The JNA mobilised citizens of all ethnic groups in Bosnia-Hercegovina to fight in Croatia, which also increased tension. The Serbs responded to a certain extent, the Muslims much less, and the Croats did all they could to avoid mobilisation. The Bosnian President Izetbegović said 'This is not our war', which all groups interpreted in the way that suited them. He was accused by the Serbs of aligning himself with Croat secessionists, and by the Croats of wanting to remain neutral in a war of aggression.

The Bosnian Serb leaders, together with the leaders of Serbia and Montenegro and the JNA command, had planned the war in Bosnia with great care ever since the first signs that the SFRJ and socialism might fall. In 1990 some Serbian villages in Bosnia-Hercegovina were armed just like those in Croatia. In September-October 1991 the Ozren Chetnik unit (Ozren is a mountain in central Bosnia) was founded to carry on the 'best' Chetnik traditions of the Second World War. As the war in Croatia proceeded and it became completely clear that the Yugoslav concept was a lost cause, the Greater Serbians approached their preparations for war in Bosnia much more openly and efficiently than they had done in Croatia. Concealing their intentions behind a barrage of demagogic statements about honouring the 'will of the Serbian people', they completely discarded the Yugoslav concept and replaced it with a Greater Serbian policy. The Serbian Democratic Party under Karadžić grew more open in its support of secession and occupation of a large part of Bosnia-Hercegovina. Preparing for war, they took control of communications and blew up bridges across the Sava to prevent supplies arriving from Croatia for Croat and Muslim units that might be created in the future.

Matters came to a head at the end of February 1992 when a referendum was called on the independence of Bosnia-Hercegovina. The HDZ was in a quandary: should it or should it not support independence? This also meant: should it support an integral or a divided Bosnia-Hercegovina? At that moment the Boban tendency wanted to lay all its cards on the table and openly stand out against Bosnian independence – and thus in favour of dividing the country – but had to hold back because Croatia was in an exceedingly delicate situation. Finally pressure from the Catholic church and the interests of Croats in central and northern Bosnia prevailed. The great majority of Croats voted for independence and their votes were decisive: the turnout was 63.7 per cent, and 99.4 per cent of the vote was for independence. The referendum was boycotted and did not even take place in areas under SDS control. In this way the Croats, with about 20 per cent of the electorate, and the Muslims managed to prevail. Bosnia thus became an independent state, but in the following years Croat politicians challenged its independence and statehood.

The SDS leadership did not recognise the referendum results and considered them sufficient for 'Serbian regions' to secede from Bosnia-Hercegovina and be annexed to Greater Serbia. With the open support of the JNA and the territorial defence staff of Bosnia-Hercegovina, they began a war to conquer as much territory as possible. In this too the threads were being pulled behind the scenes from Slobodan Milošević's office in Belgrade, as subsequently published memoirs and documents establish beyond doubt. Serbian television and all the other media under Milošević's control were full of virulent propaganda against the Muslims and Croats, designed to whip up the Bosnian Serbs. In March, soon after the referendum, élite paramilitary units of Šešelj's Chetniks and Arkan's mercenaries and volunteers came to Bosnia from Serbia. Most were 'seasoned warriors' who had massacred people in Vukovar and eastern Slavonia only a few months earlier. In March 1992 they started a reign of terror, throwing bombs and provoking incidents in Banja Luka, Bosanski Brod, Bijeljina and other Bosnian towns. On 30 March Blagoje Adžić, the JNA's chief of staff, a Serb from Bosnia-Hercegovina, said in Belgrade that his army was 'ready to protect Serbs from open aggression'. Two days later Arkan's units began a three-day-long massacre in Bijeljina, probably killing almost 1,000 people, most of them Muslims. Because of this, and also because of several smaller Serb attacks that took place at the same time, the citizens of Sarajevo organised a mass anti-war rally on 5 April, during which Serb snipers shot into the crowd. This was the first day of the Serb siege of Sarajevo, which lasted for over three years with only a few short interruptions. The next day, 6 April 1992, the EC recognised Bosnia-Hercegovina as an integral state, and the Bosnian Serbs proclaimed a separate Serb Republic. Thus began the general war in Bosnia-Hercegovina.

Croatia had already begun arming the Hercegovinian Croats in 1991 and at the beginning of 1992, anticipating the Serb actions in Bosnia. When the siege of Sarajevo marked the beginning of open war, armed Croat units were organised into the Croat Defence Council (HVO), the 'only institutional form of Croat defence' in Bosnia-Hercegovina. Soon the first major clashes between the HVO and Serb forces began. Military organisation among the Muslims did not begin till much later (formation of the army of Bosnia-Hercegovina only began in the following months), so the HVO was joined by a considerable number of Muslims. At that time many of them also joined the Croat Defence Forces (HOS) organised by rightists in Hercegovina with the help of those of similar orientation in Croatia. Although the HOS were radically nationalistic, they nevertheless supported Bosnian territorial integrity much more consistently and sincerely than the HVO.

The HVO and HOS, with help from Croatia in weapons and manpower, managed partly to hold back the Serb army, but only in Hercegovina and small areas of central Bosnia. Since the Muslims were completely unprepared for war, and the Croats outside Hercegovina were also ill-prepared and disorganised, the Serb army managed during 1992 and 1993 to wage a 'low-intensity' war with no great risk to themselves, and by moving their shock troops from one front to another they conquered about 70 per cent of the territory of Bosnia-Hercegovina with relatively few casualties. In a considerable number of places – Zvornik, Foča, Brčko, Prijedor and elsewhere – the conquest was followed by massacres in which most of the victims were Muslims but some were also Croats. Several tens of thousands of Muslims and Croats were held in concentration camps, while hundreds of thousands left their homes and became refugees out of fear or in face of open death threats. Organised plunder of Muslim and Croat property and mass rape, mostly of Muslim women, were part of a plan which had as its goal the 'ethnic cleansing' of territories under Bosnian Serb control. Most of the banished Croats and many Muslims fled to and remained in Croatia, itself devastated by the recently interrupted war and very badly placed to bear this new economic and psychological burden.

Alija Izetbegović and Franjo Tudjman had always been wary of one another but now at the beginning of July 1992, faced with a common enemy, they signed an 'Agreement on Friendship and Cooperation between Croatia and Bosnia-Hercegovina' which was also a basis for military cooperation. Often this cooperation was not harmonious, but it resulted in the gradual stabilisation of defence in what remained of Bosnia-Hercegovina. Despite the arms embargo, weapons for the Muslim army of Bosnia-Hercegovina were sent through Croatia from various sources. This arms supply grew in volume and made possible the continued defence of Sarajevo, Bihać, Tuzla, Zenica and other parts of central Bosnia. Under the pressure of international sanctions Serbia reduced and at times even completely halted the help it was sending to the Bosnian Serbs, who slowly began to lose their initial advantage. Even so, at the end of 1992, when they held 70 per cent of Bosnian-Hercegovinian territory and were sure of final victory, they pronounced the unification of the Republic of Serbian Krajina in Croatia with the Serbian Republic in Bosnia-Hercegovina, thus clearly expressing their wish to bring about the Greater Serbian concept of 'all Serbs in one state'.

## War between the Croats and the Muslims

Over the issue of Bosnia the policy of the Croatian state was unprincipled and often hypocritical. In 1991 – on 25 March at Karadjordjevo and on 15 April at Tikveš – meetings took place between Presidents Tudjman and Milošević. No detailed official statement about which was ever issued, but semi-officially they discussed how to avoid war in Croatia and throughout former Yugoslavia. However, in the first half of the 1990s people in Croatia and abroad often said that they also discussed the possibility of dividing Bosnia-Hercegovina more or less along the border drawn between the Croatian *banovina* and the rest of Bosnia according to the Cvetković-Maček Agreement of 1939.

In November 1991 the 'Croat Community of Herceg-Bosna' (*Hrvatska zajednica Herceg-Bosna*) was founded in the Hercegovinian village of Grude, as the 'political, cultural, economic and regional entity' of Croats in Bosnia-Hercegovina. Its centre was Mostar, and it included municipalities with a Croat majority or with a large number of Croats, and those where the HDZ had won in elections at the end of 1990. About 200,000 Croats lived within this territory. This was hardly a quarter of the total Croat population of Bosnia-Hercegovina, yet for the next few years Croatia's Bosnian policy complied with the aspirations of Herceg-Bosna, not with the interests of all the Croats in Bosnia-Hercegovina or with the interests of Croatia as a state.

Immediately after its foundation, the 'Croat Community of Herceg-Bosna' followed a policy that clearly showed that it considered itself to be a completely autonomous part of Bosnia-Hercegovina and closer to the state of Croatia than to that of Bosnia-Hercegovina. The Croat leadership supported this separatism of the Hercegovinian Croats politically, economically and militarily, yet at the same time they signed treaties and declarations in support of an integral Bosnia-Hercegovina. This increased suspicion and confrontation in the Croat-Muslim military alliance and led to differentiation among the Muslims: some, including their politicians, still considered themselves and the Croats to be natural allies against the Serb attackers, but others supported 'equidistance', i.e. being equally reserved towards Serbs and Croats. The thesis of equidistance had its roots in the Communist period when many people regarded the situation in Bosnia and in all of Yugoslavia to be basically good, but that some 'nationalistic' groups were stirring things up. How paradoxical such a belief could sometimes be was seen in the words of a speaker at the mass meeting on 5 April 1992 in Sarajevo, at a moment when scores of Serbian cannon and tanks were aimed at that city: 'Let all the

Serb chauvinists go to Serbia, and the Croat chauvinists to Croatia! We want to stay here together. We want to preserve Bosnia as a whole.' It seemed to the Croats that they were being given no credit for having defended Bosnia-Hercegovina and saved many Muslims in the first stage of the war.

Later most Muslims left the Croat Defence Council (HVO) to join the Muslim army of Bosnia-Hercegovina, so that there were then two armies with different commands. Instead of close cooperation in the field, misunderstandings increased and they sometimes used completely opposite tactics. In August 1992 a well-prepared HVO ambush near Mostar killed General Blaž Kraljević, leader of the Hercegovinian HOS, who supported close cooperation with the Muslims and the army of Bosnia-Hercegovina. After this, HOS units were quickly disbanded or fell apart and the HVO remained the only army of the Hercegovinian Croats. In October 1992, at a convention of the Bosnia-Hercegovina HDZ in Mostar, a new party leadership was elected. It was headed by Mate Boban, who was already President of Herceg-Bosna and HVO commander, and thus now united in one person the three most responsible offices – political, military and administrative. He sought a balance of policy with President Tudjman of Croatia and even more with the Croatian defence minister Gojko Šušak, a Hercegovinian by origin. As time passed he ceased to recognise Alija Izetbegović, the President of his country, and they gradually became adversaries.

Croat-Muslim relations became still worse when large numbers of Muslim refugees from eastern Bosnia, fleeing from the Serbs, started to settle in regions with a majority Croat population. The Hercegovinian Croats accused the Muslims and their leaders of trying to change the ethnic structure, of wanting a homogeneous, predominantly Muslim Bosnia, of fundamentalism, and of creating an Islamic state in Europe. The Muslims accused the Hercegovinian Croats in turn of breaking up the common front, of secretly parleying with the Serbs, of handing over some areas in northern Bosnia to the Serbs without a fight, and of not helping to raise the siege of Sarajevo.

At the beginning of 1993 tension came to a head and the first clashes occurred in places where the HVO and the army of Bosnia-Hercegovina came into contact. The Muslims had started a war for an integrated Bosnia, the Croats had done so for maximum independence or secession. In mid-April the first massacre took place: HVO units killed 117 Muslims, burnt 140 houses, and destroyed two mosques and schools in Ahmići near Vitez in central Bosnia. The move was planned and organised from outside the area to induce total war in a mixed community. From that moment a Croat-Muslim war raged in central Bosnia. Both sides followed up their military operations with atrocities against civilians. After initial Croat success, the initiative passed in the summer months to the Muslims. The HVO and most of the Croat population were forced to withdraw from most of central Bosnia, abandoning towns and leaving only isolated enclaves under Croat control, which could not survive in the long run.

For the Serbs the Croat-Muslim war brought a respite: pressure on them weakened. In various ways they helped first one side and then the other, depending on conditions on the battlefield and what suited them best. They preferred to side with the Hercegovinian Croats against the Muslims, and accordingly on 6 May 1993 Karadžić met Boban in the Austrian city of Graz. They haggled over the division of Bosnia-Hercegovina at the expense of the Muslims, and only reached a partial agreement on delimitation in Hercegovina.

In the Croat-Muslim war of 1993-4 over 10,000 Croats and an unknown but even greater number of Muslims were killed. Both symbolically and actually, the war reached its peak in Mostar. That town, which before the war had been inhabited by almost equal numbers of Croats, Serbs and Muslims, was to become the capital of the Croat part of Bosnia-Hercegovina in the event of a Croat victory or, in the event of a Muslim victory, proof of the wholeness and integrity of Bosnia. Each of the two opposing forces evicted, imprisoned and killed civilians of the other side. The HVO made systematic use of artillery to destroy the eastern part of the town (which remained under the control of the army of Bosnia-Hercegovina), especially the old town nucleus, and organised concentration camps nearby. For the first time the international community almost unanimously accused Croatia because there was no doubt that troops of the Croatian army were taking part in HVO operations in Mostar and in all of Hercegovina. At the peak of the conflict, in November 1993, HVO units destroyed the old bridge, a masterpiece of Ottoman architecture which, to make the paradox even greater, had been built in 1566, under the direction of Muslim architects, by Croatian stone-masons from Dubrovnik and Korčula skilled in making such sophisticated structures. The material damage was immense, and central Bosnia, where the fighting was worst, was ruined not only economically but even more from the aspect of civilisation itself. This war damaged Croatia immeasurably in another way too – it lost the Croats and Croatia the status of victim to which at earlier stages they could reasonably have laid claim.

Some Islamic groups hurried to join the war in Bosnia: they did not confine themselves to sending aid to the threatened Muslims but often promoted a clearly fundamentalist programme of re-Islamising the Bosnian Muslims who over the centuries had become greatly secularised. Islamic mercenaries and fanatics fought on the Muslim side, and took a far from negligible part in crimes against the Croats. More fuel was poured on the fire in August 1993 when the Croat Republic of Herceg-Bosna was proclaimed in Grude (again) as a 'state' of the Croats in Bosnia-Hercegovina, with Mostar as its capital. Still, in many places in central and northern Bosnia the Croat-Muslim alliance held – a mitigating fact for the Croats and Croatia. In Bihać, Tuzla and the Posavina region army and HVO units continued to fight the Serbs on the same side. In encircled Sarajevo solidarity between Muslims, Croats and about 30,000 Serbs who did not want to join the other side still continued. All this encouraged the hope that in spite of everything Bosnia's multi-ethnic nature might be preserved.

The Croats of Bosnia-Hercegovina suffered about 30,000 casualties in the war against the Serbs and the Muslims. By the beginning of 1994 almost half of the pre-war Croat population in Bosnia of about 750,000 had had to leave their homes. This was the low point of Croatia's foreign and domestic policy. Because of the war against the Muslims, Croatia was threatened with international sanctions like those already imposed on Yugoslavia, and it had no international support for the reintegration of Croatian territories not under Serb occupation.

Consensus on essential questions of national importance, which had existed in 1991, disappeared. Most opposition parties and much of the Catholic Church opposed the country's policy in Bosnia – pressure that resulted in a great fall in popularity for the HDZ and President Tudjman.

The Croats in Sarajevo and in parts of Bosnia under Muslim control suffered worst and had the most cause to be dissatisfied with Croatia's Bosnian policy. In January 1994 they founded the Croat National Council in Sarajevo, which worked out the first plan for cooperation and reconciliation between Croats and Muslims. US diplomacy quickly accepted this initiative and organised a preliminary meeting, in Vienna, of representatives of both sides, followed by a large conference in Washington of the principal representatives from Croatia and Bosnia-Hercegovina. When Mate Boban withdrew from all leading positions in February 1994, the Muslims and Croats agreed on a ceasefire and signed an agreement in Washington that brought the Croat-Muslim war in Bosnia to an end. An agreement was worked out to create a Croat-Muslim Federation in Bosnia-Hercegovina, and its confederation with Croatia. The former enemies, who had contracted not a 'love marriage' but a 'marriage of convenience', could now unite against the common enemy. There was now a very limited normalisation but despite public announcements of the new situation, few refugees have returned to their homes and it has proved difficult if not impossible to form common institutions. However, the road-blocks were removed, and the army of Bosnia-Hercegovina got weapons and other equipment more freely. The Serbs, who till then had enjoyed relative calm, were soon to face great difficulties.

### Croatia in 1992-5: from statehood to military victory

Although the ceasefire signed at the beginning of 1992 brought Croatia relief, the situation was far from normal. The UN Security Council Resolution no. 743 of February 1992 established the United Nations Protection Forces (UNPROFOR) and four UN-Protected Areas (UNPA): East (eastern Slavonia – Vukovar and Baranja, and the area around Osijek), West (western Slavonia – the area around Okučani and Pakrac), North (Kordun and Banija) and South (the Dalmatian interior). The international community agreed almost unanimously that the UNPAs were an integral part of Croatia, but insisted that all problems should be solved by agreement. The Serbs for their part supported the *status quo* and undermined any progress that was being made. For example, it had been agreed that some Serb-held Croatian areas, so-called 'pink zones', should be unconditionally returned to Croatian control, but this never happened.

The rebel Serbs created a para-state on Croatian territory, the Republic of Serbian Krajina, and with the more or less open support of the Bosnian Serbs and Yugoslavia stubbornly persisted in demanding recognition of their secession from Croatia. Their argument was that if Croatia's secession from Yugoslavia was now recognised, then 'Krajina' could achieve the same status *vis-à-vis* Croatia. However, even Yugoslavia did not recognise them. Between 1992 and 1995 the reintegration of Krajina was a question of 'to be or not to be'. In eastern Slavonia the Serbs held the richest part of Croatia for agricultural purposes, and in the central areas they blocked roads between Zagreb and Dalmatia, occupied three airports, and blocked all river traffic down the Sava and the Danube. Of the thirty largest towns, the Serbs held three and eleven were within range of Croatian or Bosnian Serb artillery.

One might have said that the Serbs had won the war, because they were holding about a quarter of Croatian territory, whereas before the war they had made up 12 per cent of Croatia's population. However, there were no victors in that war. These boundaries were insupportable for either the Croats or the Serbs. Serb-held territories in central Croatia and Dalmatia were 500 km. from Belgrade, and the connections were terrible. They had no outlet to the sea, which in some places was only a few kilometres away and no links with Western Europe. Hemmed in as they were, the Serbs in the Croatian areas they held inevitably faced poverty, emigration and a bleak future even if there had been no military threat from the Croats.

The refugees were a particularly heavy burden for both sides, both morally and materially. Croatia had about 250,000 refugees, and only a small number moved into houses and apartments vacated by Serbs. Most, initially at least, were accommodated in hotels and tourist holiday villages. In those years every political discussion started and ended with the question: when will the displaced people return home, or will they ever be able to return? Masses of Serbs also fled, and those who left areas far from the war zone tried to exchange their property for that of Croats in Bosnia or in Yugoslavia, but many Serbs, especially those from western Slavonia, moved into vacated Croatian houses in eastern Slavonia.

There were also many homeless people who moved into Bosnia and Yugoslavia, especially Vojvodina and Belgrade itself.

After the end of war operations in January 1992 Croatian tactics and strategy were always conducted on two levels: negotiation and, if negotiation yielded no results, then resort to other means. At first Croatia believed that small military surprise attacks could be used to achieve successes quickly, but after the first coup in the spring of 1992 in Baranja, the Croatian army had to return to its starting position. In the same year a complicated but successful operation liberated the western part of the Dubrovnik municipality and lifted the siege of the city. Some strategic positions from which the Serbs dominated Zadar and its surroundings were also taken, as was Miljevci, an important plateau between Šibenik and Knin. In January 1993 the Croatian army initiated the Maslenica operation and freed a small but crucial part of the Zadar interior: the strait of Masleničko Ždrilo, which had once been spanned by a strategically important bridge on the Adriatic coast road. After that they freed Zadar airport, which placed Zadar out of immediate danger. Peruča hydroelectric power plant was also freed, but it was first mined by the Serbs. This cut the electricity supply in Dalmatia, which faced major electricity shortages in the following months.

In September 1993 the Serb stronghold of Medak was attacked from the direction of Gospić, but the operation showed that not much more could be achieved by this method of local surprise attacks. It brought down on Croatia the rage of international diplomacy, which demanded exclusively peaceful solutions to all disputes. Things were made worse by the repression carried out against civilians during and after the operation, when property was burned and looted (the Croat-Muslim war was raging in Bosnia at the same time). Because of this the UN ordered the demilitarisation of the zone which Croatian units had freed in the operation, and militarily the situation returned more or less to where it had stood before the Medak operation. It was clear that Croatia would incur drastic punishment if it embarked on any further military action of a similar kind. To make matters worse, this did not cow the rebel Serbs who continued intermittently to shell Croatian towns.

Another path now had to be taken, primarily by negotiation: in the Zagreb agreement (the so-called Russian Embassy agreement) of March 1994 it was decided to strive for peace through a three-stage confidence-building process between the 'two sides' (this euphemism was used to appease the Serbian side). The first stage was to establish a stable peace, the second was to find solutions to economic questions, and the final stage would consist of dis-cussion and agreement on political issues. To implement the first stage, it was agreed to create a buffer zone 2 km. wide and move heavy artillery 20 km. back from the demarcation line. The positive aspect of this agreement was that it brought Croatia a period of relative peace, especially in central Dalmatia, and as the result the 1994 tourist season was relatively successful. On the other hand, in a way it promoted the rebel Croatian Serbs into a relevant, indeed an equal party in negotiations. Furthermore, the agreement did not give deadlines for the implementation of the stages, which opened the way for new Serb procrastination.

The strategic situation changed when a ceasefire was signed between the Croats and the Muslims in Bosnia-Hercegovina: the Serbs' military predominance was eroded and international pressure on them grew. The protracted war in Bosnia-Hercegovina and Croatia was destabilising the broader region and because of this the international community, most notably the United States, wanted to end it, but in a way which would punish the aggressor. This made the Serbs nervous and they sought a quick solution, wanting to round off their conquest. For more than two years they had held the town of Bihać in western Bosnia, on the border of Croatia, in complete encirclement, but the town itself remained under Muslim (and Croat) control, which impaired the integrity of their territory. Because of this, the Bosnian and Croatian Serbs, with the help of local Muslim defectors from the Sarajevo govern-ment, moved in the winter of 1994-5 to conquer Bihać. Croatia stated unequivocally that it would intervene. Unlike in the preced-ing three years, it intervened this time in agreement with the international community, in particular with the US government. The Bihać enclave managed to defend itself without direct Croatian assistance, but the Croatian army nevertheless sent military helicop-ters and commando units there. At the same time the Croatian army and the HVO launched small-scale operations that gradually freed territory in south-western Bosnia around Livno and Grahovo along the Croatian border. This indirectly helped Bihać, but also prepared the ground for the final liberation of Knin, around which the noose was slowly but surely tightening.

## 1995: the year of resolution

At the end of 1994 a breakthrough finally occurred in the haggling between Croats and Serbs in Croatia: 27 km. of the Zagreb–eastern Slavonia motorway that passed through UNPA Sector West (and on to Belgrade) was opened and traffic along it built up rapidly, without any serious incidents. At the beginning of 1995 the oil pipeline through UNPA Sector North became operative, an important step for Croatia's economy since it could raise total annual income to $100 million. The concessions made by the Serbs were paid for by concessions from the Croats (supply of oil derivatives, permission for civilians from UNPA Sector West to shop in surrounding Croatian shops, and so on).

The Krajina leadership still stuck to an extremist policy – it was also a blind alley. Although it was certainly clear to them that the balance of power was shifting, that Croatia was quickly arming itself and organising a professional army, and that barely 200,000 Krajina Serbs could not for ever resist the pressure from a country with 4.5 million inhabitants, they stubbornly persisted in their demand for the Krajina's statehood. They did not even consider the obvious truth that neither the Bosnian Serbs nor – even less – Milošević could help them, weighed down as they were by international sanctions and a major economic crisis. With incredible nonchalance they rejected the 'Z-4 Plan' which the US, British, German and Russian ambassadors in Zagreb had offered them and the Croatian government in 1994 in the name of their governments. The agreement called for broad Serbian autonomy in Croatia, including their own money. Croatia accepted the Plan in principle, but with strong reservations, whereas the Krajina representative Milan Martić (he called himself President of Krajina) would not even receive its text which US ambassador Peter Galbraith personally carried to Knin.

At the end of April 1995 there was a major incident along the motorway near Okučani, which the Croatian army and police used as a pretext to start Operation Flash (*Bljesak*) in which they retook all of western Slavonia (about 510 square km.) in only one and a half days. Many of the Serbs there did not stay for the encounter with the Croatian army and 18,000 of them fled, mostly to neighbouring Bosnia. Less than 2,000 remained. A day later, in retaliation, the Serb rebels fired several long-distance rockets at Zagreb, which was about 40 km. away, and at other Croatian towns. In Zagreb seven civilians were killed.

The Bosnian Serbs had been trying the patience of the international community for months and years, but when they overran the protected eastern Bosnian zone of Srebrenica in July 1995 (and Žepa in August) and then killed several thousand prisoners of war and civilians it finally snapped. At that time the Croatian army and the HVO took several more strategic points in the Bosnian mountains near Knin, making the defence of the town much more difficult. On 2 August representatives of the Croatian state and of the Krajina Serbs met in Geneva, and the Croats made proposals that, had they been accepted, would have meant the Serbs' capitulation. Suddenly the Serbs showed by certain signs that they might give in, although this would have represented a humiliation, but it was too late. The Croats had already taken the decision. The international community still supported the peaceable solution of all disputes and in principle did not condone any Croatian attack. However, it seems that the United States had given a positive signal to go ahead.

### Operation Storm (Oluja)

In the early morning of 4 August about 150,000 Croatian soldiers attacked on a 630 km.-wide front defended by about 40,000 Serbian soldiers. Already on the first day the Serbian front lines were broken in thirty places in the main path of the attack to a depth of 5-15 km. On the second morning Croatian soldiers entered Knin and hoisted the Croatian flag over the town's castle, which marked the end of the Republic of Serbian Krajina, symbolically and in fact. All Serb resistance ended two days later. After 1,201 days under siege Bihać was relieved and another of the operation's goals was fulfilled.

In the general panic and confusion that followed, most of the civilians retreated together with the Serb army: the number of refugees is estimated at about 100,000 in addition to those who had left earlier. Only 5-6,000 people remained, most of them elderly. The reasons for the Serb exodus are complex. Some had to leave because the Serb army forced them to, while others feared the revenge of the Croatian army or of their former Croatian neighbours, whom they had driven away and whose homes they had mostly looted (it was later shown that this fear was far from groundless). Propaganda also played a part because it kept hammering home the message that this was a repeat of 1941 and that the Serbs would again fall victim to the Ustasha knife. It seems that many of them remained imprisoned in the ideology that took them to their doom. After accepting the principle of a Serbian state in which no non-Serbs could live, they had effectively ethnically cleansed themselves. When they lost the territory they controlled, they applied the principle to themselves in assuming that there was no room for them in the Croatian state. The Serbian Orthodox church, as one of the main power centres promoting the Greater Serbian national programme, contributed to this attitude. Its priests departed from regions controlled by the Croats and Bosniaks, alleging that they were being threatened. A minimum number of Orthodox priests remained in parts of Croatia under Zagreb's control after 1991, and there were only two in the Muslim- and Croat-controlled parts of Bosnia-Hercegovina in 1995.

When the Croatian army entered the territory it was liberating, several hundred Serb civilians were killed and Serb property was looted and burned. The Croatian authorities were inadmissibly tolerant of these actions, and legal procedures turned into a farce when the perpetrators were known or even caught. Croatia was again seriously criticised by the international community, and the most far-fetched Serb claims about the 'genocidal' Croats seemed to have at least some foundation.

A new episode in the war and refugee tragedy happened after the Serbs fled from Croatia, moved east over the border into Bosnia and arrived in the Banja Luka region. There they drove out some 20,000 Muslims and Croats and moved into their houses. The Bosnian Croats moved to Croatia and took over the deserted Serb houses.

*The war draws to a close*

Despite the defeat of their allies in Croatia, the Bosnian Serbs continued to defy the international community. They did not honour the artillery exclusion zone around Sarajevo, once killing more than forty people with a single shell, and in September 1995 NATO began extensive air attacks against the Serb anti-aircraft installations, transmitters, warehouses and communications. At the same time a joint offensive of Croat and Muslim units was being mounted in western and northern Bosnia. The Serbs were demoralised and disorganised and quickly lost territory, sometimes retreating in panic. The HVO and the army of Bosnia- Hercegovina managed to liberate almost 51 per cent of the territory of Bosnia-Hercegovina, which complied with the proposal of the international community that it should be divided 51:49 to the benefit of the Croatian-Muslim side. The Bosnian Serbs were now forced to negotiate in earnest. All the major powers were in agreement, but the talks that began in November 1995 in Dayton, Ohio, were mostly conducted under US auspices. After about twenty days of intensive negotiations in which American intermediaries used all kinds of diplomatic pressure, a global peace accord was signed (the Croatian, Bosnian-Hercegovinian and Serbian delegations were led, respectively, by Franjo Tudjman, Alija Izetbegović and Slobodan Milošević) confirming the sovereignty of Bosnia-Hercegovina with Sarajevo as its capital. The territory was divided on the principle of 51 per cent for the Federation and 49 for the Serb entity. The right of all refugees to return to their homes was confirmed, and the international community, represented in this case by NATO, undertook to send 60,000 soldiers to supervise the ceasefire. Significant financial and other aid was promised to the sides that loyally cooperated in the peace process. The signatures of the three Presidents on the Dayton document ended the war in Bosnia-Hercegovina, but many problems remained unresolved. In later months the accord could not be consistently adhered to because of different interpretations of the document, and because of the unwillingness of one side or the other, particularly the Serbs, to comply.

While the Presidents were bargaining in Dayton, another drama was unfolding in the former war zone. The United States wanted to stabilise the peace in Croatia at the same time, and negotiations were being held about the future of eastern Slavonia, which was then all that remained under Serb control. An agreement was signed in Erdut, a small town near Osijek temporarily held by the Serbs. It called for a period of transition, lasting one or two years, during which the international community would govern the area. (The organ for this exercise was United Nations Transition Action Eastern Slavonia – UNTAES.) Croatia would then resume full power.

This ended the war in Croatia. President Tudjman has stated that in the 1991-5 war 10,668 soldiers and civilians were killed on the Croatian side. In addition 2,915 are classified as missing, and 37,180 were wounded. The losses of the other side, mostly Croatian citizens of Serbs nationality, are not known.

# 15

## CROATIA IN THE 1990S: BETWEEN THE BALKANS AND EUROPE

At the beginning of 1992 the international community recognised Croatia as an independent state. In the nineteenth century and earlier in the twentieth, many Croats dreamed the distant dream of sovereign independence, but when the Yugoslav crisis gathered momentum at the end of the 1980s an increasing number of people became convinced that democracy and economic progress were only possible outside the Yugoslav community. However, when this independence was finally achieved, new obstacles in the way of a better life appeared. The main one was certainly the 1991-5 war. The economy suffered immeasurable damage: besides the general destruction, roads and railways in Croatia were blocked for five years, and for the same period about a quarter of the national territory, with its considerable economic potential, was occupied. Because of the lack of security, Croatian tourism fell in 1992 and 1993 to 10 per cent of its pre-war volume, and foreign tourists stayed away almost entirely.

Irreparable human damage has been done with thousands of people killed and incapacitated and families destroyed. The destructive atmosphere of war poisoned ordinary social relations and contacts between the nationalities. When death and destruction become everyday facts of life, thought and discussion about ethics, honesty and work for the good of the community make little sense.

These are the objective reasons for Croatia's slowdown, but some moves were made that greatly aggravated its situation. Privatisation was carried out, with the result that a small number of people close to the centre of power acquired considerable wealth. Because these new owners lacked ability and often wanted to sell off their newly-acquired property as quickly as they could, many privatised firms went bankrupt. The fall in the standard of living was not reflected so much in lower wages as in a doubling of unemployment to nearly 20 per cent (before the war about 1,500,000 people were employed, and seven years later hardly 950,000). To this was added a dramatic increase in the number of pensioners, poorer health protection, and a great fall in house-building. Tens or maybe hundreds of thousands of people are employed in the grey economy. All the problems that once beset the socially-owned economy now burden the privatised economy to an even greater extent, with low productivity, insolvency, in-ternal debt and lack of investment. There are also problems in the capital market: banks have not been financially reconstructed, and are still under strong state control. Although the first stock markets were opened in 1992, they have not yet acquired major importance, mostly due to circumstances. The investment cycle had been broken: in 1995 the level of investment was 14 per cent of what it had been in 1990, which was already a year of crisis, and in 1997 it had not even reached half of the 1990 figures. In 1996 and 1997 investment grew, but only modestly. The ports of Split, Zadar and Šibenik were reduced to negligible local traffic for five years because the Knin railway junction was in rebel hands. After 1995 traffic increased, but it remained small. Even in Rijeka the physical volume of port traffic fell from over 12 million tons in the best years to barely 2 million in 1997. The Croatian economy has also suffered from the closure of the markets of other Yugoslav republics and the crises that have bedevilled other former socialist countries.

President Tudjman's autocratic style of government left its mark on the entire state. The President concentrates power in his own hands, even exceeding constitutional authority. The personality cult which developed was rooted in an anachronistic concept of 'universal' presidential authority and his untouchable political office, inherited from former undemocratic systems. On the other hand, there is a tendency in the Croatian electorate to seek a leader who can be relied on to lead the nation in difficult times when the future is uncertain. The government has been marginalised, its main function being to elaborate and implement strategic decisions made by the President and his advisory bodies. The *Sabor* is increasingly becoming a 'monarchist parliament' in which the majority HDZ members implements the President's decisions without discussion. The fate of government officials often depends on personal loyalty to him.

All this logically leads to complete centralisation of all state offices in Zagreb, which in turn creates resentment of Zagreb in other parts of Croatia that consider themselves neglected. The separation of state power into judiciary, executive and legislature is often not honoured. The highest state officials are protected by law, and often sue the independent media and journalists if they do not like their radical criticism or satire, demanding great sums of money as compensation for mental suffering. Although the constitution gives wide powers to the President of the Republic, he has broadened them. There is practically no field of life in Croatia in which President Tudjman does not have an influence if he wants it. He arbitrates in cultural matters – e.g. over which films are shown – and in sport. The information programme of the state-owned television, especially during election campaigns, is a party organ of the ruling HDZ.

Since 1990, the HDZ and President Tudjman have been to the polls several more times at various levels of government. In 1992 and 1997, by carefully timing elections and adapting the electoral laws to their needs, he won two five-year presidential terms in the first round of elections by winning just over 55 per cent of the vote. Similarly the HDZ won in both parliamentary and local elections. However, political and economic difficulties have led to a fall in the HDZ's popularity. From 42 per cent in 1990, when the population included at least 12 per cent of Serbs and there were minimum abstentions, it won less than 30 per cent in some constituencies at parliamentary and local elections in the following years. The number of Serb voters had greatly decreased, which automatically eliminated opposition to the HDZ, and up to 40 per cent of Croatian voters abstained. After 1990 a large number of people who would always vote for the party in power voted for the HDZ. Finally, no elections after 1990 can be considered fair because the opposition were discriminated against in many ways. In every election the government adapted the electoral law to suit its own purposes, even giving voting rights to the Croatian 'diaspora', particularly the Croats in Bosnia-Hercegovina, who voted overwhelmingly for the HDZ. In this way the HDZ still managed to retain power at the national level. It enjoys greater support in small towns and villages and in areas hit by the war. In some large towns or regions (Rijeka, Osijek, Istria) it has never won, and in Zagreb and Split it has been known to lose.

President Tudjman considers the creation of an independent Croatia to be his achievement. He is completely engrossed in national problems and judges every event according to the benefit he imagines it will give to the Croatian state. Because he is a historian, his political thinking often follows examples from history. His vision is to create a society without internal conflicts led by the HDZ, that will be a synthesis of 'all the state-building Croatian traditions' from Ante Starčević to the Croatian Communists.

Little has come of the portentously announced return of the Croatian diaspora to the homeland. Few people have returned, and only a minority of these have brought ability, experience, knowledge or financial assets. Returnees are most notable for harbouring old obsessions and intolerance.

The war has greatly increased general intolerance: there are some who publicly promote xenophobia and ethnic, religious or other prejudices, and seek to relativise the criminal character of the NDH. The authorities and to some extent the public are often inadmissibly tolerant of such outbursts, and in some cases even support them. The thesis that since the Croats were only defending themselves in the war they could not have committed war crimes has often been aired. The new conservativism has increased, and in 1992 a broadly conceived 'spiritual renewal' and return to traditional Christian values were announced. Attempts are being made to create a cult of the family, with many children and the mother as housewife, and to ban abortion. The state is actively encouraging Croatian naive art, which is already internationally known, as an 'expression of the Croatian spirit', and neglecting other more important and valuable artistic currents.

In 1990 the church generally welcomed the victory of democracy and free elections, but most of the junior clergy openly supported the HDZ, which in subsequent years has also enjoyed the direct or indirect support of the church hierarchy. This stems partly from the church's traditional position in Croatian society, where it has often been seen as the champion of national interests, and partly from the often tasteless and fawning obeisance paid to the church by the authorities. The broader public accepted the view that 'Croatdom' is to be identified with Catholicism, i.e. that the

Catholic church is one with the state and the state one with the Catholic church. Because of all this, in the early 1990s the church only offered mild criticism of social injustices. None the less, it took a more forceful stand against the attempts of Croatian politicians to divide Bosnia-Hercegovina. When Pope John Paul II visited Zagreb in September 1994 – the first pope to come to Croatia in many centuries[*] –people converged *en masse* with spontaneous enthusiasm to greet him. He met the top state officials, and at a public eucharist spoke in the spirit of ecumenism and forgiveness. Many who were present would have preferred not to have to hear what the Pope said. (He visited Croatia again – and beatified Stepinac – in 1998.) However, as the social crisis increased, the church grew more critical of social events. It seems that the nomination of Josip Bozanić, born in 1949 and thus relatively young, as Archbishop of Zagreb at the end of 1997 may be a turning-point marking a shift by the church towards a policy dominated by ecumenism and social issues, and no longer by the national element.

On the international plane Croatia's policy towards Bosnia-Hercegovina certainly did it most damage. The Croatian government always supported an integral Bosnia-Hercegovina in words, but its actions often tended in a completely opposite direction. In addition, Croatian foreign policy is rife with improvisation, mistakes and blunders. In 1993 the Central European countries – the Czech Republic, Hungary, Poland and Slovakia, later joined by Slovenia and Rumania – offered Croatia membership in the Central European Free Trade Association (CEFTA), but were rebuffed. At that time the President believed that Croatia could enter European integration directly, not in partnership with former Communist countries. The country did not fulfill international obligations that it undertook and this cooled relations with its former close allies, Germany and the United States. Promises that Croatia would enter the NATO Partnership for Peace programme and become an associate EC member were still unfulfilled in 1998, and the future prospects in this regard were unclear. The anti-European attitude in some circles close to the authorities, though only expressed by a minority, has contributed to these

[*]Pope Alexander III was in Zadar in 1177.

failures. These people opt for isolation in order not to have to accommodate Croatian standards to European ones.

The war drove over half a million Croats from their homes in Croatia and Bosnia-Hercegovina. The Croatian authorities openly supported Serbian plans for population exchange, and in 1992 Tudjman and Dobrica Ćosić, President of Yugoslavia, even signed a treaty on 'humane relocation'. Their view was that Serbs and Croats cannot live together and that those who live on the 'wrong' side of the border must move to the 'right' side, although they added the rider that they should only do so of their own 'free will'. The only issue was where the border lay. After Operation Storm in 1995 the number of Serb refugees enormously increased and this seemed the right moment for a population exchange.

However, there are also hopeful elements. In April 1996, after more than three years of waiting, the parliament of the Council of Europe accepted Croatia as its fortieth member. This happened only after Croatian representatives promised to fulfill twenty-one demands in connection with human and minority rights. Although entry to the Council of Europe was difficult, it was the first and necessary step towards membership of other European and Euro-Atlantic organisations. In September 1996 Mate Granić, the Croatian foreign minister, signed an agreement with his Yugoslav counterpart Milutinović on normalisation of relations between the two countries, which practically ended the five-year (undeclared) war. All this contributed to make the 1997 tourist season, with just over 30 million tourist nights, much more successful than the preceding one, although it was still barely 44 per cent of the best pre-war year. This represents a very high 13 per cent of Croatia's gross national income.

International pressure and the stabilisation of peace has forced the Croatian authorities to soften their attitude to the return of Serb refugees. This was connected with the implementation of the UNTAES mission in eastern Slavonia which called for the return of everybody to their homes: of the Serbs who had taken refuge in eastern Slavonia back into other parts of Croatia, and of Croats back into eastern Slavonia. A certain number of Serbs did return to their homes in Croatia, but many also remained in eastern Slavonia. The pre-war number of Serbs in Croatia has probably been halved, but the civil and minority rights of those who remain are a test for the Croatian state.

The UNTAES mission ended successfully in January 1998: Vukovar and its surroundings were reintegrated into Croatia. Thus Croatia governs all its internationally recognised territory, and the war has been left behind. The remaining war wounds are healing slowly. The peace in Bosnia–Hercegovina under international supervision, which has a direct influence on the situation in Croatia whether we like it or not, still holds. Possible destabilisation in the region, particularly in Bosnia–Hercegovina, are still threats to the country's stability. The war in Kosovo in 1998 and the NATO intervention in 1999 are discouraging Croatian tourism and international traffic through the country. Croatia again has the chance of joining Europe, something it has desired for a full 500 years. The question is, will it now make use of its chance?

# SELECT BIBLIOGRAPHY

*General works*

Banac, I. *The National Question in Yugoslavia. Origins, History, Politics*, Ithaca, NY, 1984.

Beuc, I., *Povijest institucija državne vlasti Kraljevine Hrvatske, Slavonije i Dalmacije*, Zagreb 1985.

Castellan, G., *Histoire des Balkans*, Paris 1991.

———— and G. Vidan, *La Croatie*, Paris 1998.

Dabinović, A., *Hrvatska državna i pravna povijest*, 1st published Zagreb 1940; reprinted Zagreb 1990.

Dadić, Ž., *Povijest egzaktnih znanosti u Hrvata*, Zagreb 1982.

Dedijer, V., I. Božić, S. Ćirković, M. Ekmečić, *History of Yugoslavia*, New York 1974.

Donia, R. J., and J. V. A. Fine, *Bosnia and Hercegovina: A Tradition Betrayed*, London 1994.

Frangeš, I., *Povijest hrvatske književnosti*, Zagreb – Ljubljana 1987.

Gazi, S., *A History of Croatia*, New York 1973.

Goldstein, I. (ed.), *Kronologija, Hrvatska – Europa – Svijet*, Zagreb 1997.

Goldstein, S. (ed.), *Jews in Yugoslavia*, Zagreb 1989.

Guldescu, S., *Croatia: Land, People, Culture*, Toronto 1964.

Horvat, J., *Politička povijest Hrvatske*, 2 vols, first published. Zagreb 1936-8; reprinted Zagreb 1990.

Jelavich, B., *History of the Balkans*, Cambridge 1983.

Klaić, V., *Povijest Hrvata*, 4 vols 2nd ed Zagreb 1975.

Macan, T., *Povijest hrvatskoga naroda*, Zagreb 1992.

————, *Hrvatska povijest*, Zagreb 1995.

Malcolm, N., *Bosnia: A Short History*, London 1994.

Pavličević, D., *Povijest Hrvatske*, Zagreb 1994.

Pavlowitch, S., *The Improbable Survivor: Yugoslavia and its Problems, 1918 – 1988*, London 1998.

————, *Tito: Yugoslavia's Great Dictator*, London 1992.

Peroche, G., *Histoire de la Croatie et des nations slaves du sud, 395-1992*, Paris 1992.

Sirotković, H., and L. Margetić, *Povijest države i prava naroda SFR Jugoslavije*, Zagreb 1990.

Šanjek, F., *Kršćanstvo na hrvatskom prostoru*, Zagreb 1991.

Šišić, F., *Pregled povijesti hrvatskog naroda*, Zagreb 1962.

## Up till end of 18th century

Belošević, J., *Materijalna kultura Hrvata od 7. do 9. Stoljeća*, Zagreb 1980.
Adamček, J., *Agrarni odnosi u Hrvatskoj od sredine XV. do kraja XVII – stoljeća*, Zagreb 1980.
———*et al.*, *Seljačke bune u Hrvatskoj u 17. stoljeću*, Zagreb 1985.
Bertoša, M., *Mletačka Istra u XVI. i XVII. stoljeću*, Pule 1986.
Budak, N. (ed.), *Etnogeneza Hrvata*, Zagreb 1995.
Fcrluga, J., *L'amministrazione bizantina in Dalmazia*, Venice 1978.
Foretić, V., *Povijest Dubrovnika do 1808. godine*, 2 vols, Zagreb, *1980*.
Fortis, A., *Travels into Dalmatia*, London 1778.
Goldstein, I., *Bizant na Jadranu*, Zagreb 1992.
———, *Hrvatski rani srednji vijek*, Zagreb 1995.
——— (ed.), *Zvonimir kralj hrvatski*, Zagreb 1997.
———and M. Kruhek (eds), *Sisačka bitka 1593*, Zagreb 1994.
Herman J. (ed.), *Welt der Slawen*, Berlin 1986.
Klaić, N., *Povijest Hrvata u ranom srednjem vijeku*, Zagreb 1970.
———, *Povijest Hrvata u razvijenom srednjem vijeku*, Zagreb 1975.
———*Srednjovjekovna Bosna, politički položaj bosanskih vladara do Tvrtkove krunidbe 1377. godine*, Zagreb 1989.
Pcričić, Š., *Dalmacija uoči pada Mletačke Republike*, Zagreb 1980.
Rački, F. (ed.), *Documenta historiae chroaticae periodum antiquam illustrantia*, Zagrabiae 1877.
Raukar, T. *Hrvatsko srednjovjekovlje*, Zagreb 1997.
Rendić-Miočcvić, D., *Iliri antički svijet*, Split 1989.
Suić, M., *Antički grad na istočnom Jadranu*, Zagreb 1980.
Supičić, I. (ed.), *Hrvatska i Europa*, vol. I: *Rano doba hrvatske kulture*, Zagreb 1997.
Šanjek, F., *Crkva i kršćanstvo u Hrvatskoj*, vol. I: *Srednji vijek*, Zagreb 1988.
Šidak, J., *Studije o 'Crkvi bosanskoj' i bogumilstvu*, Zagreb 1975.
Šišić, F., *Povijest Hrvata u doba narodnihvladara*, first published Zagreb 1925; reprinted Zagreb 1990.
———, *Povijest Hrvata za doma Arpadovića I*, Zagreb 1944.
Wilkes. J., *Dalmatia: A history of the Roman Province*. London 1969.
———, *The Illyrians*, Oxford 1992.

## End of the 18th century to 1918

Džaja, M. S., *Bosnien-Herzegowina in der österreichisch-ungarischen Epoche (1878-1918)*, Munich 1994.
Gross, M., *Počeci moderne Hrvatske, neoapsolutizam u civilnoj Hrvatskoj i Slavoniji 1850–1860*, Zagreb 1989.
———, *Izvorno pravaštvo*, Zagreb 2000.

266     Select Bibliography

Gross, M., and A. Szabo, *Prema hrvatskom gradjanskom društvu*, Zagreb 1992.

——, *Die Anfänge der modernen Kroatien (1830-1878)*, Vienna 1993.

—— (ed.), *Društveni razvoj u Hrvatskoj od 16. do početka 20. stoljeća*, Zagreb 1981.

Horvat, J., *Ljudevit Gaj, Biografija*, Zagreb 1974.

Jelavich, C., *The Establishment of the Balkan National States, 1804-1920*, Seattle, WA, 1977.

Karaman, I., *Privreda i društvo Hrvatske u 19. stoljeću*, Zagreb 1972.

Lovrenčić, R., *Geneza politike 'novog kursa'*, Zagreb 1972.

Pavličević, D., *Narodni pokret 1883. u Hrvatskoj*, Zagreb 1980.

——, *Hrvatske kućne zadruge*, Zagreb 1989.

—— (ed.), *Vojna krajina od 16. st. do sjedinjenja Hrvatskom 1881*, Zagreb 1984.

—— (ed.), *Dnevnik Maksimilijana Vrhovca*, Zagreb 1987.

Stančić, N., *Hrvatska nacionalna ideologija preporodnogu pokreta u Dalmaciji – Mihovil Pavlinović i njegov krug*, Zagreb 1980.

——, 'Hrvatski narodni preporod, 1790-1848' in *Hrvatski narodni preporod*, Zagreb 1985.

Strecha, M., *Katoličko hrvatstvo*, Zagreb 1997.

Szabo, A., *Središnje institucije u Sagrebu 1860-1873*, 2 vols, Zagreb 1987.

Šidak, J., *Studije iz hrvatske povijesti XIX stoljeća*, Zagreb 1973.

——, *Studije iz hrvatske povijesti za revolucije 1848-49*, Zagreb 1979.

——, M. Gross., I. Karaman and D. Šepić, *Povijest hrvatskoga naroda, 1860-1914*, Zagreb 1968.

——, V. Forctić, J. Grabovac, I. Karaman, P. Strčić, M. Valentić, *Hrvatski narodni preporod-ilirski pokret*, Zagreb 1988.

Valentić, M., *Vojna krajina i pitanje njezina sjedinjenja s Hrvatskom, 1849-1881*, Zagreb 1981.

Vranješ-Šoljan, B., *Stanovništvo gradova banske Hrvatske na prijelazu stoljeća*, Zagreb 1991.


### 1918 – end of 20th century

Alexander, S., *Church and State in Yugoslavia since 1945*, Cambridge 1979.

Beloff, N., *Tito's Flawed Legacy: Yugoslavia and the West, 1939 to 1984*, London 1985.

Bennett, C., *Yugoslavia's Bloody Collapse: Causes, Course, Consequences*, London 1995.

Bilandžić, D., *Povijest Socijalističke Federativne Republike Jugoslavije*, Zagreb 1978.

Boban, Lj., *Svetozar Pribićević u opoziciji*, Zagreb 1973.

————, *Maček i HSS*, 2 vols, Zagreb 1974.

————, *Hrvatska u arhivima izbjegličke vlade (1941-3)*, Zagreb 1985.

————, *Kontroverze iz povijesti Jugoslavije*, vols I (1987); II (1989); and III (1990), Zagreb.

————, *Hrvatska u diplomatskim izvještajima izbjegličke vlade, 1941-1943*. 2 vols, Zagreb 1988.

Deakin, F. W. D, *The Embattled Mountain*, London 1971.

Djilas, M., *Wartime*, London 1977.

Glenny, M., *The Fall of Yugoslavia: The Third Balkan War*, London 1992.

Garde, P., *Vie et mort de la Yougoslavie*, Paris 1992.

Grmek, M. D. M., Gjidara, N. Šimac, *Le Nettoyage ethnique. Documents historiques sur une idéologie serbe*, Paris 1993.

Hoptner, J. B., *Yugoslavia in Crisis, 1934-1941*, New York 1962.

Hory, I. and M. Broszat, *Der kroatische Ustascha-Staat*, Stuttgart 1964.

Jelić, I., *Hrvatska u ratu i revoluciji*, Zagreb 1978.

————, *Jugoslavenska socijalistička revolucija*, Zagreb 1979.

Jelić-Butić, F., *Ustaše i Nezavisna Država Hrvatska 1941– 5*, Zagreb 1977.

————, *HSS (u ratu i revoluciji)*, Zagreb 1983.

————, J. *Četnici u Hrvatskoj 1941-1945*, Zagreb 1986.

Kočović, B., *Žrtve drugog svetskoga rata u Jugoslaviji*, London 1985.

Krizman, B. (ed.), *Korespondencija Stjepana Radića*, 2 vols, Zagreb 1972-3.

Krizman, B., *Ante Pavelić i ustaše*, Zagreb 1978.

————, *Pavelić izmedu Hitlera i Mussolinija*, Zagreb 1980.

————, *Pavelić u bjegstvu*, Zagreb 1986.

————, *Ustaše i Treći Reich*, 2 vols, Zagreb 1988.

————, *Hrvatska u prvom svjetskom ratu i hrvatsko-srpski politički odnosi*, Zagreb 1989.

Kvaternik, E. D., *Sjećanja i zapažanja*, Zagreb 1995.

Lasić, S., *Sukob na književnoj ljevici*, Zagreb 1970.

Lydall, H., *Yugoslavia in crisis*, Oxford 1989.

Maček, V., *In the Struggle for Freedom*, London 1957.

Magaš, B., *The Destruction of Yugoslavia: Tracking the Break-up, 1980-1992*, London 1993.

Mastnak, T., 'Finis Yugoslaviae', *East European Reporter*, vol. 5, No. 1, Jan.–Feb. 1992, pp. 3-7.

Maticka, M., *Agrarna reforma i kolonizacija u Hrvatskoj 1945-1948*, Zagreb 1990.

Matković, H., *Svetozar Pribićević i Samostalna demokratska stranka do šestojanuarske diktature*, Zagreb 1972.

McFarlane, B., *Yugoslavia: Politics, Economics and Society*, London 1988.

Mićunović, V., *Moskovske godine, 1956-1958*, Zagreb 1975.

Rusinow, D., *The Yugoslav Experiment, 1948-1974*, London 1978.

Stein-Erlich, V., *Jugoslavenska porodica u transformaciji*, Zagreb 1975.
Tomašević, J., *Peasants, Politics, and Economic Change in Yugoslavia*, Stanford, CA, 1955.
————,*The Chetniks: War and Revolution in Yugoslavia 1941-1945*, Stanford, CA, 1975.
*Zbornik dokumentata i podataka o narodnooslobodilačkom ratu jugoslavenskih naroda*, 14 vols, Beograd, 1950-60.
Žanić, I., *Prevarena povijest*, Zagreb 1998.
Žerjavić, V., *Opsesije i megalomanije oko Jasenovca i Bleiburga*, Zagreb 1992.

# INDEX

269